"Zeigler models honest engagement in an environment where Christian thought is no longer the starting point for dialogue. By opening us up to rival 'life-organizing stories,' he demonstrates clearly what makes Christian hope truly unique: Jesus. With an academic mind and a pastoral heart, Zeigler offers not only a new way of thinking about Christian hope, but a new way of thinking about theology. Read this book."

—**Justin Rossow**
Senior Pastor, St. Luke Lutheran Church, Ann Arbor, Michigan

"*Christian Hope Among Rivals* invites its reader—Christian or otherwise—to self-understanding and respectful dialogue. Zeigler shows that every attempt to 'make sense' of the world that we all know results in a life-organizing story that offers hope. Zeigler helps Christians readers find emphatic contact with others who do not trust in the Triune God. He encourages Christians to live in the hope rooted in Jesus—crucified, risen, and returning—even as we invite others to embrace Jesus and become part of the story enacted and promised through him."

—**Jeff Gibbs**
Concordia Seminary, St. Louis, Missouri

Christian Hope among Rivals

Christian Hope among Rivals
How Life-Organizing Stories Anticipate the End of Evil

MICHAEL W. ZEIGLER
Foreword by Joel P. Okamoto

☙PICKWICK *Publications* · Eugene, Oregon

CHRISTIAN HOPE AMONG RIVALS
How Life-Organizing Stories Anticipate the End of Evil

Copyright © 2017 Michael W. Zeigler. All rights reserved. Except for brief quotations in critical publications or reviews, no part of this book may be reproduced in any manner without prior written permission from the publisher. Write: Permissions, Wipf and Stock Publishers, 199 W. 8th Ave., Suite 3, Eugene, OR 97401.

Pickwick Publications
An Imprint of Wipf and Stock Publishers
199 W. 8th Ave., Suite 3
Eugene, OR 97401

www.wipfandstock.com

PAPERBACK ISBN: 978-1-5326-0462-1
HARDCOVER ISBN: 978-1-5326-0464-5
EBOOK ISBN: 978-1-5326-0463-8

Cataloguing-in-Publication data:

Names: Zeigler, Michael W., author. | Okamoto, Joel P., foreword.
Title: Christian hope among rivals : how life-organizing stories anticipate the end of evil / Michael W. Zeigler ; foreword by Joel P. Okamoto.
Description: Eugene, OR : Pickwick Publications, 2017 | Includes bibliographical references.
Identifiers: ISBN 978-1-5326-0462-1 (paperback) | ISBN 978-1-5326-0464-5 (hardcover) | ISBN 978-1-5326-0463-8 (ebook)
Subjects: LCSH: Narrative theology. | Theodicy. | Storytelling—Religious aspects—Christianity.
Classification: BT83.78 .Z45 2017 (paperback) | BT83.78 .Z45 (ebook)

Manufactured in the U.S.A.   08/28/17

To my family

Theology has only one problem: *God*. We are theologians *for God's sake*. God is our dignity. God is our suffering. God is our hope.

JÜRGEN MOLTMANN, *GOD FOR A SECULAR PEOPLE*

Iam extra Iesum quaerere deum est diabolus.
To seek God apart from Jesus—that is the devil.

MARTIN LUTHER, *COMMENTARY ON PSALM 130*, 1533

Contents

Foreword | ix
Preface | xiii

1 Zombie Jesus | 1
2 Comparing Eschatologies | 16
3 Eschatology and Story | 33
4 Narrative Theodicy | 63
5 A Typology of Narrative Theodicies—After Ricoeur | 89
6 Idealist Types | 115
7 Realist Types | 140
8 Staying in the Story | 163
   Conclusion: Zombie Jesus *Redivivus* | 191

Bibliography | 199

Foreword

FOR MORE THAN A hundred years, eschatology has been a central motif across Christian theology. Johannes Weiss and Albert Schweitzer made eschatology basic to interpretation of the New Testament, a theme pressed today by such scholars as N. T. Wright. For Karl Barth in one way and for Wolfhart Pannenberg in quite another, eschatology became basic to conceiving of divine revelation. For Gustavo Gutierrez, eschatology was central to a theology of liberation, and for John Howard Yoder it was essential for understanding the politics of Jesus and, indeed, for "working with the grain of the universe."

Eschatology in modern theology has many features, but two are especially important for properly understanding and appreciating this book and its proposal. The first feature is that eschatology has been mostly an internal Christian concern. It has been concerned with what Christians should think about "the last things" and what Christians should think "eschatology" should encompass. Sometimes interest in non-Christian views on death, afterlife, history, and the future have been taken into account, but usually to clarify or distinguish a Christian view. The second feature is understanding eschatology in "either/or" terms. Either you see recognize Jesus' message as thoroughly eschatological, or you don't. Either you think "eschatology" is the last chapter of dogmatics, or you see Christianity itself as eschatology. Either eschatology has to do with the transcendent, or it has to do with the future.

In both of these respects Michael Zeigler approaches "eschatology" differently. He recognizes, as admittedly many do, that everyone has views about the future and thoughts about hope, and he acknowledges that there are some compelling non-Christian alternatives. But he sees that thinking about these views within the usual Christian concepts and distinctions—treating eschatology as an internal Christian concern—will mean that one probably will conclude, as a matter of course and not incidentally, that non-Christian eschatologies are *either* like *or* unlike Christian eschatology.

This in turn will mean that one probably will not be doing justice to our contemporary rivals. Being fair and honest about others is always important for Christians, but today the Christian Church can no longer assume recognition and respect. So the urgency for Christians to do right by all of their neighbors is apparent. This applies to views and expectations about the future—"eschatologies" in a broad but appropriate sense—as much as anything.

The operative question is how to proceed. Zeigler argues that we should understand different views about the future and thoughts about hope in terms of the "life-organizing stories" in which these views and thoughts arise. A "life-organizing story" is a story of everything: a story that encompassing not only life and death, time and space, meaning and purpose, but also defining and orienting them. One of the most important features of any such story is its ability to resolve the conflicts and confusions that threaten anyone living according to a particular story. And this feature is its "eschatology."

Zeigler's approach brings Christian theology into conversation with contemporary philosophy in three notable respects. First, he appropriates Susan Neiman's discussion on the problem of evil to characterize both the conflicts in a life-organizing story and to characterize its resolution—its eschatology—as a theodicy. Second, he interacts with John Searle on language and the mind to help explain differences between various eschatologies. Third, his approach allows him to engage some modern philosophers, including Leibniz and Nietzsche, in eschatological terms.

The result is that Zeigler persuasively argues for and successfully demonstrates a re-rendering of eschatology. Of course, this is not the last word on the last things. In fact, it is nothing like a last word, but much more a new foray.

It is about this newness that I would conclude. Christian theology in general, and not only in eschatology, has been largely an intramural activity. This has been the case even where dealing with non-Christians has been the theme, as in missions. How should we conceive of those outside the Christian community? Some will answer: As those who are lost, in darkness, in despair, blind. Others will think them as more or less equals with Christians, responding to the ineffable Divine in their finite ways just as much as Christians are in theirs. The answers themselves are different, and yet they amount to many ways to say the same thing: how they are like or unlike Christians. This is surely an important question, but when it is sets the agenda, as it usually does, it tends to close off serious self-reflection about the Church and her message and mission and also serious reflection about those outside the Church.

But it is one thing to recognize this problem, and another to have a way to work beyond it. Zeigler's approach to working beyond this problem in eschatology suggests ways for dealing with other topics and problems. As you read, I encourage you to look for and work out these suggestions.

Joel P. Okamoto
St. Louis, Missouri

Preface

THIS PROJECT IS LOCATED within systematic theology, specifically in the area of Christian eschatology. The twentieth century has been called the century of eschatology. Albert Schweitzer's *The Quest for the Historical Jesus*, first published in 1906, initiated a period of renewed interest in the eschatological nature of the Gospel. In some ways, this rediscovery culminated with Jürgen Moltmann's *Theology of Hope*, translated into English in 1967. The century of eschatology has now closed, but interest in the discussion has not run dry. Although, as I argue in this book, it is in danger of stagnating.

Here I propose a different approach to eschatology. This will entail asking different questions than are typically asked in the field. I have not tried to answer standard questions, such as, To what degree is the Reign of God inaugurated in Christ already realized, and what still remains to be done? What is the nature of the interim state of the soul between death and resurrection of the body? How much continuity is there between the original creation and the new creation? These are important questions for appreciating the antinomous attributes contained within Christian hope—antinomies found in the witness of the New Testament. There, the diverse accounts of Paul, the Synoptic Gospels, and John constitute a plurality of features that resist systemization. It is important for theological reflection on Christian eschatology to appreciate the tension in this plurality. But, that is not the focus of this project.

My approach is warranted by the question I want to answer: How is Christian hope distinct as compared to other forms of life-organizing hope? The usual answers to this question tend to emphasize the dialectic tension that is contained in Christian hope. Christian eschatology is said to be distinct because of its balanced-tension between the "already" and "not yet" of the Kingdom that has come in Jesus and the Spirit. This tension is, on the one hand, contrasted against Modernity's hope of progress, which is criticized for its "over-realized eschatology" or for how it diminishes the transcendent or "vertical dimension" in favor of what is immanent and historical. On the other hand, the well-balanced, Christian hope is contrasted against a pessimistic longing for escape, which is sometimes said to be noneschatological. This form of life-organizing hope is criticized for how it expects too much discontinuity between this life and the life to come or for the way it diminishes the non-human, spatial-material creation. Christian hope, by contrast, is said to effectively avoid these extremes. Therefore, it is suited to produce an ethic that can avoid triumphalism, on the one hand, and despair, on the other.

My contention is that these kinds of answers do not appreciate how other accounts of hope actually do offer their own variation on a balanced-tension that avoids both presumption and despair. I argue that the balanced-tension approach to Christian eschatology is not equipped to recognize these other accounts, or stories-of-the-world, as true rivals. They are rival stories that offer a persuasive, coherent vision for life and vigorously compete for the fear, love, and trust of both the Church and the people to whom the Church bears witness. Failing to see these rival hopes for what they are—failing to rightly size up the competition—diminishes the Church's ability to witness and cooperate without being co-opted by a more encompassing story.

To address this problem, my thesis is that Christian *eschatology* should be understood as the *resolution of conflict* within and all-encompassing plot. This approach, which focuses on the storied nature of Christian hope as a whole, will enable Christian eschatology to be compared and contrasted with rival stories that also generate hope. Building on that definition of eschatology, I define the *conflict* in the plot as occurring between "good" and "evil." Therefore, eschatologies can be understood as *theodicies*, and vice versa.

I am using the term theodicy after the manner of contemporary philosopher Susan Neiman, in her book *Evil in Modern Thought*. Theodicy, she argued, is not just a demand on theists. It is a demand for anyone who wants the world to make sense, who wants the world to be intelligible. She related theodicy to the problem of evil, where *evil* is anything that threatens to make your or my world unintelligible. So as not to despair, people make sense of evil by locating it within a life-organizing story. These stories are eschatological because they anticipate an overcoming of *evil* by the *good*. They elicit hope for a resolution of the conflict. They are at the same time provisional theodicies because this hoped-for resolution will justify that story's author. The resolution of the conflict will demonstrate that author as trustworthy.

This intertwining of narrative, eschatology, and theodicy is, to the best of my knowledge, what is original and significant about this project. Thus, chapters one through four are the most important part of the book. The typology of narrative theodicies explained and explored in chapters five through seven illustrates the thesis. The quadrants describe four model narratives by the way they characterize *evil* and then by the strategies they take to overcome *evil* in hopes to resolve the plot. As I argue in chapter eight, the difference of the Christian hope is the way Christians characterize evil within the story of Jesus-in-Israel-and-the-Church. The conflict in their story will resolve only when the God of Jesus brings the world to conform to the word of the promise he made to Abraham.

The four model narrative theodicies are given to say what Christian hope is not. They are presented to show that this approach to eschatology can yield something concrete. In this book, I offer a conceptual map to help post-Constantinian Christians walk the narrow way as disciples of Jesus. My appeal to fellow Christians is simply to "stay in the story."

I would like to acknowledge the help of several people who contributed to this project. First of all, I am grateful to Joel Okamoto, who tirelessly interrogated my work and helped me formulate coherent answers to his questions, all while exemplifying Christ-like longsuffering and pastoral concern. Also, I am grateful to my Charles Arand and Jeffrey Gibbs, who read and commented on an earlier version of this work. They, along with the entire faculty of Concordia Seminary, continue to shape my theological formation. I thank my colleagues for the many critical and constructive conversations, especially Michael Fieberkorn, Beth Hoeltke, Joel Meyer, and William Horton. Also, I thank Robert Stroud and Kathryn Nafzger for their gracious and meticulous efforts in helping me proofread and edit the manuscript.

Several dear sisters and brothers in Christ financially supported my family during my work on this project, to include Douglas and Ann Marie Hamilton, Louis and Christy Stewart, along with the baptized saints of the Peace Lutheran Church Guild of Natoma, Kansas. Their concern, their devotion to the Lord of the church, and their model of sacrificial giving will be a source of lasting encouragement to me.

I am deeply grateful to God's people at Epiphany Lutheran Church, whom I currently serve as pastor. They, along with the people of Timothy Lutheran Church in St. Louis, Missouri, whom I served from 2012–14 as assistant pastor with Pastor Ron Rall and Pastor Bill Wilson, have graciously given me room to learn and grow as a shepherd of God's people. I also thank my parents, Timothy and Bernice Zeigler, and my wife's parents, Rodney and Kristine Frieling, for their consistent and unconditional love. Most of all, I thank my wife Amy, who not only read and helped edit an earlier form of this book, but also, with our four children, Josiah, Elise, Titus, and Jude, continually stood by me, encouraged, and cheered me on during this project.

1

Zombie Jesus

I AM PASTOR OF a smaller, urban Christian congregation within the Lutheran tradition. I struggle to help the members of our congregation live faithfully in a pluralistic confluence of cultures within which the traditional Christian faith looks more and more like a weird mix of fantasy and delusion. When the "resurrection of the dead" came up in a recent Bible study meeting at a local coffee shop, one of our dearly-loved, regular participants, Sean—a man in his mid-thirties, the nephew of one of our elderly members—commented, "So you're basically telling us to believe in Zombie Jesus."

This book offers a Christian account of *hope in general* in order to show the distinctiveness of *Christian* hope in particular. The central question is, "How does Christian hope compare to other kinds of hope?" I assume that some readers will be more like Sean—interested, but skeptical, and perhaps even amused by the traditional Christian hope. If so, I think you will find my account of *hope in general* helpful to your purposes. Some readers will be like the others at our coffee shop Bible study—struggling to hope like a Christian and to show others how to do likewise. For you, I think my account of the distinctiveness of *Christian hope* will be helpful.

While I have attempted to investigate this question with academic rigor, my heart is also in it, something like an oncology researcher who has lost a loved one to cancer. Each week, I lead my congregation to "look for the resurrection of the dead" and publically confess their hope in him who "will come again to judge both the living and the dead, whose kingdom will have no end." I struggle to help our congregation more clearly articulate and more practically orient our shared way of life around this hope. This book is designed to help others in that struggle.

A struggle typically has two sides. I am directly addressing the Christian side. Indirectly, I address those who struggle with or against traditional Christian teaching. I offer conceptual clarity on the human capacity to hope in order to identify the distinctiveness of the hope confessed in the Christian Scriptures and re-stated in the ecumenical creeds. I answer the question, "How does Christian hope compare with other forms of *eschatological* hope?"

Eschatology is a technical term for discussion about how hope begins and where it leads. It's a term I have found useful because it allows me to focus on a particular kind of hope—not just any passing wish, such as "I hope my package arrives today" or "I hope we don't get freezing rain," but an *enduring* hope—one around which I could organize my life. Let's call it *eschatological* hope. This sort of hope is at the heart of Christian faith, but Christians aren't the only ones who hope in this way.

So how does Christian hope compare to others? If you asked this question to a hundred informed people in North America, you would get at least two kinds of answers. One answer will assume that Christian hope is beyond compare; another, that Christian hope is essentially like any other. Both assumptions work against what I present in this book, so we will address them up front. The problem is not that these assumptions are completely false. The problem is that they anticipate *a resolution of conflict* that has not yet occurred.

CONSTANTINIAN ASSUMPTIONS

Each of these assumptions was expressed by two scholars who wrote something significant about eschatological hope. The first was conveyed by Hans Schwarz, an accomplished Christian scholar who had worked for more than forty years in international and inter-denominational settings. For Schwarz, Christian hope was beyond compare. In this regard, he speaks for many conservative, evangelical, and confessional Christians. The second assumption was conveyed by Immanuel Kant. As one of the most influential prophets of the modern, secular world, he speaks—in regard to this assumption—for many people who feel aversion to the words *conservative*, *evangelical*, and *confessional*.

Assumption 1: Christian Hope Is beyond Compare

I can't imagine living without hope. That is a sentiment often expressed by those who hold the first assumption. They believe Christian hope is the true hope. Everything else is delusion. This need not be expressed in a pompous, arrogant tone. It can be an expression of heart-felt pity for those who either do not know or do not accept the hope offered in Jesus Christ. In the introduction to his *Eschatology*,[1] Hans Schwarz, an internationally respected ecumenical, Lutheran theologian,[2] exhibited this first assumption. When Schwarz said he finds it "impossible to dispense with the eschatological expectations of the Christian faith and still maintain a meaningful hope in the future,"[3] I hear him speaking in a tone of heart-felt pity for those who live without the hope of Christ. Schwarz argued that Christian eschatology "is crucial for our time" because it alone offers the hope of a meaningful and certain future.[4] Christian hope, as "proleptic anticipation,"[5] has no rival. It is beyond compare. Present-day "obsession with the present" and ancient pessimism, which was typically "confined to a cyclical understanding of time," are both *non*eschatological because they offer no "meaningful goal." And even though a modern, linear view of time promises the possibility of progress, it offers no certainty because it exchanged "God-confidence" for "self-confidence." Since self-reliance is uncertain, it yields "no ultimate hope."[6] Schwarz developed this argument in great detail, and his core assumption was constant throughout: the only choices are Christian hope or hopelessness.

This assumption is closely related to those held by the Apostle Paul. He wrote to the Ephesian converts: "Remember that you were [once] separated from Christ, alienated from the commonwealth of Israel and strangers to the covenants of promise, having *no hope* and without God in the world."[7] Although, Paul probably recognized the questionable status of his professed hope, assuming he wrote this letter "in chains" (Eph 6:20) and under Roman custody. As Luke reported, Paul had previously declared, "I stand here on trial because of my hope in the promise made by God to our fathers" (Acts 26:6). After explaining himself, Paul urged the visiting King Agrippa to

---

1. Schwarz, *Eschatology*.
2. See Schwarz, *Theological Autobiography*.
3. Schwarz, *Eschatology*, 369.
4. Ibid., 21.
5. Ibid., 370. Two definitions of *prolepsis* are the "representation or assumption of a future act or development as if presently existing or accomplished" or "the application of an adjective to a noun in anticipation of the result of the action of the verb (as in 'while yon slow oxen turn the *furrowed* plain')" (*Merriam-Webster Dictionary*, on-line ed., s.v. "Prolepsis").
6. Ibid., 2–20.
7. Eph 2:12 ESV. Unless otherwise noted, all citations of the Bible are from the English Standard Version.

endorse his claim. Agrippa responded: "In a short time would you persuade me to be a Christian?" (Acts 26:28). Paul boldly asserted that the true hope of all people, both Jew and Gentile, commoner and king, is found only in this crucified and resurrected Jesus of Nazareth. But the fact that Paul was rejected by many of his own people and was in the custody of the empire raised questions about the reliability of his testimony. "Paul, you are out of your mind," said Governor Festus (Acts 26:24). Paul's claim was not *certain* in the sense that it could be demonstrated to any rational person of goodwill. It was contested and required vindication. From the governor's seat, Paul appeared to be the one without hope.

Mennonite theologian John Howard Yoder criticized Christians in the West for forgetting the contestable and controversial nature of their claims. Ever since Christianity became the favorite of the established political and social system, the church began to assume that the Christian worldview was, more or less, common sense. Yoder's initial point is not contentious: there occurred in western history a "deep shift in the relation of church and world for which Constantine soon became the symbol."[8] By the end of the fourth century, Paul's first century context was reversed. Not only was the emperor a Christian, but so was every citizen, nominally, at least.

Yoder argued that this reversal was not without cost. To some degree, the hope that Paul so confidently confessed was compromised in the effort to cooperate with the dominant powers. To hope for something better—a more noble ruler and superior way of life—could be interpreted as a threat to the establishment. This was because the Christianized Roman Empire began to be identified with the reign of God on earth. Constantinian Christians were encouraged to spiritualize, privatize, and individualize their hope since their earthly, political future seemed secure.[9] But, Christians today no longer enjoy this favored status. Yoder's concern was not Christianity's loss of cultural privilege. Instead, he was alarmed at how the dissolution of the Constantinian synthesis left modern Christians ill-equipped to stand on trial for the apostolic hope they had received.

> Christians in the first century were a minority in a hostile world. Their ethical views were attuned to that context. In the twentieth century, Christians—especially if by that noun we refer to people voluntarily committing themselves, at some cost, to living in the light of their confession of Christ—are also a minority

---

8. Yoder, *Priestly Kingdom*, 135.

9. Ibid., 136–41. Although, it is worth noting that while King Agrippa and Governor Festus may have thought Paul was "out of his mind," they agreed that he was no threat to the common good: "this man is doing nothing to deserve death or imprisonment" (Acts 26:24–32).

in a world committed to other loyalties, yet we do not reason as the early Christians did.[10]

Stanley Hauerwas and William Willimon described the problem of sharing the context but not the reasoning of the first-century church as the "post-Constantinian situation."[11] This situation, they claimed, began for American Christians sometime between 1960 and 1980. And if Constantine served as the symbol for the beginning of the synthesis, then the Greenville South Carolina Fox Theater's showing of a John Wayne film on a *Sunday* in 1963 signaled the close. "On that night . . . the last pocket of resistance to secularity in the Western world . . . served notice that it would no longer be a prop for the church."[12]

I do not employ the analysis of Yoder, Hauerwas, and Willimon as an historical argument to portray a homogenous state of affairs between AD 311 and 1963. They don't either. Instead, I use this analysis to describe a way of assuming the questions asked and answers offered by the church are obvious to everyone. The "habit of Constantinian thinking is hard to break."[13] The church has yet to adequately respond to her new context. Having grown accustomed to being the only show in town, Christians have gotten out of the habit of confessing their hope among rivals.

We are now far removed from the setting that nurtured this assumption. To illustrate, I offer a vignette from the life of Prussian philosopher Immanuel Kant (1724–1804). When he was about 70 years old, Kant published his book *Religion within the Boundaries of Mere Reason*. In a letter to a friend, he explained that the purpose of the book was to answer but *one* question: "What may I hope for?"[14] In the book's preface, Kant appealed for a dialogue between philosophers and biblical theologians: "whether the theologian agrees with the philosopher or believes himself obligated to oppose him: let him just hear him out. For in this way alone can the theologian be forearmed against all the difficulties that the philosopher may cause him."[15]

About five years earlier, in 1788, Kant's government had updated the policy on the regulation of materials printed in the Prussian realm. To ensure compliance, state-accredited censors previewed proposed books. When

---

10. Ibid., 135.
11. Hauerwas and Willimon, *Resident Aliens*, 42.
12. Ibid., 15–16.
13. Ibid., 72.
14. Quoted in Giovanni, "Translator's Introduction," in Kant, *Religion within the Boundaries of Mere Reason*, 49.
15. Ibid., 63.

Kant submitted a portion of the work mentioned above, it was denied publication. However, Kant found a legal loop-hole and had the work approved through an authorized university. About a year after it was published, he received a letter from the king:

> Our most high person has for a long time observed with great displeasure how you misuse your philosophy to distort and disparage many of the cardinal and basic teachings of the Holy Scriptures and of Christianity; how you have done this particularly in your book *Religion within the Boundaries of Mere Reason* . . . We demand that you give at once a most conscientious account of yourself, and expect that in the future, to avoid our highest disfavor, you will be guilty of no such fault.[16]

Kant caught the king's drift and agreed not to write any more on religion. He had desired a dialogue to contest not only the dogmatic certainty of the orthodox theologians, but also that of the deistic philosophers. But instead he was silenced by the highest authority in the land. Yet, already in 1794, the Constantinian synthesis was in its twilight. A few years later, Kant reported that the restrictions were lifted when the king died and "an enlightened statesman" was appointed—one without "a one-sided predilection for a special branch of science (theology)."[17] Now that Kant's account of hope has been proleptically vindicated and our context today is thoroughly post-Constantinian, what sort of difficulties might be made for the dogmatic certainty of Christian hope?

Recall how Hans Schwarz asserted that Christian eschatology alone offers ultimate hope. This was because, unlike a cyclic understanding of time, it presented a "meaningful goal" for the future.[18] Unlike modern, scientific hopes for progress, it provided "certainty." As examples of a cyclic view of time, Schwarz described the outlook of the Indian religions of Hinduism and Buddhism along with the Greek philosophy of Plato. These, he said, are all "pessimistic" and primarily look for an ultimate "release from this world." For them, this world has "no actual value."[19] In contrast, the Judeo-Christian worldview gave history "a goal worth living for" because it looks to the "acting and active God who provided the beginning, who controls the present, and who will provide the future."[20]

---

16. Kant, *Conflict of the Faculties*, in *Religion within the Boundaries of Mere Reason*, 240.

17. Ibid., 243.

18. See also Hong, *A History of the Future*, 20, 57.

19. Schwarz, *Eschatology*, 8–9.

20. Ibid., 13.

But what difficulties are inherent in this argument? One is raised by the question, "On what basis do you decide which outlook is meaning*ful* and which is meaning*less*?" Seen from *within* Buddhism, for example, "release from the world" is not pessimism. It is a goal that provides direction and endurance through life's darkest valleys:

> Given that the ultimate goal is to bring rebirth to an end . . . some Western observers have viewed early Buddhism as nihilistic, teaching a doctrine of self-annihilation. But the texts are quite consistent in maintaining that what is annihilated is not one's "self" . . . [but] the elimination of desire and of ignorance about the nature of reality and, as a result the suffering that is otherwise endemic to sentient life.[21]

According to the Buddha, all his teaching "is impregnated with but one flavor. . .the taste of deliverance."[22] In this regard, Buddhism provides a meaningful goal for the future.

There are other questions that create difficulties for the assumed certainty of Christian hope. Can you demonstrate that the Christian God will in fact bring history to a meaningful goal? And how will this God justify the gratuitous suffering that took place along the way—especially when it is confessed that he *controls* every present moment? To voice these questions, Kant put forward not the arguments of a philosopher, but the laments of a theologian: Job. In Kant's essay from 1791, "On the Miscarriage of all Philosophical Trials in Theodicy," he noted how Job's acceptance of God's sovereignty raised more questions than it answered.[23] "God has worn me out," said Job,

> He has torn me in his wrath and hated me . . . God gives me up to the ungodly and casts me into the hands of the wicked . . . Why do the wicked live . . . and grow mighty in power? Their offspring are established . . . Their houses are safe from fear . . . Why are not times of judgment kept by the Almighty? (Job 16:7–11; 21:7–9; 24:1)

And what about the notion of "certainty" that was said to be present in "God-confidence," but lacking in humanistic "self-confidence"? On what basis should we place our confidence in God? In light of Job's complaints, *God's trustworthiness is precisely the matter in question.* When a Christian

---

21. Jan Nattier, "Buddhist Eschatology," in *Oxford Handbook of Eschatology*, 161.

22. *Cullavagga* IX.i.4., quoted in ibid., 160.

23. Kant, "Miscarriage of All Philosophical Trials in Theodicy," in *Religion and Rational Theology*, 32–33.

projects forward to the hope of the resurrection and to the new creation inaugurated in the risen Christ, the problem of certainty is raised to an even higher pitch: why are some promised an inheritance in this renewed world, while others remain under the threat of eternal loss? If the cause for exclusion is placed on humanity—even if the determining point is as small as "making a decision for Christ"—God-confidence must give way to humanistic self-confidence. What will prevent me from faltering on that decision and thereby excluding myself?

But, if the ultimate choice is God's—if salvation is by grace alone—then doubt about God's trustworthiness remains. Why some and not others? Even if I did have the certainty that "God knows his elect," how can I entrust myself to a sovereign—to quote contemporary Kantian philosopher, Susan Neiman—"who judges many of the forms of life He created to be sinful, then tortures us eternally for our brief participation in them"? These "torments of the damned, even without the doctrine of predestination, are the block on which reason stumbles." And with predestination (whether "double" or "single"), "we are led to a system choked with evil so inscrutable that we turn to modern worldviews for relief."[24] On this scandal, we do not need a philosopher to make problems for us. A theologian will do just fine. It "cannot be comprehended," Martin Luther lamented, "how this God can be merciful and just" when "he saves so few and damns so many."[25]

To be fair to Schwarz, he also admitted that answers to these questions are beyond our comprehension: "We have to acknowledge the ultimate hiddenness of God, a God who is beyond justice and love. At this point we can only *hope* without *knowing* for sure that his never-ending grace will ultimately prevail."[26] Here he described "hope" as something we do when we do not know "for sure." That is, hope is operative when certainty is lacking. Or as Paul said, "Now hope that is seen is not hope. For who hopes for what he sees? But if we hope for what we do not see, we wait for it with patience" (Rom 8:24–25).

Schwarz did not explain how this insight coheres with his assumption that Christian hope is unique because it alone gives meaningfulness and certainty. If the Christian God's trustworthiness is contested, then the goal

---

24. Neiman, *Evil in Modern Thought*, 19–20.

25. Luther, "Bondage of the Will," in *Luther's Works: Career of the Reformer*, 33:62–63. One solution to this problem is the idea that God will ultimately make all people heirs of the new creation. Luther rejects this because it would cause us to disregard God's actual threats and promises in favor of our own wishful thinking (see ibid., 138–40). Schwarz also rejects a doctrine of "universalism" on similar grounds (see *Eschatology*, 387–404).

26. Schwarz, *Eschatology*, 396–97 (italics original).

set forward in his threats and promises is, for those addressed by him, still uncertain. And with the goal in question, the meaning offered by the Christian outlook is not a given, but a claim in need of validation. It makes more sense to say that when Christians trust the God of Jesus, they *anticipate* that their God will demonstrate himself to be trustworthy. Even Schwarz admitted, this "hoped-for and expected goal is not unambiguously demonstrated in its anticipation."[27] Like Paul, Christians today bear witness to contested claims that await final vindication. Christian hope—*like all other forms of hope*—does not proceed from certainty but *seeks* certainty.[28]

This conclusion brings us back to the driving question of this book: "How does Christian hope compare with other forms of hope?" The assumption that Christian hope is beyond compare because it alone provides meaningfulness and certainty has proven false. The problems inherent in our post-Constantinian situation are aggravated when Christians continue to assume that ours is the only show in town. There are powerful, coherent, and persuasive rivals. They complicate the church's efforts to offer a clear Christian witness while cooperating to seek a common good. These rivals struggle to maintain their own constituency. They also compete for the confidence and loyalty of Christian people. Not only are they still projected liturgically in theaters and stadiums every Sunday, they are now being streamed on-line, on-demand. This situation gives rise to the need for a comparative eschatology.

Assumption 2: Christian Hope Is Essentially Like Others

If Christian hope is not beyond compare, then what about the other assumption? Is the essence of Christian hope the same as human hope in general? Immanuel Kant thought so. He offered his perspective in *Religion within the Boundaries of Mere Reason*. Kant claimed that the essence of all historical religions, including Christianity, is identical. If we compared Christian hope with any other, we would find that they are essentially the same. A friend of mine tells me that he believes the Bible is a series of parables that teach the same basic truths found in other religions. He and Kant are like-minded in this regard. Kant asserted that he could

> start from some alleged revelation or other . . . and see whether it does not lead back to the same pure *rational system* of religion

---

27. Ibid., 382.

28. Bayer, *Theology the Lutheran Way*, 234n212, argued, "At the center of Luther's theology . . . is not the *fides quaerens intellectum* (faith seeking understanding) but the *tentatus quaerens certitudinem* (the person under attack seeking certainty)."

... If this is the case, then we shall be able to say that between reason and Scripture there is, not only compatibility but also unity, so that whoever follows the one (under the guidance of moral concepts) will not fail to come across to the other as well.[29]

Kant described the Christian faith as containing both "natural religion" and "learned religion."[30] Religion that needs to be learned cannot be deduced from human reason alone. It must be supernaturally revealed (or else, invented). And if this revelation were not "publically repeated," it would "disappear from the world." Therefore, word-of-mouth religion is "accidental"—contingent on particular historical events and actors. In contrast to this is *natural religion*, of which . . . every human being can be convinced through his reason." One who holds to natural religion does not necessarily deny the possibility of a true revelation from God (only a *"naturalist"* does that). He only denies that a revealed religion can be "universally communicable." Only natural religion holds a persuasive power that is effective on all people. This is because any human being *"could and ought to have* arrived at it on their own through the mere use of their reason." Therefore, it is possible for a historical religion to contain both what is natural and what is revealed. The former is *essential*, the latter is *nonessential*. Kant believed the Christian faith is such a religion. This, of course, makes the particular man Jesus, who was called Christ, dispensable. He is merely illustrative of a rational principle.

For Kant, the critical difference between natural and revealed religion—both of which express human hope—is that "through the use of reason," any human being "can be convinced" of a hope that is "natural." The same cannot be said for a hope that is revealed. However, a hope that is revealed, that is, received by word-of-mouth, need not be scrapped. It needs only to be husked to harvest the essence.

Two questions must be asked of this argument: On what basis does Kant claim that his account of hope can and ought to be accepted as true by any (reasonable) human being? And, why go to the trouble of convincing everyone in the first place?

To answer the first, Kant argued his account of hope was "universally communicable" because it was based on the ever-present, inner testimony of the moral law. The content of this law is the categorical imperative, which is functionally equivalent to Jesus' command: "whatever you wish that others would do to you, do also to them" (Matt 7:12—a kernel of natural

---

29. Kant, *Religion within the Boundaries of Mere Reason*, in *Religion and Rational Theology*, 64.

30. Ibid., 177–79. All of the quotations in this paragraph come from these pages.

religion within the husk of the revealed). But what if this supposed inner testimony of the moral law is merely an illusion? What if it is a contingent claim no more valid than a reported revelation from God? It could be that we are motivated not by morals, but by mere survival: "Whatever we do is driven, one way or another, by the urge to perpetuate ourselves."[31] This is Susan Neiman's summary of "evolutionary psychology," which works out the anthropological implications of Charles Darwin's conclusions in *The Origin of Species*.

If Kant once claimed that rationality is the essence of religious hope, what will stop Darwinians from claiming that instinctive self-interest is the essence of so-called rational hope? Neiman, a present-day proponent of Kantian hope, answered: nothing will stop them. This is because both explanations work, "and as Kant has taught us, nothing can decide between them."[32] Evolutionary psychologists assume that it is "natural" for people to be determined by an unconscious urge to propagate the species. Kantians assume that altruistic behavior in conformity to a higher moral law is "natural" (or at least proper) for humans. Appeals to empirical data cannot decide between the two because "evidence" will be selected and interpreted according to the interpreter's assumptions. It "isn't a matter of evidence," said Neiman, "for the evidence works both ways."[33] And so "*What we are*," naturally, "is beside the point, here . . . What most matters . . . is *what we should be*." Neiman continued:

> Hence we ought to uphold whatever view of nature, and progress, best supports that. What's the minimum we need to believe about the goodness of the world in order to contribute to making it better? . . . Reason tells you to work for ideals whether or not you see your hopes take shape in reality. But if reality never answers, you will one day resign . . . Should that threaten, reason permits not a leap, just a step toward a very abstract faith . . . It's a step, not a leap, because we know just enough: We are as good as we need to be in order to act as if we are.[34]

Kant's hope is not blind optimism. He admitted that humanity has a "natural propensity to evil."[35] He does not think progress is inevitable, but only possible. This does not prove, but assumes humans, as free and rational beings, can rise above whatever hand nature has dealt. If we refuse to believe

---

31. Neiman, *Moral Clarity*, 266.
32. Ibid., 272.
33. Ibid., 283. Cf. Kant, *Religion*, 82.
34. Neiman, *Moral Clarity*, 286–87.
35. Kant, *Religion*, 83.

we are determined by biology, then we can improve ourselves. And if we can improve, then natural religion is our best bet for realizing this hope, according to Kant.[36]

To review, Kant's answer to our first question regarding the basis for claiming the universal communicability of his hope is this: morality-based hope can neither be proven nor disproven. The hope that proceeds from morality is a demand of pure, practical reason. Everyone in their right mind wants a world where people always treat others as they want to be treated. This answer leads to the second question we put to Kant: why do you want to convince everyone that this is the way things are?

Kant's answer: for the sake of unity, justice, and peace. Historical religion inevitably leads to "conflict."[37] Its demands are tribal and cannot create consensus. Kant's story of revealed religion is bleak: its "turmoil" has "wrecked the human race" and "still tears it apart." In Christianity's early days, it rendered many people "useless to the world," through asceticism. Others it blinded with "superstition." Then "the terrible voice of *orthodoxy* rose from the mouth of self-appointed canonical expositors of scripture, and this voice split the Christian world into bitter parties over opinions in matters of faith." Controversies inevitably led to "foreign wars" and "feuds among themselves." Even now, at the dawn of the Enlightenment, this strife "is kept from violent outbreaks only through political interest."

If this is the story of historical faith, then, clearly, our best hope is "the introduction of a pure religious faith, over which there can be no dissension of opinions."[38] Such faith is "an autonomous principle which is one and the same for all people."[39] The "moral predisposition in us" is the "foundation and . . . interpreter of all religion."[40] Therefore "the sacred narrative" of an historical religion like Christianity can be read as an extended parable, "a vivid representation" of its true object: "virtue." It should not be taught as a "profession of what God does or has done for our salvation," but only "in the interest of morality."[41] Biblical eschatology, according to Kant, does not anticipate historical events. Rather, it is

---

36. Cf. Bayer, *Theology the Lutheran Way*, "Kant's essay, *Religion* . . . [shows how] Reason . . . takes hold of history and draws on it; in any case, it tries to demonstrate its rationality" (195).

37. Kant, *Religion*, 146.

38. Ibid., 158–59.

39. Ibid., 153.

40. Ibid., 151.

41. Ibid., 160.

a beautiful ideal of the moral world-epoch brought about by the introduction of the true universal religion and *foreseen* in faith in its completion—one which we do not see *directly* in the manner of an empirical completion but *have a glimpse of* in the continuous advance and approximation toward the highest possible good on earth.[42]

Neiman offered a summary of Kant's hope: "progress is possible and it is up to individuals to make it actual."[43] This is not a proof drawn from the world of experience. It is a demand that reason places upon the world of experience.

For Kant, religion is an account of human hope. It answers the question, "For what may I hope?" Kant assumed that social and political unity is a project for which religion is a tool. And if hope is instrumental for a strong polity, then competing accounts of hope will need to be suppressed or subsumed in order to create unity. This insight was part of the rationale behind the "Constantinian synthesis." In one version of the "Constantinian synthesis," the primary method was the suppression of rivals. For example, affirmation of the Nicene Creed was required for citizenship in the empire; state-accredited censors blocked publications that disparaged basic teachings of Christianity. In other forms, what Yoder branded as "neo-Constantinianism,"[44] the primary method was to subsume rivals within a more-encompassing account. For example, hopes based on historical contingencies (e.g., events surrounding a first century Jew) can be reinterpreted and thereby co-opted to fit within an account that is supposedly natural and necessary. Both methods were employed to suppress and overcome rivals.

The two assumptions I've been addressing in this section are both at home within Constantinian thinking. The statement: "Christian hope has no rivals" is better understood as a social luxury often enjoyed by the Western church between 311 and 1963. It is not, as Schwarz assumed, a proposition established by Christianity's superior ability to offer certainty and meaning. Also, the statement "Christian hope is essentially like all others," has not been unquestionably demonstrated by empirical evidence or rational proof. Instead, it is an historically contingent argument formulated in eighteenth-century Europe to build consensus and unite competitors under a single vision. The first assumption is a luxury the post-Constantinian church can no longer afford. The second assumption, while not a proven fact, did produce an argument that was successful enough to unseat traditional Western

42. Ibid., 162–63 (italics original).
43. Neiman, *Moral Clarity*, 296.
44. Yoder, "Constantinian Sources," in *Priestly Kingdom*, 141–44.

Christianity from its position of social privilege and cultural authority. This reversal was effected by a gradual assimilation into that beatific vision Kant anticipated: "the victory of the good principle over the evil principle . . . in the founding of a Kingdom of God on earth."[45]

These factors contribute to making our situation today "post-Constantinian." They make the question "How does Christian hope compare to others?" an important question to ask, but a difficult one to answer. The difficulty arises from how key features of Christian hope were dissolved and recovered during the nineteenth and twentieth centuries.

As Kant predicted, the traditional Christian hope was dissolved during the neo-Constantinian reversal that began after the sixteenth and seventeenth centuries' so-called "wars of religion."[46] Christian eschatology's historical peculiarities—the return of Christ for final judgment, the resurrection of the body, and the life of the age to come—were subsumed within the optimism of the surrounding culture. For many, all that remained was the hope that things on earth were gradually getting better and that people went to heaven when they die. This critique about the dissolution of genuine Christian hope is common to current studies in Christian eschatology.[47]

The second aspect of the challenge to answering our question is often overlooked. After the peculiar features of Christian hope were rediscovered during the first half of the twentieth century, Christian discussions about eschatology mostly remained an in-house affair. Christian scholars have been less interested in comparing rival eschatologies and more interested in deciding what constituted their own. Even at the beginning of the twenty-first century, when an accomplished scholar like Hans Schwarz examined other worldviews, he still assumed that Christianity had no true rivals. The habit of Constantinian thinking is hard to break.

Now, almost two decades into the twenty-first century, as Christians struggle to consistently organize their lives—as the Apostle Paul did—around the crucified, risen, reigning, and returning Jesus of Nazareth, they do so, like Paul, surrounded by rival life-organizing forms of hope. Recently I was visiting with Wil, a ninety-year-old man from my congregation. "Pastor," he told me, "people are no longer asking the question, *What must I do to be saved?*" This faithful Christian man had spent many of his earlier years on evangelism teams that started with the assumption that most people hoped to be *saved* in the Christian sense of the word. Therefore, what they needed

---

45. Kant, *Religion*, 129–30.

46. See Cavanaugh, *Myth of Religious Violence*.

47. E.g., Wolfhart Pannenberg, "Modernity, History, and Eschatology," in *Oxford Handbook of Eschatology*, 495–97; Moltmann, *Coming of God*, 5–6.

was a *certain* hope in Jesus as opposed to an *uncertain* hope in something else, such as their own attempts at doing good or formal association with some Christian institution. The approach may have been well-suited for a time, but now, as Wil was nearing the end of his mortal life, he wanted to make sure his pastor knew that it no longer worked.

Having read this introduction, you may have concluded that what I am saying will make Christians *uncertain* of their hope. That is not my intent. I do, however, intend to challenge the Constantinian assumptions that have allowed Christians to see their hope as *uncontested*. For Christians to merely dismiss all rival forms of hope as *uncertain* is unhelpful. This approach leaves Christians uncritical of how rival life-organizing hopes offer alternative notions of salvation. If, as Wil observed, people aren't worried about being saved (in the Christian sense), Christian hope has not for them become uncertain. It has become meaningless—or laughable, like "zombie Jesus."

By critically comparing and contrasting Christian hope with its rivals, I intend to give a timely account of its meaningfulness. Along the way, in struggling with the problem of evil and the trustworthiness of God as Luther and Job did, we will unsettle what I consider a false certainty. But we will not leave it there. As a practicing Christian pastor, I am concerned, in an openly biased way, with what will ultimately make Christians *more* certain. I will advocate a hope that *seeks* certainty in Jesus of Nazareth as he is identified in the Christian Scriptures and confessed in the ecumenical creeds. Until he returns to resolve our conflict, Christians will continue to exercise their hope among rivals.

2

Comparing Eschatologies

How does Christian eschatology compare to others? A timely answer will require a conceptual approach that significantly differs from what has become typical. I argue that Christian eschatology should be understood as the resolution of conflict within an all-encompassing plot. This approach will enable Christian eschatology to be compared and contrasted with other eschatologies, whereas recent thinking in this field has been conducted in a sphere secluded from rival accounts.

In 1925, the State of Tennessee enacted legislation that made it unlawful "to teach any theory that denies the story of divine creation as taught by the Bible and to teach instead that man was descended from a lower order of animals."[1] This law prompted events leading to the bizarre and sensational "Monkey Trial" in the summer of 1925. John Scopes, the local high school biology teacher, was prosecuted and found guilty of violating the new law. He was fined $100. A year later the Tennessee Supreme Court reversed the decision on a technicality: the jury should have set the fine, not the judge. More significantly, after the case became a national sideshow, thirteen state legislatures with anti-evolution laws pending refrained from enacting them. Forty-three years later the U. S. Supreme Court ruled unconstitutional a similar law privileging the Christian story above other stories of the world.[2] The "Constantinian synthesis" was dissolving. Christians would need to be ready for a trial—and not necessarily as the prosecution.

---

1. Linder, "State v. John Scopes ("The Monkey Trial")," accessed at on Aug 18, 2016 at http://law2.umkc.edu/faculty/projects/ftrials/scopes/evolut.htm.

2. Ibid.

CHRISTIAN ESCHATOLOGY IN A POST-CONSTANTINIAN SITUATION

In this next section, I will review how present-day scholars have interpreted and contributed to the last 100 years of discussion on Christian hope. I intend to describe a consensus and demonstrate a pattern. I will frame the consensus as a *gain* and the pattern as a *deficiency*. In the second section, I will examine the work of several scholars who break with the pattern. Their insights will serve as a bridge to overcome the deficiency.

A Consensus and a Pattern

The consensus about Christian eschatology is that hope is integrated into all of the church's doctrine and practice. Furthermore, hope is held together in a tension, which has been inaugurated in the person and work of Jesus and the giving of his Spirit.[3] The pattern is that current studies in Christian eschatology tend to linger on the *internal use of attributes*.

Uses of Attributes. Here I am making the kind of distinction Immanuel Kant made in his *Introduction to Logic*. Kant reflected on how we are able to derive a picture of an object in our minds by conceptualizing its distinct features. Inversely, we can identify that object in front of us by recognizing those features. Kant referred to this practice as the "internal use of attributes."[4] The difference between *internal* and *external* does not denote two sets of attributes. It is the same plurality of features, but seen from a different perspective and identified for a different *use*. According to Kant, a "clear idea" is also a *distinct* idea when we are conscious "of the plurality" of attributes contained in it.[5] He considered attributes from the perspective of a "twofold use, either *internal* or *external*." The "*internal* use consists in *derivation*," which conceptualizes a thing itself "by means of attributes as ground of cognition." But, the external use "consists in *comparison*, inasmuch as by means of attributes we can compare one thing to another," that is, whole to whole.[6]

The following is an illustration of Kant's distinction. I will list some features of an object and you picture it in your mind: "grip, barrel, trigger,

---

3. See also Horton, *Covenant and Eschatology*, 5.
4. Kant, *Introduction to Logic*, 25. My use of Kant's logic is deliberate, demonstrating a Christian adaptation of a resource arising from a rival life-organizing story.
5. Ibid.
6. Ibid., 49.

clip, spring." Let's say you imagined a 9mm, Beretta Pistol. If so, you would have done it by considering a plurality of features in order to derive a clear conception of the particular object that consists of those features. That was an internal use of attributes. However, when I said, "grip, barrel, trigger, clip, spring," someone else may have imagined a spray nozzle attachment for a power washer.

Mentally place these two objects side by side to compare them: the pistol and the spray nozzle. We have now moved into the external use of attributes. As we compare one thing to another, whole to whole, it is more helpful to ask, "What problem does *this* object aim to solve as compared to *that* one? What kind of solution does it offer in contrast to that one? It is less helpful to ask, "How are their various parts compared?" When mentally comparing a pistol with a spray nozzle, it does not add much conceptual clarity to list features. Features alone might even lead you to confuse the one with the other. It would be more productive to compare the distinct *problems* each is offered to address: "violent crime" vs. "dirty car"; or, the *solutions* that each anticipates: "deterrent-by-lethal-force" vs. "grease-removal-by-pressurized-water-stream." When making an external use of attributes, we think of how each object fits into a different setting and sequence of events that begins with a problem and moves toward a solution.

Internal Use of Attributes. This distinction is helpful for understanding the current story told about Christian eschatology. Scholars today generally interpret the eschatological reflection that began with Albert Schweitzer's *The Quest for the Historical Jesus* and continued through Jürgen Moltmann's *Theology of Hope* as one-dimensional or unbalanced. In the last 40 years, effort was devoted to two tasks: synthesizing the various dimensions of Christian eschatology in order to derive a balanced whole; and analyzing the constituent parts in relation to the whole. The purpose for studying these *internal attributes* was to bring a balanced hope to bear on the life of the church. But as the church continues to find herself in a post-Constantinian situation, more work of a different kind is required.

Current studies in Christian eschatology focus on internal rather than external features—that is, on derivation, rather than comparison. Geoffrey Wainwright and Christoph Schwöbel are two authors who follow this pattern. Although Schwöbel wrote his essay 30 years after Wainwright, he essentially duplicates his method and conclusions. Schwöbel stated that the twentieth century was the "century of eschatology."[7] He used this phrase in the title of his essay, which served as a conclusion to a selection of proceedings from

---

7. Schwöbel, "Last Things First?," 217.

the conference of the "Society for the Study of Theology held at the University of Edinburgh in April, 1999."[8] Schwöbel's article is representative of many turn-of-the-century overviews of Christian eschatology.

The story Schwöbel and others tell transpires in at least three stages: *dissolution, discovery,* and *derivation*. The period of *dissolution* occurred mostly during the nineteenth century. During this time, the distinctive Christian hope was gradually lost amid the optimistic cultural outlook of enlightened Europeans and North Americans. This stage is significant because "Twentieth-century reflection on eschatology cannot be understood without the background of nineteenth-century views,"[9] well-represented by Kant's views summarized above.

The beginning of the second stage commenced around 1906, when Albert Schweitzer first published *The Quest for the Historical Jesus*.[10] This period of (re)*discovery* continued through the publication of Jürgen Moltmann's *Theology of Hope* in 1967. Various dimensions of the peculiar eschatology of the Christian faith were re-learned in this period but not yet fully synthesized into a complete whole. Schweitzer reminded us of the future and transcendent features of Jesus' apocalyptic message of the imminent Kingdom of God. Karl Barth, Rudolf Bultmann and C. H. Dodd, each in their particular ways, rediscovered the present-tense dimension—whether in the eternity of God, the ultimacy of the human consciousness, or in the already-accomplished ministry and deeds of the historical Jesus. Next, Oscar Cullmann, A. T. Robinson, and Walter Kreck synthesized the present and future aspects into a now-and-not-yet tension in the person of Jesus and in the completed, yet still future action of the Christ-event. Finally Teilhard de Chardin, Wolfhart Pannenberg, and Jürgen Moltmann balanced out an undue focus on the vertical or supra-historical dimension with their horizontal or historical emphasis on the transcendent power of the "future as the unifying perspective for all dimensions of reality."[11]

After the widespread impact of Moltmann's early writings, others began to work out the implications of this "turn to the future." Eschatology "after Moltmann"[12] initiated the third segment of the story: *derivation*. Schwöbel places himself in this stage by surveying the discoveries and selecting "lessons" in the interest of deriving the whole by keeping these antinomous attributes in a balanced-tension.[13] The synthesis is said to hold together in

8. Fergusson and Sarot, *Future as God's Gift*, ix.
9. Ibid., 220.
10. Cf. Moltmann, *Theology of Hope*, 37.
11. Schwöbel, "Last Things First?" 233.
12. See Volf, "After Moltmann," in Bauckham, *God Will Be All in All*, 233.
13. Voelz, *What Does This Mean?*, 253n10, used the term "antinomous" to describe

"the matrix of the Christ event."[14] Maintaining it will keep twenty-first century theologians from coming out of balance by succumbing to the fallacy of "*one-dimensional eschatologies.*"[15]

Schwöbel's essay follows a widespread pattern of critiquing the twentieth century's discoveries for how they singled out one feature of Christian hope, thus isolating it from the whole. Scholars in the last 40 years have generally understood their task *either* as synthesis (drawing these co-ordinate features into an aggregate) *or* as analysis (clarifying each constituent part in relation to the whole). Whether as a synthesis to re-construct a distinctly Christian hope or as an analysis of what was constructed, the focus has been on *internal attributes*. These are attributes employed for the derivation and maintenance of a complex whole.

Thirty years before Schwöbel authored his essay, Geoffrey Wainwright presented an overview of the period of eschatological rediscovery from Schweitzer to Moltmann.[16] The likeness between Wainwright's and Schwöbel's interpretations is striking. If the division between the periods of *discovery* and *derivation* is accepted as an apt description of twentieth-century reflection on hope, then Wainwright's *Eucharist and Eschatology* represents the turn to *derivation* in its early stages. Various forms of his *balanced-tension* approach are assumed by most scholars working to derive a distinct Christian eschatology.

In his preface Wainwright stated, "This book is one man's answer to the call at Aarhus in 1964 by the World Council of Churches . . . for a study of the eucharist in the eschatological perspective."[17] In part, the task was inspired by Western Theology's "rediscovery of the eschatological dimension of the gospel" in both "biblical and systematic theology."[18] He wanted to bring this eschatological awareness to bear on the church's understanding of the Eucharist. At the same time, he believed that reflection on the Eucharist could help balance out eschatology. Given the nature of his task,

---

how three distinct eschatological perspectives are held together in tension. They are the "inaugurated" or "proleptic eschatology" of the Synoptic Gospels and Acts, the realized-but-hidden eschatology of John's gospel and the realized-in-Christ eschatology of Paul. The term "antinomy" is helpful because it expresses the situation of two (or more) incongruous, but not contradictory explanations of a single state of affairs.

14. Schwöbel, "Last Things First?" 237.

15. Ibid., 238–41. Schwöbel includes other fallacies ("*misplaced continuities and discontinuities,*" "*premature temporalisation*" and "*moralisation*" of eschatology), all of which he describes as "one-dimensional" in some way.

16. Wainwright, *Eucharist and Eschatology*, 7.

17. Ibid., Preface, vii.

18. Ibid., 5–7.

synthesizing and analyzing the findings during the period of rediscovery was a necessary first step.

As Wainwright reviewed nearly all of the authors mentioned by Schwöbel (and many others not mentioned), he developed some constitutive concepts. First, there was the idea of "realization," which addresses the question: to what extent did Jesus' first advent, ministry, death, and resurrection establish and fulfill the promised reign of God?[19] One answer to this question was offered by Oscar Cullmann, with the concept of *Heilsgeschichte*, or "salvation history."[20] This approach described the Reign of God as arriving over the course of time and moving progressively from a foundational, but contestable status (in Israel, Jesus and the church) to a manifestly incontestable status (in the second advent of Jesus).

Wainwright referred to Cullmann's approach as the "horizontal" model because it presents "a *purely* linear conception of the relation between present and future." He claims that it needs to be off-set by "the more 'spatial' image of an eternal heavenly kingdom *on high*," that is, by the "vertical" model. In the vertical model, the dialectic between divine eternity and creaturely temporality is dominant. In the horizontal model, the dialectic is mainly between the "already-now" and the "not yet." Both dimensions are needed: "The eternal invades time in a moment, the supernatural breaks into the natural, the heavenly bursts upon the earthly scene" (vertical). Nevertheless, "time goes on: the *parousia* of Christ is still awaited, we are not yet in our resurrection bodies, the perfect community does not yet rejoice together in the unclouded vision of God" (horizontal).[21] By way of conclusion, Wainwright advocated a dynamic tension between the two: "'Vertical' categories . . . are a necessary aid to expressing the eschatological tension, but they must not be allowed to displace the 'horizontal' from the picture."[22]

Wainwright's work to derive a well-balanced eschatology has become paradigmatic. Analysis of the constituent parts gleaned from the period of rediscovery aimed to recognize the synthesized whole and apply it to all facets of life. Gerhard Sauter's research in *What Dare We Hope?* reproduced the approach of both Wainwright and Schwöbel, but with increased intensity.

Sauter discussed three "storms" during the twentieth century rediscovery. The first was *konsquente* (or consistent) *Eschatologie*, which Schweitzer attributed to the immediate apocalyptic (and from Schweitzer's perspective, failed) expectation of the historical Jesus. The second began after the First

---

19. Ibid., 9.
20. Cullmann, *Christ and Time*, 27.
21. Wainwright, *Eucharist and Eschatology*, 13–14.
22. Ibid., 15.

World War with Barth and Bultmann's *radical eschatology*, which had no expectation for the future, but looked only to the eternal present. The third began after World War II, with Moltmann and Pannenberg's *theology of history*, which appealed to the meaning of Jesus' resurrection as the key for reinterpreting history along the lines of proleptic hope.[23] A central contention of *konsequent Eschatologie* is that hope manifests itself by ethical action *within* history.[24] Central for the radical type is that Christian hope comes from *beyond* history—from the eternal God, who is qualitatively (vertically) distant and close to all times.[25] And for eschatology as theology-of-history, it is that Christian hope *for* history means Christians can identify God's work of renewal within history (horizontally). Looking to the future of the risen Christ, they can help it along the way.[26] Faced with irreconcilable differences between these accounts of Christian hope, Sauter resolved to keep them in tension by placing them in dialogue. This is because "they do not rule each other out. Each has a corrective effect on the others."[27]

Hans Schwarz's *Eschatology* also reproduces the derivation-through-balanced-tension approach, with no less rigor than Sauter. Accounting for all of the contentions in Sauter's three "storms," Schwarz first assumes the connection between hope and ethical action; second, he maintains that Christian hope springs from the eternal God; and third, that Christians have been freed to participate in God's work within history.[28] As he surveys a dozen approaches to eschatology, he strives to be "neither exclusively individualistic nor exclusively otherworldly in orientation." This is achieved only "in continuous tension between concern for the individual and the community . . . between this world and the world to come."[29]

The pattern in Schwöbel, Wainwright, Sauter, and Schwarz can be observed throughout the various quarters of Christian theology. Here are six examples: (1) From a German-speaking *Roman Catholic* perspective in 1977, (pope-emeritus) Joseph Ratzinger stated that "the task of contemporary eschatology" is "to marry perspectives, so that the person and the community, present and future, are seen in their unity."[30] This means that "we need to integrate the opposing elements in the light of the Christian center,

---

23. Sauter, *What Dare We Hope?* 25.
24. Ibid., 40–41.
25. Ibid., 97–108.
26. Ibid., 9, 17–18.
27. Ibid., 22.
28. Schwarz, *Eschatology*, xiii.
29. Ibid., 128n59.
30. Ratzinger, *Eschatology*, 12.

to strike a fair balance."³¹ (2) From a *Black American* perspective in 1982, Gayraud Wilmore likewise advocated a "balancing viewpoint," which brings these contrasting perspectives "together in a mutually corrective way."³² Then he offered "the central paradox of black eschatology" as instructive for maintaining this view: "The authentic faith of the black folk community brought together this world and the next in a creative tension . . . the ecstasy of a vision of paradise at one moment, and in the next it drove believers into the streets to give that vision material actuality."³³ (3) From a French-speaking *Eastern Orthodox* perspective in 1986, Boris Bobrinskoy spoke of an "inaugurated" eschatological perspective in the liturgy and the Eucharist, citing Alexander Schmemann and John Zizioulas, "The eucharistic liturgy actualizes this eschatological presence of Christ." Bobrinskoy viewed the *eschaton* in both its "qualitative as well as its linear content."³⁴ These mirror Wainwright's vertical and horizontal models. These two dimensions of the *eschaton* are held in tension in the church "through the blessed and painful alternations of [Christ's] absence, His expectation, His coming, His presence in the Eucharist."³⁵ Thus, the ancient Eucharistic prayer *Maranatha* (1 Cor 16:22) is simultaneously "expectation," "announcement," and "realization."³⁶ (4) From a *Confessional Lutheran* perspective in 1993, John Stephenson argued that the "Book of Concord does justice to the themes of both inaugurated and realized eschatology."³⁷ (5) From a *Hispanic* perspective in 1996, Justo González echoed Bobrinskoy's eschatological insights on Christian worship: "Latino worship is a fiesta. It is a celebration of the mighty deeds of God . . . Our people . . . celebrate God's future in the midst of an oppressive and alienating present."³⁸ (6) From a *Reformed-Evangelical* perspective in 2004, Russell Moore examined the "new eschatological consensus . . . reflected in systematic projects that span the ideological fissures of contemporary evangelical theology." This comes from the general agreement on an "inaugurated eschatology" grounded in an "already/not yet" view of the reign of Christ.³⁹

31. Ibid., 15.
32. Wilmore, *Last Things First*, 53.
33. Ibid., 88.
34. Bobrinskoy, *Mystery of the Trinity*, 168–69.
35. Ibid., 172–73.
36. Ibid., 188.
37. Stephenson, *Eschatology*, 29.
38. González, "Hispanic Worship," 20, 22.
39. Moore, *Kingdom of Christ*, 37.

Examples of this "eschatological consensus" mentioned by Moore could be cited *ad nauseam*.[40] This holds not only for systematic theology, but is also a theme in New Testament exegetical studies.[41] After the "century of eschatology," just about everything that *could* be said *has been* said. For eschatology "after Moltmann," during the period of *derivation*, the goal was to keep everything in balance—making room for the vertical dimension without crowding out the horizontal; embracing a realized hope, but not *over*-realized, with *both* continuity *and* discontinuity; neither succumbing to premillennial despair nor postmillennial presumption; keeping one eye on personal implications and the other on ecological and cosmic implications; emphasizing God's action *as well as* human participation. And the list goes on.

The strength of the balanced-tension approach is its comprehensive coverage. It is well-suited for appreciating the plurality within Christian hope and maintaining this complex whole. But, in terms of answering the question (What is distinct about Christian hope compared to others?), it is deficient. Listing features does not help compare and contrast Christian hope with its rivals. A different approach—one that focuses on the *external use of attributes*—is needed.

Consensus. To construct this approach, I will draw on a consensus about two critical internal attributes highlighted from the period of *derivation*. Both are mentioned by Richard Bauckham in his interpretation of Moltmann's eschatology.[42] More recently, Bauckham restated these in the conclusion to the *Oxford Handbook of Eschatology*. Any "Christian eschatology in the twenty-first century that aims at faithfulness to the theological heart of the gospel . . . is likely to show these characteristics."[43] They are "Christological" and "integrative" eschatology. The first has to do with the "Christological foundation and criterion of Christian hope," which is "contested by few who write intentionally Christian eschatology."[44] The second has to do with the "holistic vision of redemption and transfiguration for the whole of God's creation."[45] This integration of creation, Christology, and final redemption

---

40. E.g., part 2 of *Oxford Handbook of Eschatology*, "Eschatology in Distinct Christian Traditions and Theological Movements," 215–339, where every essayist invokes some form of the "now" and "not yet" tension.

41. See Frey, "Introduction," in *Eschatology of the New Testament*, 28.

42. Bauckham, *God Will Be All in All*, 1–34.

43. Richard Bauckham, "Conclusion," in Walls, *Oxford Handbook of Eschatology*, 672.

44. Ibid.

45. Ibid, 673.

is what makes the Christian account of the world "a comprehensive story, encompassing all other stories, with an ending that will be the common ending of all stories."[46] In the sense of being integrative, eschatology is no longer seen as the loosely-attached appendix of Christian doctrine, but as its medium or character.[47] This aspect of the consensus can be detected by taking note of how often contemporary scholars in all fields use the adjective "eschatological" to describe Christian homiletics,[48] sacraments,[49] ethics,[50] politics,[51] and nearly everything else.[52]

A Bridge to Overcome the Deficiency

I offered the preceding discussion on the state of Christian eschatology to demonstrate a consensus and illustrate a pattern. By claiming that recent scholarship has settled into a pattern of applying the internal use of attributes, I am not claiming that all scholars limit their inquiries in this way. In fact, the external use of attributes in the study of Christian hope is a minor theme along with the major emphasis of deriving and maintaining the balanced whole.[53] This minor theme is a timely candidate for initiating the next stage in the story of Christian eschatology since the nineteenth century: dissolution, discovery, derivation, *comparison*.

The dissolution of Christian hope within the currents of nineteenth century optimism can be understood in relation to the larger flow of the "Constantinian synthesis." When it ran dry, Christians labored to re-conceptualize the distinctive features of biblical hope. This was and remains an important task. But now this re-conceptualized hope must find its way amid a plurality of other views. An internal focus, which simply poses Christian questions and offers Christian answers, will not help the church respond to

46. Ibid., 679.

47. Bauckham's use of the term "integrative" focuses on holding together creation and redemption. My use includes Bauckham's, but also Schwöbel's more expansive use, when he speaks of the need for eschatology to be "integrated into the doctrinal scheme of Christianity," which helps "avoid the dangers of an isolated treatment of eschatology" and "consists in developing a Christian eschatology as a trinitarian eschatology," Schwöbel, "Last Things First," 238.

48. Long, "Preaching God's Future," 191–202.

49. Just, *Heaven on Earth*.

50. McClendon, *Ethics*, vol. 1 of *Systematic Theology*, 242–75.

51. Yoder, *Original Revolution*, 60–64, 83.

52. Peter C. Phan, "Roman Catholic Theology," in Walls, *Oxford Handbook of Eschatology*, 217–18.

53. See Walls, "Introduction," in *Oxford Handbook of Eschatology*, 4.

the "post-Constantinian situation." An external perspective, which places one hope-generating account alongside another, is more likely to yield the conceptual resources needed for our present context. The work of several scholars has touched on the task of comparative eschatology. Their insights will form a bridge to overcome the deficiency.

Toward an External Use. There is a common but too often passing reference to the external use of attributes in discussions of Christian eschatology. The hope of Christianity is regularly contrasted against the hope of "escape" and the hope of "progress."[54] Another common reference, which we noted in Schwarz's account, is the "cyclical" versus "linear" view of time and the worldviews with which they coordinate.[55] These comparisons are frequently made, but not explored in depth. At times they simply serve as another segue into more statements about the need to maintain an internal tension. And so it is said that the idea of escape contains too much "vertical dimension" and "discontinuity." Or, that the idea of progress is "over-realized" eschatology and doesn't leave enough room for the "transcendent" dimension.[56] Less often are these ideas perceived as representing incommensurate, conflicting accounts of the world.

Eschatological Rationalities. As mentioned in the prior section, Gerhard Sauter was a major figure during the period of *derivation* after Moltmann's *Theology of Hope*. His book *What Dare We Hope?* is a well-rounded synthesis of the "three waves" of (re)discovery during the outset of the twentieth century. It is an in-depth analysis of the plurality of features found in Christian hope. While this work mainly employs internal attributes, his book *Eschatological Rationality,* especially the last chapter, gives a nod toward the external use of those attributes.

Reflecting the consensus on "integrative eschatology," Sauter links hope with the theological enterprise as a whole. Eschatology is discourse about the final future God has decided to give in Christ. It "provides an exemplary opportunity for extracting basic determinations of what theology is from the inner structure of theological statements."[57] One such vital statement is from 2 Corinthians 1:20: "For all the promises of God find their Yes in [Jesus]. That is why it is through him that we utter our Amen to God

---

54. E.g, Moltmann, *Coming of God*, 45–46; 58–62; also, N. T. Wright, *Surprised By Hope*, 79–88.

55. E.g., Löwith, *Meaning in History*. See also, Wilkinson, *Christian Eschatology*, 7.

56. Richard Bauckham, "Conclusion," in Walls, *Oxford Handbook of Eschatology*, 679.

57. Sauter, *Eschatological Rationality*, 173.

for his glory." Sauter believes that this is "a key proposition . . . in Christian theology." It is so because it states that all faithful orientation toward God is directed toward his promises fulfilled in Jesus. The church responds, "Amen"—"this is the way it is and no other."[58] The concept "promise" is not merely God's future-oriented word, but God's "Christ-oriented word." And "promise" becomes "the basic category of faith."[59] The hope of faith is oriented towards God's past, present, and future action in Jesus. Therefore, while Christian theology does indeed have eschatology as but one of its many *loci*, even more so, the Christian way of life is itself eschatological:

> To exist theologically is to be a person under the promise and in expectation of new life. Under this promise one is called, one is inserted into the situation before God that is opened up by God's condemning and saving judgment. One is inserted into the hidden history of Jesus Christ in the world. That *is* the living space in which our being human is "located" and "takes place." "For you died, and your life is hidden with Christ in God." (Colossians 3:3)[60]

This new eschatological situation before God means that Christians think and speak with a "special semantic incommensurability (*Gebrochenheit*) peculiar to [their] hope." Therefore "translation" of Christian "promissory concepts" (e.g., justice, peace, life) will not seek to make Christian thought and speech "plausible" to other culturally developed forms of thought and speech.[61] In his conclusion, Sauter briefly gestured toward the *external use* of this plurality of features. Because of its "semantic incommensurability," Christian theology "has stood from the beginning in the middle of other religions, other ways of believing, other hopes. Thus it cannot be understood as one . . . stage of development in the history of religion, or as an . . . optimal . . . realization of the possibilities of 'religion' in general." All of this is because of the "contingency of God's act in Jesus Christ."[62]

Once more we see the consensus about Christian hope's unique, internal attributes: it is integrated and Christological. God's plan for creation is centered on this first century Jew. He is indispensable. These same attributes have external implications. They constitute a unique and holistic way of being human—a peculiar, "eschatological rationality" that is fundamentally incommensurate with other rationalities.

58. Ibid., 173.
59. Ibid., 174.
60. Ibid., 197–98.
61. Ibid., 176–77.
62. Ibid., 198–99.

Where Sauter glanced, Moltmann had turned and explored. In his ground-breaking *Theology of Hope*, I find a clear departure from the patterned use of internal attributes in Christian eschatology. Unfortunately, Moltmann is too quickly dismissed by recent synthesizing scholarship as one-dimensional. His early work is placed in its 1960s historical context with the challenge posed by neo-Marxism in post-war Europe. His theology is said to diminish the transcendent or vertical dimension in service to what is immanent, horizontal, and historical.[63] While this may be true to some degree, his work can also serve as a good example of the external use of attributes to compare Christian hope with other forms of hope.

Incompatible Modes of Experience. In *Theology of Hope*, Moltmann contrasts between the "god" of the "eternal present" and the "God of promise."[64] These claimants for deity draw their followers into a "process of struggle between two mutually incompatible forms of faith."[65] The first offers security through contact with the transcendent ground of reality-as-is. It is derived "entirely" from the "thought forms of the Greek mind" and is manifested in the "transcendental eschatology" of Kant, Barth, and Bultmann. This thinking, according to Moltmann, is not a balancing agent on behalf of the vertical realm. Rather, it is at total odds with the "language of promise."[66] The God of promise is the God of exodus and resurrection, who "announces the coming of a not yet existing reality" from the future of the crucified and risen Jesus of Nazareth.[67]

For Moltmann, transcendental eschatology, which offers no "goal of history," but only the "goal of the individual human being," is not merely a one-sided, incomplete exposition of Christian hope. Instead, it is the "self-surrender of the faith."[68] The same can be said for the "scientific and technological millenarianism" of the "modern age (*Neuzeit*)," which "seeks the end of history in history." Theses rivals generate a distinct kind of hope that "could either regard this world as itself the fulfillment, or else in gnostic fashion transcend [it] into the supra-worldly realm."[69] This is because "world-picture and faith are inseparable"—the "very mode of our experience of the world is not adiaphorous."[70]

63. E.g., Sauter, *What Dare We Hope?* 132–38.
64. Moltmann, *Theology of Hope*, 30–31.
65. Ibid., 96.
66. Ibid., 41–46.
67. Ibid., 84–85.
68. Ibid., 62, 41.
69. Ibid., 92–94.
70. Ibid., 69.

Even if some of Moltmann's arguments are questioned by scholars who have interpreted his work, his external use of the distinctive features of Christian hope is instructive for the task of comparative eschatology. His contrast between Greek or gnostic "escapist" eschatology and Modernity's "progressive" eschatology—each differentiated from Christian eschatology—helps us conceptualize a line between *derivation* and *comparison*. At some point, we can no longer hold antinomous attributes in tension. Recognizing this line, it makes little sense to take the "vertical" and "discontinuity" elements in the hope for escape along with the "horizontal" and "continuity" elements in hope for progress and then synthesize them into an amalgam called "Christian hope." Moltmann's difference in *Theology of Hope* is evident in the distinction between the internal and external use of attributes—that is, in the difference between deriving the whole versus comparing one whole to another.

The Provisional Nature of Truth. Pannenberg is another important exception to the pattern. As seen in Schwöbel's essay, Moltmann and Pannenberg are often grouped together under the category of "theology of history" or future-directed eschatology.[71] Pannenberg's use of eschatology's external attributes will complete the bridge from the current focus on deriving a balanced, internal tension to a comparison of rival eschatologies. When Moltmann compared attributes of rival eschatologies in *Theology of Hope*, he contrasted finding hope in the structures, resources, and powers already discernibly present in reality (a feature common to both escapist and progressive hopes) against finding hope in the promise of the still-outstanding future of the crucified and risen Jesus (the distinctive feature of Christian hope, according to Moltmann). Pannenberg, in his *Systematic Theology*, likewise contrasted the Christian God of promise against the Greek notion of an "eternal present behind the flux of time." The latter seeks the "true" behind or above the transience of historical life. The former waits for it *in spite of* the contingency of time. Both are peculiar forms of hopeful faith.[72]

Drawing on Luther's notion as to how "faith in the heart" makes either God or an idol, Pannenberg described the necessity of faith as the "ec-centric form of human life." This means that we all must come to "rest on something outside ourselves. We have no choice. We can only choose on what to rest."[73] And, because all people experience reality as a ceaseless flow of events, we continually live in "anticipation of the totality of the

---

71. For the first, see Sauter, *What Dare We Hope?* For the second, see Braaten and Jenson, *The Futurist Option*.

72. Pannenberg, *Systematic Theology*, vol. 1, 54, 177–88.

73. Ibid., 113.

truth which will be complete only in the future."[74] Even those who seek an eternal present beyond time must wait for the truth of this orientation to be validated in the course of time. Every form of ec-centric resting is always historical and provisional. History becomes the field of religious rivalry as "the gods of the religions must show in our experience . . . that they are the powers which they claim to be."[75]

According to Pannenberg, *all* truth claims are eschatological, not just Christianity's.[76] This is the case in the sense that every account of the world is subject to a "not yet." An over-arching eschatological proviso gives rise to the preliminary and provisional character of all truth.[77] What Christian hope has in common with other forms of hope is that it must await either its ultimate disappointment or vindication.[78] This "Not Yet . . . implies a brokenness of the knowledge of revelation in the context of ongoing debatability and the power of doubt that constantly assails believers."[79] The difference of Christian hope is that it is based on the expectation that "the God of the Bible will prove himself to be the one God of all people." This is identical to the confession that he "has already shown himself to be this one God in Jesus Christ."[80] Pannenberg's external use of attributes reaches further than Sauter's and Moltmann's. His work exemplifies how Christian hope can be compared and contrasted with others.

A CASE FOR COMPARING ESCHATOLOGIES

Why compare Christian hope with others? Moltmann's comment that "world-picture and faith are inseparable" helps say why. Our era is marked by a "conflict of interpretations" about the way things go in the world.[81] To accept a particular interpretation, to allow this account to become a source of meaning and hope, is "to have a god." This is how Luther explained faith in *The Large Catechism*.[82] Or, as Moltmann said, the "very mode of our experience of the world" is not a matter indifferent to the Christian faith.

---

74. Ibid., 253.
75. Ibid., 167.
76. See also Ladrière, *L'espérance de la raison*, 118–23.
77. Pannenberg, *Systematic Theology*, vol. 1, 116, 158.
78. Ibid., 331.
79. Ibid., 250.
80. Ibid., 196.
81. Bayer, "Theology in the Conflict of Interpretations," 495.
82. Kolb and Wengert, *Book of Concord*, 386, 388.

To compare eschatologies is to get at the heart of what differentiates rival accounts. Our ability to grasp the coherence and meaning offered in them is obscured by the Constantinian kinds of assumptions we encountered in the introduction. Pannenberg's point about the provisional nature of all truth addresses the assumption that the Christian hope is unrivaled. All claims about what is true in the present have implications for what can be said about the future. Regardless of whether someone calls these claims "optimistic" or "pessimistic," they are *eschatological* because they make truth claims that presently reside within a conflict of interpretations and await either vindication or disappointment.

In this sense, Christian hope is not unique. It is like all others. However, to admit a common provisional *status* is not the same as assuming a common, essential *content* or *character*. Sauter's concept of "eschatological rationality" makes this point against the second assumption. It is not that Christian hope contains rational elements common to all and irrational elements unique to its tradition. It is not that the Enlightenment sorted out the truly rational hopes from the arbitrary ones. Rather, Christianity has its own sort of rationality, just as Immanuel Kant had his peculiar eschatological rationality. "It is not 'the' pure reason that comes to an understanding of itself in the *Critique of Pure Reason*, but Immanuel Kant from Königsberg who writes and evaluates."[83]

Constantinian thinking keeps us from seeing these matters clearly. As with the venerable Tennessee lawmakers of 1925, it can lead Christians to presume theirs is the only show in town. At the same time, it leaves Christians ignorant of how rival accounts lay claim to their loyalty. The internal/external attributes distinction was a rather technical way of describing the shift in thinking Christians need to respond to the conceptual demands of a post-Constantinian situation. One does not adequately respond to these demands by an exclusive use of attributes internal to Christianity. This is because it gives the impression that a "balanced tension" between the "now" and the "not yet" is what distinguishes Christian hope. When this impression becomes a default position, it will always yield the same formal diagnosis of opposing eschatologies: they are "unbalanced."

A comparative approach to eschatology illuminates the distinctive, external attributes of other accounts of hope. It neither identifies them as Christian heresies to be corrected, nor as complementary dimensions to be synthesized. Instead, it presents them as coherent, competing accounts. Doing so, it enters into a critical and respectful dialogue with those who

---

83. Bayer, *A Contemporary in Dissent*, 68. This is Bayer's interpretation of Hamann's response to Kant's work. Hamann was a friend and critic of Kant.

offer them. This will introduce new challenges for eschatologies constructed primarily to answer Christian questions, which fewer and fewer North Americans are asking. At the same time, the dialogue can equip Christians to bear witness to Christ when called to stand on trial for their hope.

3

Eschatology and Story

I DROVE BY THAT construction site over the course of several months. It was difficult to detect any progress. Seeing the caverns the backhoes were carving into the ground, I concluded it was an ambitious project. Yet for most of the winter, it looked like a giant mud hole. But, once the foundation work was complete, the steel, concrete, and brick walls went up quickly.

This next chapter is foundation work. I recount the depth of the footings, the dimensions of the rebar, the hardness of the concrete, and the spacing for the fasteners. The main thesis is this: *comparing eschatological hopes entails comparing life-organizing stories.*

Thus far, I have made a case for Christians to engage in comparative eschatology. The Constantinian synthesis has dissolved. Christians daily encounter other forms of hope—whether that of traditional religions, secular philosophies, or the amalgam that is Western spirituality. Lingering Constantinian assumptions can lead Christians to dismiss other hopes outright (our hope is beyond compare). Or they might allow for Christian hope to be dissolved into a general optimism (our hope is like any other). Against the first assumption, I argued that Christian hope is not beyond compare, because it shares a common provisional status. Like others, its claimants are not yet certain. They are on trial and await vindication. Against the second, I framed Kant's account of a common rational core of hope as part of a "neo-Constantinian" strategy aimed to achieve social unity and political peace without biblical, creedal, and confessional Christianity. This project was *not* based on case-closed "facts" about human nature or the origin of species. But it was a persuasive argument, which contributed to the dissolution of a distinctly Christian hope during the nineteenth century. Studies in the field of Christian eschatology have since focused on the rediscovery and derivation of this peculiar Christian hope. However, more needs to be said about how it compares and contrasts with others. Kant stated that the whole of *Religion* is concerned with answering the question, "What may I hope?"[1] My approach to eschatology assumes post-Constantinian Christians must also ask another question "How does our hope compare with others?"

Comparing hopes entails comparing stories. Not just any stories, but the stories that shape human lives. Every person, in as much as he or she lives in a society and wants to make some sense of the world, inhabits a *life-organizing story*. People grow to interpret their lives in terms of what they come to find ultimately desirable and undesirable. They evaluate experiences by how these come into conflict or approach harmony with their desires. A life-organizing story offers a plotline projected toward a future in which resolution is expected. Hope for a *resolution of conflict* in a life-story is the kind of hope I intend to analyze. I will do so by comparing the Christian story with other stories of the world. To compare Christian eschatology with other eschatologies is to compare how the conflict resolves within a given life-organizing story.[2]

Narratively defined, *eschatology is discourse on how the conflict resolves within an all-encompassing plot*. Therefore, the purpose of this chapter is to present and defend "story" as a notion for comparing eschatologies. Along the way, I take up the notion of a "speech act," which I will use to characterize the storied hope of Christians and to distinguish between rival stories.

In my defense of *story* as means to compare eschatological hopes, I address two objections, one nearer to the Christian tradition and one further from it. The first objection is voiced by German-born, New Testament scholar and historian, Rudolf Bultmann (1884–1976). Bultmann would argue that my approach to comparing Christian eschatology with others is mistaken. From his perspective, the essence of Christianity does not depend on any particular story or worldview. For Bultmann, the key to understanding the Christian hope is not the Christian story as narrated in the Bible. The key is present-moment proclamation in the name of Christ. Thus, the story must be "demythologized" for the sake of meaningful proclamation today.

My method for responding to Bultmann will be to show that his notion of proclamation still assumes some life-organizing story. It's just not the plotline given by the narratives of the New Testament. This response

---

1. Kant, *Logik*, accessed March 8, 2013, http://www.textlog.de/kant-logik-philosophie-0.html.

2. Cf. Francis Clooney, "Comparative Theology," in Webster, Tanner, and Torrance, *Oxford Handbook of Systematic Theology*, 654; and Tilley, *Story Theology*, xix.

follows from my basic assumption that where human hope is concerned, story is inescapable. I will conclude that Bultmann takes up a different hope by inhabiting a different story. Since I am following my assumption to its conclusion, this will not be a direct argument against Bultmann. But, by engaging the issues that occupy him as a theologian, I intend to show that his concern for proclamation can be met from within the Christian story, thus making his demythologizing program unnecessary.

After addressing Bultmann's objection, I consider another attempt to transcend stories. This objection to my approach comes from the Enlightenment tradition. Like the Christian one, this tradition is diverse and contains conflicting schools of thought. For now, I will simplistically account for the tradition as a whole by the way it tried to transcend the stories and myths of pre-modern peoples. My response to this tradition will parallel my response to Bultmann. The Enlightenment did indeed transcend the stories of pre-modern peoples. But, it did so by telling another story—one that was thought to be better because it discarded "self-imposed immaturity"[3] in favor of real hope.

I reframe Bultmann and the Enlightenment in terms of the stories they tell in order to show how they offer hope to those who inhabit them. These hopes are different from Christian hope not because they are more or less meaningful, factual, or certain. They are different because they arise out of rival life-organizing stories. They can be compared to the Christian hope, because it too is a storied hope. It arises from the resolution anticipated by the story centered on Jesus of Nazareth, recorded in the Bible and confessed in the ecumenical creeds.

LIFE-AND-WORLD-ORGANIZING STORIES

What, if anything, does Christian hope have in common with other forms of hope? A life-organizing story[4] is an appropriate concept not only for understanding the external character of Christian hope, but also for comparing it with other eschatological hopes. Inasmuch as people inhabit a life-organizing story, they take up an eschatological hope. Therefore, to compare the Christian hope with others is at the same time to compare the story of Jesus-in-Israel-and-the-Church[5] with other stories of the world.

---

3. Kant, "Was ist Aufklärung?," 145.

4. Cf. Hays, *Faith of Jesus Christ*, 18–19, "Paul's gospel *is* a story, and it *has* a narrative structure, but it is not *a* narrative except when it is actually narrated, as in Phil 2:6–11."

5. Cf. Jenson, *Story and Promise*, 3–12.

The Narrative Character of Christian Faith

Recall the consensus about the internal features of Christian eschatology. It was said to be both "Christological" and "integrative." This means that the Christian convictions about the sequence of events from creation to the eschaton are integrated together in the person of Jesus. As Richard Bauckham said, the Christian account is treated as "a comprehensive story, encompassing all other stories." Its anticipated ending is held to "be the common ending of all stories."[6] This observation is also at home in what has come to be called "narrative theology." Robert Robinson called it "a broad and disparate movement" marked by a "unifying appreciation for the ability of narrative to present the relationship between God and man" in a "fitting" way.[7] What is meant by "narrative" is a set of events organized along a temporal frame and a spatial setting. These events are linked together in a "plot." A narrative moves forward with the intertwining of plot and character so that action reveals character and character advances plot. Characters and plot move forward until the conflict is resolved. It is this resolution of conflict that finally makes the story.[8]

In addition to the narrative features of setting, character, and plot, Gabriel Fackre noted the role of author or narrator. It is the "narrator," who "self-consciously" controls the vision "in which the flow of events becomes a plot, and participants become characters in a storyline made by conflict and moving toward resolution." In the Christian account of the world, the author, and narrator, who "gives this overall signification is, finally God."[9] Fackre also observed that "the hope theologies of Moltmann" and others are "variations on the narrative theme of biblical faith."[10] And so another way to perceive the twentieth century's insights on Christian hope is to see them within a broader consensus about the narrative character of the Christian faith.[11] Christian doctrine contains the locus eschatology and is itself eschatological because Christians tell a story which anticipates a resolution. They claim it as *the* story. Its world-plot is moving toward an *eschaton* that has proleptically occurred in the crucified and risen Jesus.[12]

---

6. Richard Bauckham, "Conclusion," in Walls, *Oxford Handbook of Eschatology*, 679.

7. Robinson, "Narrative Theology," 689–93.

8. Cf. McClendon, *Ethics*, vol. 1 of *Systematic Theology*, 328–56.

9. Fackre, *Christian Story*, 5.

10. Ibid., 6.

11. See David Ford, "System, Story, Performance," in Hauerwas and Jones, *Why Narrative?* 191–215.

12. See Jenson, *Story and Promise*, 110–13.

The Narrative Quality of Experience

The influence of the concept of "story" has reached beyond the bounds of Christianity. A cross-disciplinary consensus on the "narrative quality of experience"[13] in general recommends story as a suitable mode of comparison between Christian hope and other forms of hope. In 1981, Alasdair MacIntyre, in his well-known book *After Virtue*, argued philosophically for a narrative understanding of human life in general. A "central thesis" of his book is that man—"in his actions and practice, as well as in his fictions"— is "essentially a story-telling animal." MacIntyre intended this as a descriptive observation, not as a metaphysical statement about the essence of humanity. Man "is not essentially, but becomes through his history, a teller of stories that aspire to truth."[14] And since "we all live out narratives" and "understand our own lives in terms of the narratives that we live," the form of narrative "is appropriate for understanding the actions of others."[15]

Consider the common sentiment: "This isn't how things ought to be." Whether it's because of something trivial like your computer crashing, or something horrifying, like Elie Wiesel's account of the crematoriums in Auschwitz[16]—the lament that things are *not right* is widespread, if not universal. People generally have a keen sense of conflict between what they imagine life *ought to be* and what life actually *is*.

Susan Neiman, in her book *Evil in Modern Thought*, argued that this sentiment is one way of talking about the problem of evil.[17] Facing this conflict between *is* and *ought*, people commonly deal with misfortunes by locating their lives within a larger story. These stories have been handed down at dinner tables, sanctuaries, and lecture halls. They encourage us to see ourselves and others as real-life characters who interact within a setting or context, whose cumulative interactions form a definite plotline, which we see leading to some hoped-for resolution. A critical element of this perceived plot is conflict. Our sense of conflict in the stories of our lives surfaces every time we say, "This isn't how it's supposed to be." Sensing a conflict between *is* and *ought*, we direct our thoughts and actions toward rectifying it on some scale. In doing so, we conceive ourselves as following a storyline and making progress toward a goal, *eschaton*, or *telos*. Here is how MacIntyre said it:

13. Crites, "Narrative Quality of Experience," 291–311.
14. MacIntyre, *After Virtue*, 216. See also Milbank, *Theology and Social Theory*, 259.
15. Ibid., 212.
16. Wiesel, *Night*, 32.
17. Neiman. *Evil in Modern Thought*.

> We live out our lives, both individually and in our relationships with each other, in the light of certain conceptions of a possible shared future, a future in which certain possibilities beckon us forward and others repel us, some seem already foreclosed and others perhaps inevitable. There is no present which is not informed by some image of some future and an image of the future which always presents itself in the form of a *telos*... toward which we are either moving or failing to move... like characters in a fictional narrative we do not know what will happen next, but nonetheless our lives have a certain form which projects itself toward our future.[18]

Though these observations are not earth-shattering, they are compelling. They are an attempt at "scrutinizing some of our most taken-for-granted, but clearly correct conceptual insights about human actions and selfhood in order to show how natural it is to think of the self in a narrative mode."[19] We make sense of our lives by means of a story. This story has a goal, which is desired, believed to be possible, but as yet unattained and therefore uncertain.[20] Inhabiting such a story defends against despair. The story makes hope possible. Inversely, hope implies a story. Thus, where hope is concerned, story is inescapable. According to MacIntyre, "Mythology, in its original sense, is at the heart of things."[21]

BULTMANN'S ATTEMPT TO TRANSCEND STORIES-OF-THE-WORLD

MacIntyre believed that "mythology," in the sense of making sense of the world through a life-organizing story, is at the heart of being human. To some extent, Rudolf Bultmann would agree. But, he would clarify by saying that it is at the heart of human being enslaved to "the anxiety in which we seek to hold on to ourselves and what is ours in the secret feeling that everything, including our own life, is slipping away from us."[22] In short, mythologizing represents sin—inauthentic existence, which is opposed to faith. Therefore, by Bultmann's reckoning, the purpose of Christian proclamation is to transcend the need for any story of the world, including the one given in the New Testament. The "significance of [the] story lies in

---

18. MacIntyre, *After Virtue*, 215–16.
19. Ibid., 206.
20. See Searle, *Intentionality*, 35, for a definition of hope as an "intentional state."
21. MacIntyre, *After Virtue*, 216.
22. Bultmann, *New Testament and Mythology*, 17.

what God wants to say to us through it."²³ Demythologizing is a method for determining what God wants to say. Thus, Bultmann would object to comparing Christian eschatology to others by means of their stories. This is because the distinctiveness of Christian hope is that it needs no story to support it. Instead, it rests solely on the proclamation of the gospel—God's personal address in Christ.

I have drawn the preceding points from Bultmann's 1941 essay, "New Testament and Mythology." Shubert Ogden thought it was "perhaps the single most discussed and controversial theological writing of the [twentieth] century."²⁴ Richard Hays called its author the "great adversary" and the "unnamed elephant in the room."²⁵ His shadow looms over each of the three eschatological theologians in my bridge in the prior chapter (Sauter, Moltmann, and Pannenberg). "The task of theology," according to Bultmann, is "to demythologize the Christian proclamation"²⁶; or as Hays called it: to "de-narrativize."²⁷

By choosing to describe Christian hope in narrative terms, my method is in conflict with Butlmann's. After considering the deep concerns of his demythologizing program, I will respond by analyzing his notion of proclamation and the form of hope it inspires. By appropriating some elements of John Searle's philosophy of language, mind, and society, I will show how Bultmann's account of Christian proclamation nonetheless assumes a certain life-organizing story—one that is in conflict with the story to which the biblical narratives bear witness. Though I will eventually reject Bultmann's "de-narrativizing" program, his emphasis on proclamation rightly challenges Christian expositors of narrative theology. Christian hope is not simply an aspect of a worldview. Rather, it is a response to God's personal address in Jesus.

Stories in Conflict

In that controversial essay from 1941, Bultmann maintained that it would be both pointless and impossible to ask modern men and women to accept the New Testament myth—that is, the characters, setting, and plot of the story as presented in the text. This is especially the case with the plot's

---

23. Ibid., 33.
24. Ogden, preface, in Bultmann, *New Testament and Mythology*, vii.
25. Hays, *Faith of Jesus Christ*, xxv-xvi.
26. Bultmann, *New Testament and Mythology*, 3.
27. Hays, *Faith of Jesus Christ*, xxvi.

resolution. Bultmann explained that in the New Testament, the resurrection of God's Son is said to be

> the beginning of the cosmic catastrophe through which the death brought into the world by Adam is annihilated . . . demonic powers of the world have lost their power . . . The risen one has been exalted to heaven . . . He will return . . . in order to complete the work of salvation; then will take place the resurrection of the dead and the last judgment . . . finally sin, death, and all suffering will be done away . . . And this will happen at any moment.[28]

Bultmann thought this "mythical eschatology is finished" because "world history continues and—as every competent judge is convinced—will continue." It is pointless to cling to this story because there is nothing specifically Christian about it. It is simply an artifact of "a time now past," which "was not yet formed by scientific thinking." And it is impossible to demand its acceptance, because "no one can appropriate a world picture by sheer resolve, since it is already given with one's particular historical situation."[29] Modern people know too much. "We cannot use electric lights and radios and, in the event of illness, avail ourselves of modern medical and clinical means and at the same time believe in the spirit and wonder world of the New Testament."[30] To the modern ear, the hoped-for resurrection sounds like zombie-fiction. A "corpse cannot come back to life or rise from the grave."[31]

Whether or not we accept Bultmann's pronouncements about what can or cannot be believed, his description of the clash between the New Testament "myth" and the "myth" of Modernity is apt. If we are concerned with the question, "Which story discloses the real world?" then we must acknowledge the persuasive power of the story about scientific-technological progress. Now, you might say, this was 1941—before the wonders of quantum physics, the horrors of Auschwitz, and the failures of the environmental crisis shattered the modern myth. Bultmann responded to this sort of argument in a 1952 essay. He agreed that recent breakthroughs "with respect to atomic processes" have "relativized" the "law of causality." But it is naïve to

---

28. Bultmann, *New Testament and Mythology*, 2.

29. Ibid., 3–5.

30. Ibid., 4.

31. Bultmann, "Case for Demythologization," in Jaspers and Bultmann, *Myth and Christianity*, 60.

think that this "opened the door to the intervention of transcendent powers! Has natural science today given up experimentation?"[32]

Sixty some years later, the same could be said. Let it be granted that the unpredictability of matter and the environmental crisis have now become features of Modernity's story. Nevertheless, the basic assumptions of the modern scientific method still hold: the universe is naturally determined and closed to "supernatural" intervention. And the proprietors of this method are still authorities in the eyes of the public. As for Auschwitz, it only reinforced the idea that human progress was not inevitable, but only possible, and sometimes deceptive. All of which Kant knew well. Besides, the horror of war and genocide during the twentieth century pose just as many problems for the Christian story, with its confession that God is the author, who consciously creates the flow of events that become a plot. If the Christian and modern stories do have anything in common, it is the way they continue to be plagued by the problem of evil. We will explore this connection in the next chapter.

Transcending Story through Proclamation

Even though our path will lead us to part ways with Bultmann, he had a deeper concern that should give us pause. It begins with a common accusation against him: demythologizing tries to make the gospel scientifically respectable "by trimming the traditional Biblical texts." Bultmann answered: on the contrary, it makes "clearer to modern man what the Christian faith is." It removes a false stumbling block in order to make way for the *real* scandal: God's *kerygma*, the personal "summons to man," which "entails the sacrifice of all security attainable by his own unaided efforts."[33] The scandal is being confronted with "God speaking directly to me." The offense is not the mythology, but "the claim of the Christian faith to absoluteness." Bultmann does not want the Christian *kerygma* to be domesticated as something valuable to culture. Rather, it must be received as the exclusive word "that is concretely addressed to me."[34]

His debate with Karl Jaspers brings out the character of Bultmann's concern especially well. Conservative theologians often brand Bultmann a "liberal." Jaspers thought otherwise: "In Bultmann I find nothing of a

---

32. Bultmann, "On the Problem of Demythologizing," in *New Testament and Mythology*, 96.

33. Bultmann, "Case for Demythologization," in Jaspers and Bultmann, *Myth and Christianity*, 59–60.

34. Ibid., 71.

Lessing, a Kant, a Goethe, none of the liberal spirit, but something of their opponents."[35] Liberal faith "strives to keep itself open, ready to recognize the language of the godhead in everything that is real." Bultmann's assertion that God speaks openly through Christ does violence to this. Freedom "forbids absolute obedience to the words of sacred text . . . because [according to liberal faith] every man can be in direct relation to the godhead in his freedom and reason, which constitute a higher authority."[36] Against this, Bultmann claimed the absoluteness of God's act in Christ. He believed that demythologizing served this claim.

Another objection is that demythologization makes God completely subjective—no longer having any reality outside of believers. Not true, said Bultmann. The point is that "God's act is hidden from all eyes other than the eyes of faith."[37] "God is not visible outside of faith," but this "does not mean that God is not real outside of faith." Consider the experience of being loved by another person. The true character of this relationship cannot be scrutinized from the outside. It can only be perceived "by me myself as the one affected by it."[38] In the same way, Christian faith "is not knowledge possessed once and for all, not a 'world view.' It can only be an event."[39]

> I am not talking merely about an idea of God, but am at pains to talk about the living God in whose hands our time is held and who encounters each of us in our time . . . God encounters us in the word, namely, in a specific word, in the proclamation established with Jesus Christ . . . not as a possession that we can secure for ourselves by knowledge but only as the address that encounters us again and again.[40]

All this must be believed against objective occurrences in the world. Demythologizing "destroys every false security." Those who "believe in God as their God need to know that they have nothing in hand on the basis of which they could believe."[41]

According to Bultmann, the problem with any myth—New Testament or otherwise—is that it objectifies God. Myth aims to objectify ultimate reality in order to gain control over it. Myth enables "action calculated to

---

35. Karl Jaspers, "Myth and Religion," in ibid., 40.

36. Ibid., 43.

37. Bultmann, "On the Problem of Demythologizing," in *New Testament and Mythology*, 111.

38. Ibid., 114.

39. Ibid., 111–12.

40. Ibid., 119.

41. Ibid., 122.

influence the attitude of the deity by averting its wrath and winning its favor."[42] Likewise, science calculates to manipulate the world for human purposes. But "demythologizing wants an understanding of scripture free of every world picture projected by objectifying thinking, whether it is that of myth or that of science."[43]

Bultmann's critique raises important questions about the suitability of a life-organizing story to account for Christian hope. Is the Christian story simply about disclosing the real world? Is Christian faith primarily assent to one account of the world over and against others? Some narrative theologians seem to present it as such. David Ford's essay on "System, Story, Performance" says much about "the primary perspective on reality," in terms of "the right assessment of [Jesus]."[44] Reading Ford's Christian appropriation of narrative, I hear him demand "the labor of a plausible ontology as part of the testimony to the Gospel," and call for "performance in line with the content . . . of the gospel story."[45] But I do not hear about a *personal address* from God. Likewise, in an essay from the same volume on narrative theology, Hauerwas and Burrell describe Christian faith as "assent" which involves accepting "a story as normative by allowing it to shape one's own story."[46] But again, no attention is given to how first-person discourse from God elicits faith, hope, and love, thereby creating Christian identity. Recall Bultmann's point: Christian faith is not properly knowledge "about." It is not a "worldview." This reminds me of the Epistle of James: "You believe that God is one; you do well. Even the demons believe—and shudder!" (James 2:19). The living faith that is the Christian life is more than knowledge.

Bultmann has brought something important to our attention. Drawing from his Lutheran tradition, he has recalled the Reformation's distinction between faith's content or articles and the faith which *trusts* the God of Jesus. In *The Apology to the Augsburg Confession*, Phillip Melanchthon clarified what he and the Wittenberg theologians meant by justifying faith: "Our opponents imagine that faith is only historical knowledge" (even the demons have this). But, the "faith that justifies . . . is no mere historical knowledge, but the firm acceptance of God's offer promising forgiveness of sins and justification."[47] Bultmann's demythologizing has this concern in

42. Ibid., 99.
43. Ibid., 102.
44. David Ford, "System, Story, Performance," in Hauerwas and Jones, *Why Narrative?* 198.
45. Ibid., 201–3.
46. Hauerwas and Burrell, "From System to Story," in Hauerwas and Jones, *Why Narrative?* 184–85.
47. Melanchthon, "Apology of the Augsburg Confession," art. IV, para. 48, in Tappert, *Book of Concord*.

mind. He thought he was applying "justification through faith alone without works of the law" to "the field of knowledge."[48] While I reject Bultmann's attempt to sever faith as personal trust from any particular worldview, his objection calls for an account of the Christian story that grounds faith and hope in God's personal address through Jesus.

RESPONSE TO BULTMANN: SPEECH ACTS IN CONTEXT

I am arguing that a notion of life-organizing story is appropriate for comparing the Christian hope with others. However, Bultmann has challenged me to say more clearly how story can do justice to the centrality of Christian proclamation. Christian hope is not simply a matter of having a different description of reality. Rather, it is a response to definite speech acts received from God. Therefore, I will correlate speech act theory with the concept of a life-organizing story, thus responding to Bultmann's objection without his "de-narratizing" program.

How Words Do Work

Speaking, in normal usage, does not merely provide information and dispel ignorance. It does inform, but that's not all it does. The point of speaking is to have an effect on the hearer(s)—to elicit in them a response (e.g., assent, trust, anticipation, intention to obey or to cooperate). This sort of language is what John Searle calls "speech acts."[49] His teacher, J. L. Austin, called them "illocutionary acts."[50] They argued that the point of language, in everyday-usage, is a way of *doing* something. They called this the "illocutionary point." It is how the utterance "counts as" an act.

The illocutionary act needs to be distinguished from the "perlocutionary act."[51] The latter is the actual result or consequence of the speech act. For example, if my favorite on-line store *promised* they would deliver the book I purchased, that would be a speech act, or illocutionary act. My *having hope* would be the perlocutionary act, or effect. The bookseller's communication with me "counts as" a promise whether I respond in hope or not. All that is required is that it registers with me as a promise—as a commitment to make the world fit with their intention, which also happens to be my desire.

---

48. Bultmann, *New Testament and Mythology*, 122.
49. Searle, *Speech Acts*.
50. Austin, *How to Do Things with Words*.
51. See Searle, *Mind, Language, and Society*, 136–39.

Such a speech act carries with it the intention of eliciting my trust and hope. Similarly, the illocutionary point of making an assertion is to elicit belief. The illocutionary point of a command is to elicit intention to obey.

Speech acts aim to elicit certain states of mind (hope, belief, intention to act). Thus, language and mind are interrelated. "What we have," said Searle, "is not just the mind on one side and language on the other, but mind and language enriching each other until, for adult human beings, the mind is linguistically structured."[52] And the linguistically structured mind is related to the outside world. Searle argued that language and mind are connected to the world in one of two ways: either as description or prescription. With this distinction, he employed the phrase, "direction of fit."

Directions of Fit. The notion of *direction of fit* will be immensely important for presenting the book's case, so we will invest some time developing it. It begins with the simple observation that a person can use language to accomplish at least one of two goals: they can *describe* or *prescribe*. In description, the speaker fits (conforms) the words to match the world; In prescription, the speaker fits (or intends to fit) the world to match the word.

To illustrate, Searle told a parable about two men, each with a list.[53] The first man received a list from his wife. This list *prescribed* to him which groceries to buy. The second man also had a list. He was a private investigator hired to spy on the first man. The detective went to the market and marked on his list the items the husband had bought: "butter, bacon, beer." His list *described* a certain state of affairs in the world. The detective's list had a "list-to-world direction of fit." But the husband's had a "world-to-list direction of fit." To see the importance of this difference, you need only consider the following scenario: When the detective tailed the man into the store, he initially put down "cheese" instead of butter. But, when he watched him check out, he realized his mistake, crossed out cheese, and wrote "butter." Later, the husband arrives home and has his groceries inspected by his wife. She exclaims, "Honey, look at your list again. I wrote *beets*, not beer!" Now, imagine his wife's response if he were to "correct" his mistake by crossing out beets and writing "beer." This would not bode well for him because each list succeeds in different ways. They have different conditions of satisfaction. The detective's list must match the world. But the world must come to match the husband's list.

A Taxonomy of Speech Acts. From these two "directions of fit," Searle accounted for five basic kinds of speech acts: (1) "assertives," which always

52. Searle, *Mind, Language, and Society*, 152.
53. Ibid., 100–104. This is my adaptation of the parable.

have a word-to-world direction of fit (e.g., statements, explanations); (2) "directives," which have a world-to-word direction of fit, with the responsibility of "fit" imposed on the hearer (e.g., commands); (3) "commissives," which also have a world-to-word direction of fit, but with the responsibility of "fit" assumed by the speaker (e.g., threats, promises). With commissives, the speaker prescribes to himself responsibility to act. The last two categories are special. They have a more complex connection to the world: (4) "Expressives" have a "null" direction of fit. These are a unique case because the point of this kind of speech is not to relate to the world. The statement, "I love you," neither describes nor prescribes, but expresses. Such a statement is satisfied if it is sincere. There are no states of affairs in the world that need to correspond with or bend to it. Yet, a connection to the world is nevertheless assumed. When I say, "I love you," I take for granted that there is, in fact, a "you" to be loved. So, while the explicit connection to the world is "null," an expressive assumes a word-to-world direction of fit, same as an assertive. Finally, (5) "declaratives" have a dual direction of fit. Here, the "point is to bring about a change in the world by representing it as having been changed." Common examples are "I pronounce you man and wife" or, when an umpire declares, "You're out!" The direction is "double" because the world is made to match the word at the moment the word matches the world. This kind of speech act generally requires some external institutional support for it to "count as" a declaration (e.g., the institution of marriage, the game of baseball).[54]

Mind, Language, and World. Like language, states of mind also have a direction of fit—they have a connection to the external world: either a mind-to-world or a world-to-mind direction of fit. Belief and desire are two fundamental "intentional states" of mind, according to Searle. They are instances of consciousness called "intentionality." This should not be associated with the verb "to intend." The appropriate verb is "to direct." Intentionality does not always involve intention to act. Intentionality is a more general description of the mind being "about" or directed at something.[55] For example, belief, like the detective's list, aims to make the mind correspond to the external world. Desire, like the wife who wanted groceries, aims to make the world correspond to the mind. Searle argued that these two directions of fit are given with the biology of the human being—the sensory nervous system enables us to fit mind-to-world and the motor nervous system empowers us to fit world-to-mind.[56]

54. Searle, *Mind, Language, and Society*, 146–52.
55. John Searle, *Intentionality*.
56. Ibid., chaps. 2 and 3.

Hope as an Intentional State. Hope is an instance of intentionality that includes both *belief* and *desire*. It involves my *desire* that the world fit to the state of affairs I have in mind. Thus, it has a world-to-mind direction of fit. It also presumes a *belief* (mind-to-world fit) that I live in a world where such a state of affairs is possible. But, since it is yet unattained, it also includes uncertainty as to whether the hoped for state of affairs will actually be the case.[57]

In some cases, the *desire* element in hope can be satisfied simply by my coming to see the world in a new light. In other cases, I must take action to manipulate the external world to match my desire. In other cases still, I must wait on the action of others. With regard to my on-line book order, my hope was evoked by a promise. The speaker committed to make the world fit the word of promise. As a recipient of the promise, I can anticipate its arrival, lament its delay, but must more or less patiently await its fulfillment. The Christian hope has a similar character. It is an intentional state of mind directed at a particular state of affairs given in the last line of the Nicene Creed: "we look for the resurrection of the dead and the life of the age to come."[58]

The Story about a Promise

To link speech acts and story, I will begin by returning to the trial of Paul depicted in the book of Acts. When Paul made his final defense before the governor, the visiting king, and the crowd, he stated, "I now stand here on trial because of my hope." This was not hope in general, but the "intentional state" assumed by Paul in response to a particular speech act committed by God and addressed to the Jewish people: ". . . my hope in the promise made by God to our fathers" (Acts 26:6). For Paul, the focal point of both his hope and God's promise was "that God raises the dead"; more specifically, that the Messiah was "the first to rise from the dead" (Acts 26:23). Robert Tannehill explained:

> the hope and promise of which Paul speaks in 26:6-7 is not merely a hope for individual life after death but a hope for the Jewish people, to be realized through resurrection . . . It is hope for the Messiah's promised reign, which is established through resurrection and characterized by a resurrection life corporately shared.[59]

57. Ibid., 35.
58. Kolb and Wengert, eds., "Nicene Creed," in *Book of Concord*, 23.
59. Tannehill, *Narrative Unity of Luke-Acts*, 2:320.

The event of God's ancient promise established Israel's identity: "You are the sons ... of the covenant that God made with your fathers, saying to Abraham, 'And in your offspring shall all the families of the earth be blessed'" (Acts 3:25, Gen 12:3). Elsewhere, Paul had summarized the content of God's speech act as "the promise to Abraham and his offspring that he would be heir of the world" (Rom 4:13). As a son of Abraham, Paul spoke to some of those "families of the earth" in Athens. He pointed them toward the final fulfillment of the promise—toward the day when God "will judge the world in righteousness by a man whom he has appointed; and of this he has given assurance to all by raising him from the dead" (Acts 17:31).

The fulfillment of God's promise was still outstanding and yet at the same time vouchsafed and guaranteed by the resurrection of Jesus. These words and deeds—remembered, recounted, and still anticipated—gave Paul's world a narrative shape by eliciting a concrete expectation of how the story-of-everything would turn out. The still-unfinished plotline had been full of disappointments, reversals, proleptic resolutions, and lingering uncertainties. Nevertheless, it continued to structure life for Paul and his people. In other words, a life-organizing story engendered by a particular *commissive speech act* formed the basis of Paul's hope. If no promise were made, there would be no story to narrate. But because God *did* make a promise, because God *did* fulfill it proleptically by raising Jesus from the dead, there is now a story to tell. At this point, Richard Hays's distinction between "story" and "narrative" becomes important. The story—the actions of agents ordered in a sequence—is logically prior to any *narration* of that story. "Paul's gospel *is* a story, and it *has* a narrative structure, but it is not *a* narrative except when it is actually narrated."[60] God and the sequence of God's speech-actions preceded the narration of those actions. The story occasions the narrative.

In Hays's "Introduction to the Second Edition" of his influential book *The Faith of Jesus*, he summarized his earlier work and gave an updated account of what he thought was Paul's "foundational story." In its most basic form, Paul's story is the story of Jesus: "*In a mysterious way, Jesus has enacted our destiny, and those who are in Christ are shaped by the pattern of his self-giving death. He is the prototype of redeemed humanity.*" This means that "Jesus is not merely a good moral example; rather, his story transforms and absorbs the world. The old world has been crucified and new creation has broken in through Jesus' death and resurrection."[61] But how does this relate to the story of the promise God made to Abraham?

60. Hays, *Faith of Jesus Christ*, 19.
61. Ibid., xxix.

The Abraham story is for Paul taken up into the Christ-story, and the Christ-story is understood, with the hindsight of narrative logic, as the fit sequel to the Abraham story. Looking back upon the Abraham story from the world established by the Christ-story, Paul perceives the proleptic character of Abraham as the recipient of a promise that was inherently unfulfillable in Abraham's own lifetime, a promise destined for fulfillment only in his seed.[62]

The two are related as "prefiguration and fulfillment."[63] According to Hays, it is a story *about* a promise. But in his polemic against Bultmann, Hays does not give a response to Bultmann's objection as I have presented it. A proper response to Bultmann would need to explain how the story is *both* a world-establishing report about the faithfulness *of* Jesus *and* God's personal summons, which aims to elicit personal faith *in* Jesus, as the embodied voice of God. To make an analogy to Searle's comment on language and mind—it's not that we have promise on one side and story on the other. Rather, the two are interdependent. The promise occasioned the story. And since the story recounts the promise, telling it becomes a form of "narrated promise."

The Story That Makes a Promise

Ronald Thiemann used the phrase "narrated promise" in his book *Revelation and Theology*. He drew on Austin's and Searle's account to explain how narratives "can have a variety of illocutionary forces." For example, the story of "Little Red Riding Hood" has illocutionary force. The narrative functions as a warning. The story *does* something.[64] Next he used speech-act theory to spell out the illocutionary force of a promise:

> Promise is a relational category which requires both a speaker and a hearer but grants primacy in that relation solely to the one who promises . . . The promiser specifies the future act, expresses the intention to perform that act, undertakes the obligation implied in the promise, exhibits the requisite trustworthy behavior, and alone can perform the action which will fulfill the promise. The hearer, on the other hand, though he or she would

62. Ibid., 197–98.
63. Ibid., 198.
64. Thiemann, *Revelation and Theology*, 103. See also Wolterstorff, "Promise of Speech-act Theory for Biblical Interpretation," 82.

"prefer" that the promiser fulfill his obligation, cannot, if the act is to remain a promise, compel the promiser so to act.[65]

Thiemann continued by linking promise and narrative in his notion of a "narrated promise." This term expressed his conviction about the illocutionary point of the biblical narrative. The narrative continues to serve as a promise "to the readers of the text."[66] And since a promise commits to accomplishing a state of affairs in the world—since it has a world-to-word direction of fit—the narration of that promise necessarily makes a claim upon the world. Unlike the tale of Little Red Riding Hood, the biblical narrative *establishes* the world. It implicitly says to the reader: "You live in this storied world. You live within the world that has been pledged to Abraham's family. You live within the world that will be judged by the crucified and risen Jesus, the heir of Abraham." The story discloses the world and continues to proclaim God's vow to bring the world into conformity with his word.

Thiemann supported his claims about the illocutionary force of the biblical narrative by performing a literary and theological analysis of the New Testament book of Matthew:

> The word *promise* . . . never appears in the Gospel of Matthew. Yet the notion of promise hovers like an enormous parenthesis surrounding the entire narrative . . . [Matthew] associates Jesus, Son of God, with the Israelite heritage, thus identifying him as Son of Abraham and Son of David, i.e., as inheritor of the two great covenantal promises . . . Matthew constructs his narrative in such a way that his readers are led to identify with the disciples . . . the narrative serves as both report and proclamation . . . Matthew's story appropriately ends with Jesus' *promise*, for this narrative, functions for its readers . . . as the *narrated promise* of Jesus of Nazareth.[67]

Jeff Gibbs, who offered a more rigorous narrative reading of this gospel, echoed Thiemann in this respect: "Matthew . . . wants his readers/hearers to know that in Jesus, the ancient promises of God . . . have found their fulfillment."[68] Thus, the story "aims to plant real faith in its reader and to create faith's response of committed discipleship."[69] Gibbs summarized how the narrative pulls this off:

---

65. Thiemann, *Revelation and Theology*, 110.
66. Ibid., 69–70.
67. Ibid., 134–36.
68. Gibbs, *Matthew 1–11:1*, 52.
69. Ibid., 35.

The Gospel of Matthew proclaims that the end-time reign of God has drawn near in Jesus and that the time of the fulfillment of the Scriptures' promises has begun. The time that God ordains until the consummation of all things in Christ is the time for the church to live and move out in mission. Matthew's gospel leads every hearer/reader . . . to ask how he can participate in that mission . . .[70]

To lead the hearers in this way, the narrative aims to evoke two distinct but inseparable intentional states: assent to the world of the narrative *and* trust in the God of the narrative. Thiemann and Gibbs both acknowledged the reciprocity between these two states: "The gospel narrative can be God's promise to me if, and only if, he has [actually] raised Jesus from the dead."[71] Likewise, trusting God's promise means believing "that the 'world' presented in Matthew's narrative, along with its values and truths, is actually the *real* world."[72] The narrative evokes belief, which has a *mind*-to-narrated-*world* direction of fit. Within this narrated world, the God of Jesus makes a promise, which elicits hope. This hope has a narrated-*world*-to-promise-formed-*mind* direction of fit. Jesus' resurrection from the dead signals that the narrative lays claim to the bodily-organic-social setting that has been claimed by rival stories. Other storied-worlds are false. They are under judgment. These too will eventually be "fit" to the promised world—to the one over which Jesus has received "all authority" (Matt 28:20).

Gibbs commented on this implicit narrated *threat* in Matthew's gospel. The God of Israel makes his promise within his greater "work of reestablishing his kingship over his fallen creation." God's kingly words and deeds include both promise and threat, both judgment and salvation. The "coming of God's reign in Jesus to a world in rebellion signifies that God is committed fully to reclaiming his creation and restoring it, to removing the effects of satanic power and human sin."[73] The narrative's promise is always contrasted against its threat of judgment—the condemnation of rival attempts to "story" God's world. The hearer's faith *toward* the promise is continually paired with a turning *from* the threat of judgment.

Thiemann does not comment on this dual aspect of the narrative's illocutionary stance. Since Matthew's gospel issues a threat and a promise, we must ask whether Thiemann's term "narrated promise" is still appropriate. Holding the two together, the narrative still functions as a "commissive

---

70. Ibid., 59.
71. Thiemann, *Revelation and Theology*, 146.
72. Gibbs, *Matthew 1–11:1*, 35.
73. Ibid., 50.

speech act," to use Searle's term. The God who speaks within and through the story vows to make the world "fit" to his intentions. This includes God's intention to "gather out of his kingdom all causes of sin and all law-breakers" (Matt 13:41). The hearer is thus confronted with the threat of being sent "into the eternal fire prepared for the devil and his angels" (Matt 25:41). But since this day has not yet occurred, there is still room for the narrative to function as a promise upon every new hearing—as "good news" for "all nations" (Matt 24:14). The threat and the promise intend to evoke the same intentional state: the hope that believes God's promise has found fulfillment in Jesus and desires it to come to fruition, even as it remains uncertain. The story may prove to have two perlocutionary effects: judgment or salvation. But it has only one illocutionary point. The point of the threat is not to evoke the unbelief that leads to final condemnation. The point of the threat is to evoke repentance, trust in Jesus, love for God and neighbor, and hope that leads into the promised reign of God. Therefore, since the threat serves the promise, Thiemann's designation "narrated promise" is an appropriate summary term.

Kerygma Assumes a Story

Although others could be cited,[74] the works of Thiemann and Gibbs illustrate how Bultmann's objection can be met without "de-narrativizing" the New Testament. Proclamation and the story are inseparable. The narrative "counts as" a speech act. It establishes a world in which the God of Jesus is an actor who continues to take on the rights and duties of a speaker engaged in discourse. The commissive speech acts of threat and promise are critical because they are not simply God's "self-communication." They do more than reveal God's character. By them, God directly and personally addresses the hearers and commits himself to future action. By threatening final judgment against evil and promising the renewal of creation, God has pledged to "fit" the world disclosed in the biblical narrative to a yet outstanding state of affairs—the "life of the age to come."

Now we are in the position to scrutinize Bultmann's notion of "proclamation." What he meant by the "personal address" of God was not a commitment to future action. Bultmann's proclamation is an "expressive," not a promise. It has a "null" direction of fit, analogous to the statement, "I love you." Its illocutionary point is not to evoke hope as belief and desire for the speaker to carry out his stated intention. At most, it evokes a non-descript

---

74. See Jenson, *Story and Promise*, 1; also, McClendon, *Ethics*, vol. 1 of *Systematic Theology*, 336.

hopefulness or elation. The important thing to remember about "expressives" is how they imply a word-to-world direction of fit even if their explicit connection to the world is "null." If God says, "I love you," the statement assumes there is a "you" to be loved. The question is, "Which you?" The "you" identified and narrated by a story of Modernity or Postmodernity? Or the "you" inscribed by the story of the crucified, risen, and returning Jesus?[75] Bultmann's proclamation can fit within either, but it cannot float disconnected from all stories. Even if it derides every notion of a *telos* for world history, it still assumes a personal *telos*. For Bultmann, this was plotted as the lonely and courageous quest for personal authenticity.[76] Therefore, any effort to "demythologize" the New Testament *kerygma* always entails "remythologizing" it into another life-organizing story.

I have met Bultmann's concern for God's "personal address" by correlating speech-act theory with a narrative analysis of the story of Jesus told by Paul and Matthew. Now I will simply assert that what goes for them goes for the whole biblical narrative.[77] Bultmann can be answered as follows: The so-called "myth" of the New Testament is not a man-made attempt at self-justification by fitting God into man's world as an object to be manipulated. Rather, the story of Israel continued and completed by the New Testament is the result of God's self-chosen involvement within the world he created. Because God's involvement occurs in the form of threat and promise, God sets and fulfills the conditions of his actions. God's narrated promise elicits both the faith that he is trustworthy and the hope that he will fulfill his commitment to act. Understanding the story in this way enables the church to participate in the mission of Jesus by continuing to speak in his name—issuing commands, threats, and promises on God's behalf.[78]

However, since God has not yet fully realized his intentions to act, the story is still unresolved. "The justifiability of one's trust in the truthfulness of a promise is never fully confirmed (or disconfirmed) until the promiser actually fulfills (or fails to fulfill) his . . . promise."[79] Bultmann was right when he said that Christians have nothing "in hand" upon which to base their belief that God will prove trustworthy. They only have a narrated promise in which to hope. Until the promise is fulfilled, the conflict with rival stories cannot be ignored.

---

75. Cf. Blundell, *Paul Ricoeur*, 175.
76. See Bultmann, *History and Eschatology*, 155.
77. Cf. Gibbs, *Matthew 1–11:1*, 10; also, Wright, *Jesus and the Victory of God*, 130.
78. See Wolterstorff, *Divine Discourse*, 38–51.
79. Thiemann, *Revelation and Theology*, 94.

ENLIGHTENMENT ATTEMPTS TO TRANSCEND ALL STORIES-OF-THE-WORLD

In a 1977 essay, Stanley Hauerwas and David Burrell made a striking claim: "All our notions are narrative-dependent, including the notion of rationality."[80] Twenty years later, this essay and others were collected by Hauerwas and L. Gregory Jones into a single volume titled *Why Narrative?* The purpose of this collection was to "suggest that narrative is neither just an account of genre criticism nor a faddish appeal to the importance of telling stories; rather it is a crucial conceptual category." This point restated the claim from the 1977 essay: "what is significant" about narrative is "that rationality, methods of argument, and historical explanation have, at least to some extent, a fundamentally narrative form." This was a use of "narrative centered on epistemological issues."[81] That is to say, answers about how we know what we know always assume and are filtered through a grand story. Whether we acknowledge it or not, we all inhabit some "narrative to give our life coherence."[82]

These claims conflict with other accounts of rationality that seek to transcend the particularities of any given story and subjective points of view within those stories. In this section I will address one such attempt to transcend stories: the Enlightenment tradition. Following Hauerwas and Burrell, I will frame the Enlightenment as an attempt to transcend other stories by telling a more encompassing, more persuasive story of the world. This point is less of an argument against the Enlightenment and more of recognition that its story comes into conflict with the Christian story. In doing so, it offers a rival hope by naming a different kind of conflict in the world plot and anticipating its own sort of resolution.

The Enlightenment Vision

In their 1977 essay, Hauerwas and Burrell addressed the "narrative born of the Enlightenment," which has been presented as historical fact. They suggested that the "basic story underlying the standard account" was "of more ancient lineage, namely, humankind's quest for certainty in a world of contingency." Here is their summary of the Enlightenment story:

---

80. Hauerwas and Burrell, "From System to Story," in Hauerwas and Jones, *Why Narrative?* 168.
81. Hauerwas and Jones, *Why Narrative?*, 3–5.
82. Hauerwas and Burrell, "From System to Story," in ibid., 177.

> The plot was given in capsule by Auguste Comte: first came religion in the form of stories, then philosophy in the form of metaphysical analysis, and then science with its exact methods. The story he tells in outline is set within another elaborated by Hegel, to show us how each of these ages supplanted the other as a refinement in the progressive development of reason. So stories are pre-scientific, according to the story legitimizing the age which calls itself scientific. Yet if one overlooks that budding contradiction, or fails to spell it out . . . then the subterfuge has been worked and the exit blocked off.[83]

The Enlightenment vision, then, is a story that presents itself as historical truth. Every narration of it could be introduced like this: Here's how we grew up and left behind superstition.

In his book, *Mind, Language, and Society*, John Searle explained his philosophical starting point: "I accept the Enlightenment vision," which "assumed the universe was completely intelligible and that we are capable of a systematic understanding of its nature . . . within the limits set by our evolutionary endowments."[84] As a logical out-working of this starting point, modern people have moved to a position that is "beyond atheism."

> For us, the educated members of society, the world has become demystified. Or rather, to put the point more precisely, we no longer take the mysteries we see in the world as expressions of supernatural meaning. We no longer think of odd occurrences as cases of God performing speech acts in the language of miracles. Odd occurrences are just occurrences we do not understand. The result of this demystification is that we have gone beyond atheism to a point where the issue no longer matters in the way it did to earlier generations.[85]

The key word in Searle's story is "demystified." This does not mean that "educated" people know everything about the world that can be known. It's not even that they know everything they still want to know. Instead, it means that Searle's community takes it for granted that there are no aspects of reality that are utterly mysterious, that are formally beyond finding out.[86] We might not know about it now. Perhaps our limited evolutionary endowments will keep us from ever knowing. But this does not mean it cannot in principle be discovered. The vision of the Enlightenment is to

---

83. Hauerwas and Jones, *Why Narrative?*, 174–75.
84. Searle, *Mind, Language, and Society*, 1–4.
85. Ibid., 34–35.
86. See Searle, *Mind: A Brief Introduction*, 192.

overcome the conflict created by ignorance, superstition, and illusion. The hope for overcoming this conflict is realized through objective, impersonal knowledge.

Rival Stories of Enlightenment

Describing the Enlightenment vision as a story does not refute it. However, it does break its spell of objectivity. It allows us to imagine rival accounts. The Christian story was its original rival, but others have presented themselves. Many of these narrate different versions of a *post*-modern story. To understand the relation between Modernity and Postmodernity, think of how Paul claimed that the story of Jesus encompassed and fulfilled the story of Abraham. This is close to the relationship Postmodernity has with Modernity. The postmodern is not a rejection of the modern story. It is a *fulfillment* via an unexpected twist in the plot. A narration of the postmodern story might start like this: Here's how we grew up and left behind superstition *and then arrogance as well*.

Story and Reality. John Crossan, in his book *The Dark Interval: Towards a Theology of Story*, narrated a version of the postmodern story. He claimed that "we live in story like fish in the sea."[87] Crossan is an ex-Roman Catholic priest, a skeptical New Testament scholar, and a co-founder of the equally skeptical Jesus Seminar. According to N. T. Wright, Crossan "seems incapable . . . of thinking a boring thought or writing a dull paragraph."[88] Like many proponents of the postmodern, he invokes names like Nietzsche, Wittgenstein, and Lévi-Strauss.

In *Dark Interval*, he posed the following question: "is story telling us about a world out there objectively present before and apart from any story concerning it, or, does story create world so that we live as human beings in, and only in . . . story?"[89] Going with the latter, his main adversary became the modern story of scientific progress. Assuming the argument of Kuhn's *The Structure of Scientific Revolutions*, Crossan aimed to debunk the mythical agents of this progress: the all-seeing eye of reason and the totalizing intent of cumulative knowledge. With these mythical agents vanquished, the game they hunted—Objective Reality—now looked to be an illusion.

Crossan also defended against a common modernist charge that this loss of "objectivity" leads to groundless, rudderless relativism, which knows

---

87. Crossan, *Dark Interval*, 47.
88. Wright, *Jesus and the Victory of God*, 44.
89. Crossan, *Dark Interval*, 9.

nothing "true" but only "true for me." Crossan argued that the charge overlooked a third option: "relationalism." "Reality is neither *in here* in mind [idealism] nor *out there* in the world [realism]; it is the interplay of both mind and world in language. Reality is relational and relationship. Even more simply, reality is language."[90] Here Crossan is not too far from Searle's position: ". . . it would be a misunderstanding to suppose that there are separate, isolated classes of brute facts and institutional facts. On the contrary, we have complex interpenetrations of brute and institutional facts."[91] Crossan would simply say that the relations are so tight the two cannot be distinguished. Whether we call them "institutional" or "brute," all facts emerge from stories.

Searle and Crossan agree on the interrelation between language and the external world. However, they represent two rival schools of thought within the Enlightenment tradition. Searle contended against an "antirealist" perspective.[92] He explained how attacks on external realism are not new. They go back centuries. They all present themselves as a form of intellectual humility ("Here's how we left behind arrogance."). For example, Crossan's problem with Modernity's story was not that it was false, but presumptuous. It boasts "that we are capable of getting outside story to an objective reality."[93] Searle thought this humility was a façade:

> I do not think the various challenges to realism are motivated by the arguments actually presented; I believe they are motivated by something much deeper and less intellectual . . . many people find it repugnant that we, with our language, our consciousness, and our creative powers should be subject to and answerable to a dumb, stupid, inert material world. Why should we be answerable to the world? Why shouldn't we think of the "real world" as something we create, and therefore something that is answerable to us? If all of reality is a "social construction," then it is we who are in power, not the world.[94]

Searle's problem with antirealists is that they no longer see themselves as "answerable." By declaring—"No story can stand in judgment over another!"—they have given up on seeking a "true" story. They have ceased to be accountable. Searle would not object to the notion of life-organizing story *per se*. He only rejects an unaccountable willfulness that has no concern for

90. Ibid., 37.
91. Searle, *Mind, Language, and Society*, 131.
92. Ibid., 15.
93. Crossan, *Dark Interval*, 18.
94. Searle, *Mind, Language, and Society*, 33.

the truth—for the way reality works independently of any story. Again, this is an aspect of the Enlightenment Vision—to transcend conflicting stories by means of universal, impersonal truth.

Literary critic Stanley Fish offered an interesting take on this debate. He would tend to side with Crossan, while also addressing Searle's demand to be "answerable." In 1976, Fish wrote a fascinating essay titled, "How to Do Things with Austin and Searle: Speech Act Theory and Literary Criticism." In it, he began by using speech act theory to offer an interpretation of Shakespeare's tragedy *Coriolanus*. To relay the force of his argument, I need to give a synopsis of the play: Caius Martinius, a Roman general later named Coriolanus, returns home to be lauded a war hero. His mother encourages him to run for office. He is not eager to do this, but bows to her wishes. After he begrudgingly asks for the people's vote of confidence and attains senatorial support, he looks to be a shoe-in for the consulship. But his enemies stir up the people to oppose him. Faced with the riotous crowd, he betrays his contempt for the procedure of attaining office by popular vote. His enemies call for him to be exiled from Rome as a traitor to his words. Fish explained what comes next: "In any production, [this] scene is the centerpiece, the climax to which everything before it has been building."[95] The citizens shout, "Let him away: he's banish'd." Then, breaking all established conventions, Coriolanus responds with a declarative speech act: "I banish you . . . !"[96] Astoundingly, he creates a new state of affairs. The world is made to fit his words at the same moment his words fit the world.

The declarative speech of Coriolanus illustrates Fish's central contention: Speech Act theory is about "language and its power: the power to make the world rather than mirror it, to bring about states of affairs rather than report them, to constitute institutions rather than (or as well as) serve them."[97] Typically declaratives don't work unless the speaker has the proper status within a previously existing institutional reality (e.g., it doesn't *count* when a fan yells, "Strike three!"). But Coriolanus turned the existing institution on its head. This suggests that it "is not that words are in force only so long as long as the institutions are, but that institutions are in force only so long as the words are . . . institutions are no more than the (temporary) effects of speech act agreements."

Fish considered the ontological implications of this: "if declarative utterances . . . alter states of affairs, what brings about the state of affairs in which a declarative . . . is endowed with its intended force? The answer is,

---

95. Fish, "How to Do Things," 995.
96. Shakespeare, *Tragedy of Coriolanus*, Act III, Scene iii.
97. Fish, "How to Do Things," 1024.

another declarative utterance." And no matter how far back you push the inquiry, this is the answer you will have to keep on giving.[98] It's speech acts all the way down.

> It might be objected that to reason in this way is to imply that one can constitute a state simply by declaring it to exist. That of course is exactly what happens: a single man plants a flag on a barren shore and claims everything his eye can see in the name of a distant monarch . . . another man, hunted by police and soldiers, seeks refuge in a cave, where, alone or in the company of one or two fellows, he proclaims the birth of a revolutionary government.[99]

These declarations establish new storied worlds, such as: "In the beginning there was a demystified universe." "In the beginning there were our stories." "In the beginning, God . . ."

Coriolanus, after banishing the Roman state, said, "There is a world elsewhere."[100] He had overturned the prior world and created a new one. Next, he finds an enemy of Rome, convinces them to make him their general, and returns to Rome to seek revenge. He has become "what he always wanted to be, a natural force whose movement through the world is independent of all supports . . . He is complete and sufficient unto himself . . . His is the declarative of divine fiat, the logos, the *all*-creating word."[101]

As Coriolanus's army lays siege to the imperial city, his mother, wife, and son are sent out to beg for his mercy. Coriolanus, overcome by the power of their bids, settles for a peace treaty and leads his army home. But on the way, they turn on him. For his betrayal, they kill him. Fish comments on the play's closing words spoken by the collective voice of Rome: "He shall have a noble memory." "The irony is unrelenting. The man who scorned the word of the community . . . now depends on that word . . . for the only life he has." His speech act community reclaims him "as inescapably its own when he provides the strongest possible evidence that he is neither a God nor a machine. He dies."[102]

The Standard Story. From Fish's analysis, I will draw out some connections between the rival versions of the Enlightenment Story I have represented with Crossan and Searle. Crossan was concerned with intellectual humility

---

98. Ibid., 997.
99. Ibid.
100. Shakespeare, *Coriolanus*, Act III, Scene iii.
101. Fish, "How to Do Things," 998–99.
102. Ibid., 1001.

in the sense of being honest with ourselves. All we have is our stories and the hope that they won't lead us too far astray. We do not have anything beyond story to justify our positions. But Crossan also aims to transcend these other stories. He admits that he has subsumed them by means of a new "master story."[103] This plot advances by overcoming arrogance and intolerance by ironizing and subverting all myths in a lonely and courageous quest for authentic "transcendental experience."[104] Searle criticized this sort of self-made story as a "will to power," an unwillingness to be answerable.[105] While this diagnosis may be true, staying "unanswerable" is easier said than done. The case in point is General Caius Martinius Coriolanus.

All facts are institutional facts because institutions stipulate what "counts as" fact—what is "pickoutable." And the "real world" is simply "a story that has been told *about* the real world."[106] However, no one person can pick out any story he or she pleases—at least not for long.

> Some stories . . . are more prestigious than others; and only one story is always the standard one, the one that presents itself as uniquely true . . . Other, non-standard, stories will of course continue to be told, but they will be regarded as non-factual, when in fact, they will only be non-authorized.[107]

A standard story depends on a distinction between fact (authorized) and fantasy (unauthorized). As the story that has the capacity to organize life for individuals and collectives, the standard story generates hope and not mere wishful thinking. It can do so because it has the authority to disclose the "real world." The story establishes what counts as good (ultimately desirable) and what counts as evil (ultimately undesirable). It determines what is truly possible and what is an illusion. Therefore, it creates the conditions for imagining, anticipating, and achieving the victory of the good and the overcoming of evil. In this way, a life-organizing story gives rise to hope.

Because the standard story discloses what is real and possible and factual, it interprets all things on its own terms. This includes other stories. Whether these stories are judged to be useful or immoral, subversive or amusing—they will all be subsumed. They must be subsumed if *the* Story is going to keep on organizing life and offering hope to its participants. Normally it takes a collective intentionality, a communal "we" to author a

---

103. Crossan, *Dark Interval*, 47.
104. Ibid., 45–46.
105. Searle, *Mind, Language, and Society*, 19–20.
106. Fish, "How to Do Things," 1021.
107. Ibid., 1019.

standard story. Even Coriolanus, with his all-creating, declarative utterance, was eventually rendered silent and returned to the standard story authorized by his speech act community. An individual cannot impose his will without the consent of the collective because he will eventually yield his voice to the assembly and be silent. He will die.

But, if he were to rise from the dead? That would be another story . . .

SUMMARY

The notion of a life-organizing story is foundational to this project. Inasmuch as humans hold to a hope that defends against despair, they take up a life-organizing story. Part of what makes our situation post-Constantinian is the proliferation of stories. Because of their nature, they do not simply co-exist. They also compete. They are either co-opting their rivals or being co-opted by a more persuasive, more encompassing account. For this reason, Christians, if they are to continue to hold on to *Christian* hope, must understand these other accounts. More specifically, they must understand them as *rivals*. My strategy in this chapter has been to do just that. I have presented Bultmann, Searle, and Crossan not to defeat them once and for all, but to acknowledge them as narrators of stories that are irreducibly at odds with the Christian story. Each story internally defines conflict and establishes the plot on its own terms. Each holds out the hope of ultimately resolving this conflict.

Just like any other potential life-organizing story, the Christian story interprets all things on its terms. It understands rival accounts not simply as rivals, but as false accounts that will ultimately be judged by the one true God and brought under his rule and reign in Jesus. At the same time, the Christian account acknowledges that even these false stories are compelled to bear witness to the truth in a fragmentary way. This is because they necessarily spin their stories with the setting and characters supplied by the Christian story. And since they must use God's creation and creatures to offer their accounts, Christians will always have a basis for conversation, cooperation, and even opportunities to learn from those who inhabit other stories. But this basis, or common ground, is not neutral in any way. It does not exist apart from a story. Rather it is given with the Christian story. This story establishes the world. Within it, Christians have also received a commission from their Lord to call everyone to align themselves to God's future—to "the common ending of all stories."[108] It is in the interest of this

---

108. Richard Bauckham, "Conclusion," in Walls, *Oxford Handbook of Eschatology*, 679.

disciple-making commission that Christians ought to ask, "How does our hope compare with others?"

The notion of a life-organizing story provides a means to compare Christian eschatology with rivals. My aim is to help Christians compare and contrast their hope with others—to put forward the Christian story as both a coworker and competitor among other would-be standard stories. This will involve conversing with proponents of those stories and seeking to understand them in a way that respects their concerns.

Christians need not be hostile in this regard. These rival accounts typically afford some overlap within which to seek cooperation. At the same time, they remain rivals. They claim to disclose what is of ultimate significance—what is real as opposed to illusion. Like the Christian story, they make declarations that aim to evoke trust. They intend to establish where our loyalty lies. All who place their faith in such declarations must anticipate their vindication and thereby exercise eschatological hope. But now we must ask: "Is the authority that makes the declaration reliable?" In other words, "Can the author of the standard story be trusted?" I turn to this question in the next chapter.

4

Narrative Theodicy

THERE WAS ONCE A man who was a character within a story.[1] One day—inexplicably—he heard the voice of his author narrating him in the omniscient third person—explaining his actions, describing his feelings, foreshadowing his future. It began to dawn on him. His life was in someone else's hands. And not his life alone, but all around him—living, deceased, yet to be born—all were characters in this author's story.

The man shuddered as he thought about the awful things he and his fellow characters had endured. The violence suffered and committed seemed to somehow flow from this author. And so the man condemned the story as unfit to be told. No happy ending could justify it. Then, perhaps as a way to cope, he began to wonder whether or not the voice he was hearing wasn't his own. Maybe he had imagined the whole thing? Perhaps there was no author in the first place.

So he decided to author his own story. Whatever sense that might be made of his life was up to him to create. But the question, "Can this story be justified?" did not go away. It found a new target. He bore the burden. He considered passing the buck, but then realized the awful burden would remain regardless of where authorial responsibility came to rest. Whether shouldered by him, his community, his country, or humankind as a whole, the question of justification was unavoidable.[2] The meaningfulness of his life could not be maintained without a story. And there can be no story without an author. But which author could he trust?

---

1. This parable was inspired by the film *Stranger than Fiction*, directed by Forster, written by Helm (Columbia Pictures, 2006).

2. Cf. Bayer, *Living by Faith*, 1–8.

ESCHATOLOGY AND THEODICY IN NARRATIVE TERMS

To compare forms of eschatological hope is to compare life-organizing stories. This thesis challenges the assumption that non-Christian hopes are non-eschatological and therefore hopeless, or non-theological and therefore uncertain, or unbalanced and therefore over-realized or one-sided. Moving beyond this default use of attributes internal to Christianity, we can compare Christian hope with others and not merely dismiss them as "unchristian." In some sense, this is just good manners. More importantly, understanding rival stories of the world is essential for both Christian discipleship and mission.

Human hope arises from a life-organizing story. This is the story that shapes the lives and establishes the loyalties of its participants. Eschatological hope is given with and plotted by a life-organizing story, which establishes its own storied world. Each of these versions of reality is established by declaration: "Let there be." This utterance is creative (or possibly fictive). It makes the world fit the spoken word at the same moment the word fits the experienced world. History is narrative discourse about events which have occurred within this authorized, storied world.

Oftentimes, experiences threaten to make the reigning story unintelligible. Faced with unintelligibility, it can be revised, rejected, or reclaimed. If rejected, a new story is told and the original is subsumed within it. But even these new versions are faced with what plagued the original story: inexplicable occurrences that threaten to render the story unintelligible. They may not be the same kinds of experiences that discredited the initial story. Nevertheless, events will transpire that threaten the story's viability. No matter how often and on what scale they are re-written, the threat remains. This is *the problem of evil*. In order for the story to be told and to retain its authority, its participants must already anticipate its resolution. It must be told in hope. Therefore, eschatology can be defined as discourse on the resolution of conflict within an all-encompassing plot.

The hoped-for resolution in every case is a kind of *theodicy*—a demonstration that the implied author of the standard story is trustworthy. The trustworthiness of the author is attested through the movement of the story. This is because the author is the agent of "emplotment."[3] Here I am using the word *author* with a theological force. This does not require a *theos* in the sense of philosophical theism. Neither does it require a personal and providential Creator in the sense of the Abrahamic faiths. It only requires, as

---

3. Cf. Ricoeur, *Time and Narrative*, vol. 1, 31.

Martin Luther wrote, something "on which your heart relies and depends."[4] The author is the authority that presents the standard, world-establishing story as uniquely true. This authority could be the God of Abraham, the scientific academy, a postmodern narrated self, a pre-modern metaphysicist, or the Buddha. These authorities *emplot* life stories that are expected to yield some hoped-for resolution to the human predicament, however so defined. These stories are narrated to elicit faith, hope, loyalty, and perhaps even love for their authors. To have hope is to participate in one of these stories, to anticipate its resolution, and to proleptically accept that its author's status is justified.

This is why it makes sense that eschatology should be understood as theodicy and vice versa. Both are forms of discourse that assume, narrate, and defend a life-organizing story told in spite of *the problem of evil*. I relate the two in literary terms—after the manner of author and plot. "Eschatology" speaks to the point in terms of the plot. "Theodicy" addresses it in terms of the agent of emplotment. Both forms of discourse have the same purpose: justification of the author. Eschatology and theodicy are two names for one kind of discourse. Thus, to compare eschatological hopes is to compare competing narrative theodicies.

In this chapter, I intend to establish and elaborate on this claim. In the first half, I define key terms and then give a hearing to the *anti-*theodicy appeal made by some contemporary writers. In general, they characterize theodicy as oppressive discourse that ultimately masks evil and silences the sufferer. Therefore, they call for theodicy to be abandoned. This appeal is a challenge to my assumption that theodicy is inescapable where human hope is concerned. In constructive and critical dialogue with the anti-theodicy appeal, I introduce some distinctions between different forms of theodicy. In the second half of the chapter, I develop a method for distinguishing between these different forms in terms of how they characterize conflict and anticipate its resolution. My purpose is to say how the hope engendered by the Christian narrative theodicy is different from its rivals.

Definitions of Constitutive Features in a Narrative Theodicy

Theodicy is narrative discourse because it involves telling a story. In order for the story to be justified, it must *intelligibly* resolve the conflict internal to its plot. That is to say, it must overcome its own peculiar *problem of evil*. Since the final resolution makes the story, narrative discourse is also

---

4. Luther, "Large Catechism," in Kolb and Wengert, *Book of Concord*, 386.

eschatological discourse. *Eschatology* and *theodicy* speak to the same point: justifying the story, which is to render the author reliable.

In the prior paragraph I used italics to indicate the technical nature of these terms. I use them in a somewhat novel way. These same terms are applied in a variety of ways by other writers. During the course of this chapter, I will align and offset my usage with theirs. For now, I will define them in a preliminary way. I set the terms to fit the purpose of comparing Christian hope as one theodicy among rivals.

Eschatology is discourse on the narrative logic of a life-organizing, hope-eliciting story. Narrative logics are distinguished by how the conflict in the plot resolves. Resolution first requires a characterization of the conflict and then a manner of overcoming it. Since these stories establish the "real world," they are still in progress and unfinished as long as that world endures. Thus, every eschatology has a proleptic or now-and-not-yet character. The resolution can only be anticipated. If the story is accepted, then it is assumed that the residual conflict in its plot will not render it unintelligible. In this way, evil is expected to be overcome. Thus, the story's author will be accepted as reliable.

Intelligibility is the quality of a story that allows it to be a story. An intelligible story is more basic than a story as such. An unintelligible story is a failed candidate for the status of an intelligible story.[5] Because life-organizing stories are unfinished, because life goes on, no story can indisputably claim to already possess intelligibility. All stories-of-the-world continue as candidates for an intelligible story. In time, they will either be condemned or vindicated. Therefore intelligibility is only experienced proleptically. It remains for now an object of hope. To narrate and participate in a story is to anticipate and await its vindication.

The *Problem of Evil* is the conflict resident in the plot of a life-organizing story. Not all negative occurrences are experienced as "evil." It is only those experiences that threaten to make life unintelligible, thus unraveling the story which had until then made life meaningful. Also, not all life-organizing stories will be problematized by the same negative experiences. Driven by declarative speech acts, the story itself characterizes what counts as good and what counts as evil. Whatever is characterized as evil is a threat in the story, but not necessarily a terminal threat. Because it is a story of good overcoming evil, the participants within that story trust that evil will not prevail. Good will triumph and thus hope is in order. Negative experience, or evil, only becomes a problem when it undermines trust in the story's implied author and makes participation in that story unsustainable.

---

5. Cf. MacIntyre, *After Virtue*, 208–9.

Theodicy is discourse that seeks to demonstrate the author's reliability. Spoken from within a given life-organizing story, this discourse declares evil to be "evil" and good to be "good." Additionally, it can either describe (theoretically) or prescribe (pragmatically) how "evil" is to be overcome. Thus, theodicy is always narrative discourse. It is identical to eschatology in the sense that both argue for, speak of, reflect on, and anticipate the resolution of conflict within an all-encompassing plot. Eschatology and theodicy both aim to elicit trust in the author by telling the story in the midst of conflict and anticipating its resolution.

To summarize, eschatology and theodicy are two ways to characterize one activity: telling, inhabiting, critiquing, revising, and clinging to a life-organizing story. Such a story presumes a trustworthy author and an ultimate resolution to its plot. By defining theodicy like this, I am expanding a widely accepted, but narrow definition of theodicy as a theoretical enterprise "to give positive, plausible reasons for the existence of evil in a theistic universe."[6] I am following several scholars who have expanded the word to include non-theistic discourse. I will briefly mention three: a theorist of literature and religion, a philosopher, and a sociologist.

Theodicy in the Broad Sense

Larry Bouchard explored how evil is portrayed in both drama and in religious thought. He used the term "theodicy" broadly to express the human desire for coherence in the face of evil. "Theodicy," for his purposes, "refers not only to theological justifications of evil and the 'ways of God to man,' but to any endeavor, theological or otherwise, to bring coherence to the problem of evil and thereby justify humanity to itself."[7]

Susan Neiman framed modern philosophy as an extended attempt at theodicy, which has a narrow and a wide definition:

> Theodicy, in the narrow sense, allows the believer to maintain faith in God in face of the world's evils. Theodicy, in the broad sense, is any way of giving meaning to evil that helps us face despair. Theodicies place evils within structures that allow us to go on in the world.[8]

After Neiman narrated her alternative history of philosophy, she noted how theodicy came to an end, "over and over, throughout the eighteenth and

---

6. Peterson, *Problem of Evil*, 8.
7. Bouchard, *Tragic Method and Tragic Theology*, 1–2.
8. Neiman, *Evil in Modern Thought*, 239.

nineteenth centuries, only to reappear in other forms. Its persistence in the face of attack testifies to the fact that theodicy meets some deep human needs."[9] What keeps theodicy going is the "need to face evil in the world without giving in to despair."[10] It is an expression of humanity's refusal to live without hope.

Writing more than thirty years before Neiman, sociologist Ernest Becker raised a similar argument in his book *The Structure of Evil*. He stated that the "central problem" posed by the modern scientific revolution, which "is still ours today," is "*the problem of a new theodicy*." After Newton declared the world demystified, something "entirely different had to be done to explain evil in the world." Humanity "could not put the burden on God . . . The new theodicy had to be a natural one, a 'secular' one . . . an 'anthropodicy.'"[11] This theodicy no longer had to account for *all* suffering. Instead, "it would limit itself to the use of human powers effecting whatever they can to overcome avoidable evil."[12] Other forms of suffering were deemed unavoidable and thereby vanquished in the very act of coming to see them in a new light. Death by "natural" causes, earthquakes, the occasional illness—these could all be easily explained by a people that no longer looked for divine intervention in the world. As *natural* disasters they no longer formed a part of the conflict in the plot. They were just part of the narrative setting.

A commonality among these theodicies is that they offer a positive response to the question: "Is this author trustworthy?" For Enlightenment philosophers, the original Source of the universe was no longer seen as the "author of all things." Whether it was a distant designer or impersonal evolutionary forces, the Origin of life merely provided the setting. As David Hume's Philo concluded, the "original source of all things is entirely indifferent . . . and has no more regard to good above ill than heat above cold."[13] If there was to be any emplotment, any resolution, any hope, modern humanity would need to be its author. With the deity factored out, the burden of authorship falls on mortals. But, as Luther said, this is exactly what it means to have a *god*. And since every storied world is still plagued by a proleptically-resolved problem of evil, trust in any author anticipates a successful theodicy.

Christian doctrine, especially in the Lutheran tradition, has recognized that alongside "the true faith that corresponds to the one true God

---

9. Ibid., 288.
10. Ibid., 291.
11. Becker, *Structure of Evil*, 20.
12. Ibid., 376.
13. Hume, *Dialogues Concerning Natural Religion*, 169.

there is false faith, or trust in idols. Of both it is true that whereon our heart hangs and relies is our God." But to call one God "true" and another "false" is itself a *theodical* claim that must await *eschatological* vindication. The claim itself "does not decide who is the true God."[14] Hindus, humanists, evolutionary psychologists, and Christians alike must, for the time being, "live with provisional answers."[15] They all inhabit standard stories that are not yet complete. They experience conflict that is not yet resolved. They trust authorities whose reliability is contested. Thus, comparing other forms of eschatological hope with Christian hope involves comparing rival narrative theodicies.

The Anti-Theodicy Appeal

At first glance, the approach I have introduced is contrary to the work of several scholars. These writers, both Christian and non-Christian, share a common objective: remove theodicy from both every-day and academic discourse. Terrence Tilley, a Roman Catholic scholar, is notable among them. In 1991, He presented a book-length argument to this point: "theodicy is a discourse practice which ought to be abandoned."[16] Appeals such as Tilley's typically begin with a precise definition: "Theodicy refers to attempts to justify God when the logic of theism is at risk: (a) God is omnipotent; (b) God is all good; (c) there is evil. Theodicy tries to hold all three together and explain how *a* and *b* are still true even in the presence of *c*."

Carol Lakey Hess used this definition in an article from 2009.[17] She argued that realist and tragic literature should play a prominent role in religious education. Though Hess did not reference Tilley's work, she was continuing his anti-theodicy agenda almost twenty years later. Hess did, however, reference a scholar to whom Tilley was also indebted: Kenneth Surin, specifically his 1986 book *Theology and the Problem of Evil*.[18]

Hess's complaint against theodicy was that it "often seems like a mop up task when the grime and grit of life leaves tracks all over our polished abstract theological presuppositions."[19] She thought tragic and realistic literature can counteract these abstractions because a "tragic novel is frequently an experience that destabilizes theodicy, and it pressures us to re-ask the

---

14. Pannenberg, *Systematic Theology*, 1:113.
15. Ibid., 116.
16. Tilley, *Evils of Theodicy*, 220.
17. Hess, "Come Here Jesus," 354n1.
18. See ibid., 356 and Tilley, *Evils of Theodicy*, 251n1.
19. Hess, "Come Here Jesus," 356.

questions that produced tidy justifications of God."[20] Later Hess related theodicy to "comedic theologies," which presume a "movement from the real world to the ideal" and thereby "obscure the tragic nature of life." This is because "they affirm God's providence and abundance but then 'punt' to eschatology when it is clear that God's abundance is too far in the distance." Comedic theologies are distinguished from a "tragically structured theology," which "focuses more on describing the world as it is and less on justifying God and projecting triumph."[21]

Hess's argument implies that realistic, tragic theologies reject theodicy and are essentially noneschatological. For tragic theologians, questions like "Why do people suffer?" or "Where is God in suffering?" do not simply go away. But unlike comedic theologians, tragic theologians would address these questions with the aim of keeping them open and morally productive.

Hess offered "realist literature" as a way from comedic to tragic theology. She explored works by F. Scott Fitzgerald and Toni Morrison because both challenge "the peculiarly North American theodical narrative—the 'Rags to Riches' Myth" and "its corollary the American Dream." These life-organizing stories "slide into theological triumphalism and become an implicit form of justifying God—suggesting that those with enough discipline and determination will prosper . . . and neither God nor social forces are to blame if they get lost in history's waste."[22] This storied theodicy teaches its hearers to avert their eyes from suffering. Hess critiqued the theologies arising from it: "This religion of progress has produced triumphal theologies that lack a provision for disillusionment and failure."[23] But tragic theologies can correct this.

Hess suggested that philosophy and theology were "starting to take clues from literature" by moving away from "theorizing about evil" toward "telling stories" (fiction and nonfiction) that recount experiences of suffering. "Such stories do not reduce evil to an abstract rationale or calculation," but rather "enlarge and increase our capacity for reflection about what constitutes evil and suffering."[24] These stories are valuable because through struggling with them the readers "gain a more honest gaze and an enlarged moral vision." Hess applied this to reading biblical narratives in the context of religious education. Stories from the Bible should be read "not to

---

20. Ibid., 357.
21. Ibid., 372, 374.
22. Ibid., 356.
23. Ibid., 371.
24. Ibid., 373.

decipher what the text 'says' as much as to consider what goes on in the readers as they engage in the event of reading."[25]

Drawing on Reader-Response Criticism, Hess focused on how Bible stories can be employed in forming moral character. This is not radically different than Kant's reading of the biblical narratives, which I noted in the book's introduction. In a Kantian reading, the biblical vision of Israel's God's unilateral triumph over sin and suffering was, at best, a moral object lesson. At worst, it was a charter for quietist resignation. Fearing the worst, Hess urged religious educators not to "punt" to biblical eschatology.

Hess does not comment on what can be construed as an *alternative eschatology* at work in tragic theology. This eschatology derives from a story about growing up, which includes a different sort of triumph over evil. It is triumph through disillusionment. Its resolution includes becoming "more human," and having "theologies less convinced of their divinity." It begins by removing the "white lace doily of triumphalism." Once stripped of these false consolations, the protagonist is ready to face the real world. Tragic stories are employed to create experiences within the reader that will result in an enlarged and fortified moral vision. Triumph over evil does not occur in the renewal of the cosmos but in the renewal of the interpreter and the interpretive community. The story's ultimate resolution is proleptically experienced when tragic stories "make us gaze at suffering," and then, "by their pathos . . . make us want to make things otherwise."[26]

The life-organizing story invoked by a tragic theology can be read as a narrative theodicy. It is, no doubt, different from the theoretical theodicy that resolves only after a conceptual quest in search of a solution to a propositionally stated problem of evil. It would involve a different form of discourse. The *tragic* narrative theodicy has the illocutionary point of a *directive*: "Become a person who wants to make things otherwise." It intends to overcome evil by ridding the hearer of his or her idealistic illusions—to make the interpersonal world fit to the directive word: "Grow up." The *classic* form of theodicy tells a story with the illocutionary point of an *assertive*: "This is the best of all possible worlds and here is why." It intends to overcome evil by making the explanatory word fit to the world "as it really is" despite all appearances.

It is tempting to differentiate between the two by saying the tragic theodicy is "limited" but the classic theodicy tries to be "comprehensive." But this misses an important point. Both are comprehensive within the context of the story they tell. The tragic story seems more limited because

---

25. Ibid., 374–75.
26. Ibid., 375.

it does not designate sin-and-suffering in general as "evil." These are just matter-of-fact features of the "real" world. The world "is what it is." The problem of evil, for the tragic story, is the *illusion* that these experiences can be explained or reconciled by reference to an ideal world. Whichever way evil is defined, participants in both stories experience already-but-not-yet forms of resolution. Both claim to establish reality by telling an intelligible, standard story—a story by which all others should be judged. Both stories are backed by a particular authority, an implied author. But the question remains, which author to trust?

Like Hess, Terrence Tilley sought to counter theodicy as assertive, theoretical discourse. They both relied on Surin's *Theology and the Problem of Evil*. Surin contrasted between "theodicies with a theoretical emphasis" and "theodicies with a practical emphasis."[27] Although this distinction is fundamental to Surin's argument, neither Hess nor Tilley incorporated it into theirs. Tilley restricted his project to campaigning against "theodicy proper," which emerged during the Enlightenment and constructed "the problem of evil as a problem to be solved by a cool and detached explanation, not by a commitment to actions undertaken in order to alleviate the various particular evils."[28] For Tilley, Surin's "theodicies with a practical emphasis" is a misnomer. "Theodicy is a discourse practice which is 'impractical.'"[29] Tilley gave a reason for his focused terminology. He thought broad, or "extended uses" of the term *theodicy*

> blind one to the unique problems and power of the Enlightenment practice of theodicy proper, a practice which serves to marginalize all other discourse about God and evil. Indeed, once one stops collapsing all discourse about God and evil into one form, the difference between dry, measured, cool, calm, abstract academic voices and nonacademic voices are obvious.[30]

What if we heeded Tilley's warning about collapsing all discourse into one form, but at the same time, pursued Surin's insight that theodicies come in different forms? We do not need to assume the label "theodicy" only applies to one form of speaking about God and evil—the theoretical kind. As I inferred with the tragic theology invoked by Hess, it is possible to organize one's life around a *tragic* theodicy. This story overcomes evil by accepting the tragic nature of the world and then by resolving to become a better kind

27. Surin, *Theology*, chaps. 3 and 4.
28. Tilley, *Evils of Theodicy*, 2.
29. Ibid., 229.
30. Ibid., 2–3.

of person in spite of the world. The evil overcome here is not the tragic world, but the false consolations that mask injustice and silence sufferers.

From Tilley's perspective, the tragic narrative does not warrant the label "theodicy" because it is not an Enlightenment theodicy "proper." However, there is nothing in Tilley's approach that would formally dissuade a more "extended" use of the term, so long as theodicy is qualified in some other sense. Tilley and other anti-theodicists like Hess might justifiably question such an extension: Why drag the Christian tradition into an Enlightenment problem? Answer: the biblical narrators are too concerned about declaring and lamenting Israel's God's contested righteousness for this to merely to be an Enlightenment problem.

The Possibility of a Properly Christian Theodicy

The anti-theodicy appeal typically targets one specific mode of discourse. Theodicy, for Tilley, was theoretical, impractical, assertive declaration. As indicated above, I am enlarging the term to include other forms of narrative discourse, especially forms that are appropriate for telling, inhabiting, and enacting the Christian story. As a Christian, Tilley argued against the theoretical form of theodicy because it is, in the first place, inappropriate *for Christians*. This is because it promotes a rival life-organizing story. By saying that, I have reframed Tilley's anti-theodicy appeal. He is not against theodicy *per se*. He is against an Enlightenment story that set up a world in which many forms of evil were concealed. To counter this story, he challenged many of the Enlightenment's categories for discourse on God and evil. But his narrow focus kept him from addressing how a properly Christian theodicy would be different. In the next section, I extend his approach as a means to compare rival narrative theodicies, with special reference to the Christian narrative theodicy, which is the source and expression of Christian hope.

A Speech Act Approach. In the first part of his book, Tilley applied Speech Act Theory to discourse practices within religious traditions. He explained that a speech act approach can be used to compare various forms of religious discourse. Such a comparison can be made without assuming a universal religious experience, such as a "consciousness of being absolutely dependent," that is, "being in relation with God."[31] Tilley believed that a speech act approach "provides a way beyond the impasse between what Lindbeck has categorized as the cultural-linguistic and experiential-

---

31. Schleiermacher, *Christian Faith*, 12.

expressivist approaches."³² Like the cultural-linguistic view, a speech act approach insists that religious language is used according to intra-systematic rules. This intra-textual grammar is "neither reducible to nor justified by some common religious experience." But, like the experiential-expressivist, a speech act approach "presumes that religious practices are comparable." But it "does not presume that a basic experience, attitude, or entity is a *foundation*" for such practices.³³ My approach, similar to Tilley's, presumes that analogous discourse practices (e.g., recounting, criticizing, defending, and proclaiming a life-organizing story) can be found in various traditions and "provide a bridge for comparisons."³⁴

Theodicy by Assertive Declaration. In the final chapter of his book, Tilley concluded: "Theodicy proper, as a resolution to the problem of evil, is a discourse practice . . . which emerges in the Enlightenment."³⁵ By "theodicy proper," Tilley meant what Surin called "theodicies with a theoretical emphasis." Tilley's account of the rise of theodicy "proper" follows Surin, who argued that new forms of theoretical reflection during the Enlightenment created a new problem of evil. With the "cognitional individualism" introduced by Descartes, "the 'project' of theodicy" became "a work of solitary reflection," something that could be engaged in "by any individual who has the requisite capacity to judge."³⁶ As Becker said, the problem of evil for an eighteenth-century European deist was how to reconcile suffering with the existence of a "gentleman God," who "ran the universe in regular, lawful ways, not angry, cataclysmic ones."³⁷ Tilley then summarized: "These theodicy projects make sense [for Christians] only on the presumption that Enlightenment theism is the expression of belief in God proper to Christianity." But this is problematic if doctrines of the Trinity, Christology, and soteriology are considered "auxiliary to basic theism, but as constitutive of Christian belief in God."³⁸ And as Surin suggested, it is doubtful that the

32. Tilley, *Evils of Theodicy*, 5n1. Cf. Lindbeck, *Nature of Doctrine*.

33. Tilley, *Evils of Theodicy*, 5n1. Also, Tilley, "Incommensurability, Intratextuality, and Fideism," 87–111.

34. Ibid., Tilley, *Evils of Theodicy*, 5n1.

35. Ibid., 225.

36. Ibid., 20.

37. Becker, *Structure of Evil*, 5.

38. Tilley, *Evils of Theodicy*, 228. For examples of modern theodicists, he referenced the prototypical theodicy of Leibniz, *Theodicy: Essays on the Goodness of God, the Freedom of Man, and the Origin of Evil* (1710); the soul-making theodicy of John Hick, *Evil and the Love of God* (1978); the process theodicy of David Griffin, *God, Power, and Evil: A Process Theodicy* (1976); and the natural law theodicy of Richard Swinburne, *The Existence of God* (1979). Surin also included the free-will "defense" of Alvin Plantinga, *God, Freedom, and Evil* (1974).

"Cosmic Actualizer" defended by modern theodicists is "even telescopically identifiable as the Holy One who is the Father of Jesus Christ."[39]

Tilley identified modern theodicy discourse as "assertive declaration." He assumed the basics of John Searle's taxonomy of speech acts I described in chapter 3. Speech acts attain in the form of *assertives, directives, commissives, expressives,* and *declaratives*.[40] Tilley classified theodicy as a "hybrid" speech act, which has "multiple forces, depending upon their content, context, and purpose."[41] At first glance, modern theodicy seems to have only an assertive illocutionary point. Theodicists try to "show how things really are (despite appearances)."[42] But, theodicists do more than describe how evil is somehow necessary or beneficial to the bigger picture. They *declare* a new reality in which good and evil can be identified and sorted out. "Those who write theodicies declare what evil is." Moreover, "the purpose of theodicists' declarations is to find God not responsible for, not guilty of, what they declare evil . . . as if the theodicist were rendering a verdict on God."[43]

Earlier in the book, Tilley noted that such a communicative act "requires a narrative setting."[44] By doing so, he connected this insight to his prior work in narrative theology. He cited his 1985 book, *Story Theology*, where he discussed stories that "set up worlds" (myths), "upset worlds" (parables), and "set in worlds" (actions, or realistic narratives).[45] In *The Evils of Theodicy*, he likened Enlightenment theodicy to a story that "sets up" a world.[46] This story began with a declaration: "Let there be an absolute, impersonal ideal that governs the universe." The conflict in this storied-world is human ignorance as to how all things, even negative experiences, fall in line with the ideal, like the darker, unsightly pieces in a larger, beautiful mosaic. The conflict in this plot is resolved via one's conceptual journey to see the world aright. The negativities are transcended and thus fit into an increasingly clear view of the "divine plan" or the "big picture."[47]

39. Surin, *Theology*, 74.
40. Tilley, *Evils of Theodicy*, 10–15.
41. Ibid., 241.
42. Ibid., 232.
43. Ibid., 236–39.
44. Ibid., 19.
45. Tilley, *Story Theology*, 53, Tilley noted that his work was "deeply influenced" by Crossan, *Dark Interval: Towards a Theology of Story*.
46. Tilley, *Evils of Theodicy*, 241, "The emergence of a tradition of theodicy . . . fits as an effect of a successful declaration . . . the world with which we have to do is/becomes what the declarer says it is."
47. Cf. Graham, in *Evil and Christian Ethics*, 165–74, who called this search for the big picture a "synchronic theodicy," which he contrasted with a "diachronic theodicy."

Tilley urged resistance to this assertive-declaration of the Enlightenment's story. Its evangelists mis-declare some evils and efface others in order to make all negative experiences fit logically into a "systematic totalization."[48] "In the end, theodicy is a declaration which cannot but be a falsifying declaration which is either destructive or incoherent." It "effaces the difference between the world that theodicists wish to be . . . and the world that is."[49] Theodicy itself is evil because it silences the sufferers lest they disrupt the theodicist's enjoyment of the view.

Disrupting Theodical Assertions. Part of Tilley's strategy to disrupt this myth was to re-read several texts which have received canonical status among modern theodicists. Following the accepted strategy of assertive-declaration to overcome evil, they tend to read these texts in that light. They are thought to assert the propositions that set the terms of the debate. I will briefly review how Tilley used speech act analysis of the biblical book of *Job*, David Hume's *Dialogues Concerning Natural Religion*, and Augustine's *Enchiridion* to contradict these assertions.

Tilley observed that theodicists tend "silence Job's voice" and "ignore the text."[50] This is because it is a threat to a systematic totalization of how God relates to creatures. "The Book of Job shows a God to whom human practices and concepts of justice are irrelevant."[51] Luther, in his preface to the book, lamented with Job at how "God torments even the righteous without cause."[52] What is the illocutionary point of this? Some focus on Job's restoration at the end and take it as assertive declaration about the justice of God's ways: All suffering is a test of faith and all the faithful will eventually be rewarded. But Tilley reminded his reader,

> God's restoring Job is not a result of Job's speaking or other actions . . . Both torment and restoration are unrelated to anything Job does . . . The Book of Job, then, as a speech act, cannot answer a reader's questions about the meaning of suffering or direct a reader to act in a specific way . . . In sum, "gratuitous restoration," in disconnecting crime from punishment, reward from merit, provides no positive solutions to problems readers bring to it.[53]

---

48. Ricoeur, "Evil," 635.
49. Tilley, *Evils of Theodicy*, 248–49.
50. Ibid., 89.
51. Ibid., 104.
52. Luther, *Word and Sacrament I*, in *Luther's Works*, 35:251.
53. Tilley, *Evils of Theodicy*, 105.

Job should be heard as a negative *directive*. It is not prescriptive but *proscriptive*. It "warns against neglecting suffering when trying to understand the way things really are or standing outside of the realm of suffering and telling the suffering how they could solve their problems."[54] The discourse of Job delivers an extended, dramatic, simple charge: Don't try to justify God.[55]

Later Tilley turned to David Hume's *Dialogues Concerning Natural Religion*. Within this dialogue between Demea, Philo, and Cleanthes, it was Philo who posed the question that is usually taken as the classic statement of the Enlightenment problem of evil:

> Is [the Deity] willing to prevent evil, but not able? then he is impotent.
> Is he able, but not willing? then is he malevolent.
> Is he both able and willing? whence then is evil?[56]

Most theodicists, according to Tilley, construe Hume as a skeptic challenging religious belief. "Then they try to meet that challenge by constructing a theodicy." But this is "inadequate and irrelevant" to Hume's real challenge.[57] It is common to understand Hume as making twin arguments against classical theism by invoking both the logical and evidential problem of evil. The standard interpretation takes the skeptical Philo as Hume's mouthpiece who defeats both a metaphysical theist (Cleanthes) and a mystic (Demea). Tilley thought this was mistaken. He heard Hume's voice in the *Dialogues* as a whole. If this is the case, what speech acts did he perform? Clearly the work deconstructs both philosophical and religious certainty, but there is more to it than that. Tilley found two points: first, a warning against building a claim for God's goodness upon a foundation of empirical evidence; second, a "challenge to the reader to become aware of the weaknesses and strengths of nonfoundationalist faith."[58]

Reading the *Dialogues* has provoked many a theist to respond to what they took as a generalized, propositional problem of evil. But the problem Hume raises is not merely for philosophical theism, but for all claims about the way things "really are," including his own. Hume portrayed a persistent rivalry among the three—foundationalist, skeptic, and nonfoundationalist.

---

54. Ibid., 109.

55. Cf. Luther, *Career of the Reformer I*, in *Luther's Works*, 31:10: "Man is by nature unable to want God to be God . . . Indeed, he himself wants to be God, and does not want God to be God."

56. Hume, *Dialogues Concerning Natural Religion*, 157. Hume's Philo calls these "Epicurus's old questions."

57. Tilley, *Evils of Theodicy*, 166.

58. Ibid., 183–84.

Each tells his own tale with his own narrative logic, none of which is able to incontestably establish his claims against the others.

In a similar fashion, Tilley surveyed misappropriations of Augustine and again responded with a speech act analysis. First he outlined what is generally accepted as an "Augustinian" theodicy: The all-powerful, good God created rational, morally good beings with whom he could relate. To do so, it was logically necessary for him to endow these beings with free will. But some of them irrationally exercised their will and placed themselves, rather than God, at the center of their affections. Through this sinful choice, their nature was distorted. These became the devil and his demons. Then, through the satanically-inspired sin of Adam and Eve, this corruption spread to all humanity. Having become sinful by nature, all deserve both temporal and eternal punishment. But God chose to save some through a gift of unmerited grace.

> Hence, all evil in the world is a result of sin. Natural evils, including much human suffering, result from angelic sin, and moral and spiritual evils from human sin. Those who are damned deserve eternal punishment because they sinned. Their punishment restores order to the universe.[59]

By this explanation, God's justice is said to have been demonstrated. But, according to Tilley, this "*is not Augustine's theodicy*; it is an amalgamation."[60] It has been constructed by theologians who have mined Augustine's writings for a means to exonerate God by the standard of Enlightenment theodicy, which is foreign to Augustine's thought.

Tilley criticized the way modern theodicists extract and homogenize content from Augustine's varied works. They assume this content can be characterized as an explanation of why there is evil in the world. They use it to assert the fundamental soundness of their theistic system. Having reached the summit on a mental journey from ignorance to clarity, they bear witness to the view: "Trust me," they say. "It's not as bad as it seems. I've seen the big picture. All evils are necessary evils. They serve a greater good." Tilley contended that this is not the form of Augustine's discourse. He reviewed Augustine's *Enchiridion* to make his case. Though this work is often taken as an *assertive declaration* giving an explanation for evil, Tilley regards it as an "instruction" to guide the catechumen's intellect and will. The ancient catechism conveys "the essentials of the Christian creed." Thus, it is an

---

59. Ibid., 114.
60. Ibid., 116.

"institutionally bound assertive."[61] Augustine assumed the world disclosed by the biblical narrative(s) and aimed to make his words fit that storied world. Within the context of the catechism, this world was not contested, and so no *declaration* was necessary. Unlike modern theodicies, Augustine's *Enchiridion* does not speak forth a new storied world where good and evil enjoy a proper balance as greater good and necessary evil. As Surin argued, "For Augustine . . . the solution of the 'problem of evil' must await God's triune revelation of himself. It cannot be sought anywhere else."[62]

Augustine's *Enchiridion*, according to Tilley, does not make declaration of what counts as evil and what counts as good. Rather, it assumes such declarations from the biblical narrative. Within the world established by the Bible, Augustine *states* "what should be believed, what should be hoped for, what should be loved,"[63] assuming the Christian story is the case. When this doctrine is challenged by a problem of evil (Why does God allow any evil? Why are some saved, but not others?), Augustine asserts a *defense*, but not a *theodicy*.[64]

The difference between defense and theodicy is the lack of declaration. A *defense* only disarms the challenger's discourse by suggesting possibilities for how the Christian story is not rendered incoherent by the challenge. A *theodicy* goes further by declaring a new storied-system in which questions that were not answered within the original story can now be answered. In contrast, the *defense stays in its native story*. It is content to block the attack with a hypothetical explanation. It is "not the real solution of the problem of evil. That solution lies elsewhere."[65]

A Defense Implies a Narrative Theodicy. A theodicy aims to provide a basis for belief, whereas a defense assumes another basis is already in place. The distinction between theodicy and defense is important even if we are unsure whether or not it can hold under pressure. It is important because of what it implies: if a defense is not supposed to be the basis of Christian belief,

---

61. Ibid., 117. "Institutionally bound" should be understood as nonfoundationalist, intra-systematic discourse.

62. Surin, *Theology*, 12.

63. Augustine, *Enchiridion*, in *On Christian Belief*, 274.

64. Tilley, *Evils of Theodicy*, 130–33.

65. Ibid., 125. For another explanation of a defense versus a theodicy, see Plantinga, *God, Freedom, and Evil*, 28, "A theodicist . . . attempts to tell us why God permits evil." But a defense does "not say what God's reason *is*, but at most what God's reason *might possibly be*." Note how Plantinga locates both defense and theodicy in the realm of theory. For debate on Plantinga's (and Tilley's) distinction between theodicy and defense, see Walls, "Why Plantinga Must Move from Defense to Theodicy," in Peterson, *Problem of Evil*, 331–34.

then that basis must lie elsewhere. This raises a critical question: Should this basis be understood as a kind of theodicy? I think it should be—if theodicy is defined more generally as *discourse intended to elicit trust in the author of a life-organizing story*. In contrast to Tilley, I argue that this more encompassing definition of theodicy is needed for two reasons: first, because Christian faith is based on the trustworthiness of the God of Jesus; and second, since participation in other life-organizing stories is also based on the trustworthiness of their implied authors, a broad notion of theodicy will be useful for comparing them with the Christian story. With Tilley, I assume these theodicies should not be collapsed into one form of discourse.

HOW THEODICIES CHARACTERIZE CONFLICT AND ANTICIPATE RESOLUTION

Life-organizing stories count as theodicies. They declare a conflict with evil and speak toward the resolution of this conflict. But not all stories speak in the same manner. Narrative theodicies seek to justify their authors in different ways, and it would be helpful to have a method for sorting them out. Such a method would enable us to identify the narrative logic by answering questions like, what is the conflict that drives this story? And, how is this conflict supposed to be overcome? The method I develop in this chapter is fitted for answering these questions. It distinguishes between different forms of narrative theodicy by how they characterize conflict and anticipate resolution. I will use these distinctions to construct a typology of narrative theodicies in the following chapter. For now, I introduce them and explain how they identify the narrative logic of a life-organizing story.

To understand the narrative's logic, at least two questions must be asked of the story: (1) How is evil characterized? (2) How is the conflict with evil hoped to be resolved? For the sake of simplicity, I assume each question has a binary set of answers. For the first, evil can be characterized either *idealistically* or *realistically*. For the second, evil can be overcome either *theoretically* or *pragmatically*. To elaborate these distinctions, I draw from the work of several scholars, most notably Susan Neiman, Oswald Bayer, and Kenneth Surin.

As I construct this method, I continue to assume the basics of Tilley's speech act approach. I take a characterization of evil as a *declarative* speech act. Both idealists and realists make creative declarations when they say what counts as evil and what counts as good. They make the world fit the word at the moment the word fits the world. This discourse "sets up" a new storied world. But then this new world suffers conflict. In order for the world to hold together, the conflict must be resolved. The strategy for overcoming conflict involves issuing more speech acts. The conflict can be overcome theoretically, by the participants fitting their words to the world as it actually is over and against how it appears. Or, the conflict can be overcome pragmatically, by participants making the present world come to fit their words. The theoretic strategy intends to overcome evil by making better *assertions*. The pragmatic strategy works to overcome evil by issuing successful *directives* or *commissives*.

Characterizing Evil

Eschatology is discourse on how the conflict in the plot of a life-organizing story resolves. Theodicy is discourse that attempts to justify the author of such a story. Both speak to the resolution of conflict within an all-encompassing plot. Both aim to elicit trust in the author by telling the story in spite of the conflict. Therefore, characterizing the conflict in a given story is imperative for comparing its hope to Christian hope.

Conflict is created by a declarative speech act which calls a certain state of affairs "evil." According to Susan Neiman, "designating something as evil is a way of marking the fact that it shatters our trust in the world."[66] The *effect*, not the term, is the crucial element. If something "shatters trust" in a storied world, then it has the impact of "evil" whether or not the signifier "evil" is used. The basic form of the response is: "This (evil) ought not be."

Since the character of this declaration is a criterion for comparing theodicies, I place these declarations into one of two general categories. Without this generalization, we would need to treat the various declarations of each speech act community on their own terms. While that might be interesting, it would not offer conceptual clarity as to how Christian hope is distinct from others. Therefore, I appropriate Susan Neiman's generalizations for my purposes. Hers are helpful because they make sense of many philosophical authorities in the modern western tradition. Dialog with this tradition is critical for understanding a post-Constantinian situation. Also, Neiman's categories are broad enough to make sense of many pre-modern and non-western traditions.

How does a given narrator characterize evil? Using Neiman's classification, I assume two formal possibilities: an *idealist* declaration or a *realist* declaration. The idealist declares, "Reality is not what it seems." The realist responds, "It is."[67] The prior speaker begins by trying to find some

66. Neiman, *Evil in Modern Thought*, 9.
67. Ibid., 203.

hidden "order in addition to the miserable one presented by experience." He continues with the desire to transcend or transform our given reality in some way by making the self or the world conform, in some mode or measure, to an ideal of the good. In contrast, the realist looks for no such order. He begins with a critique of the idealist and is inclined to "abandon every search for ideals . . . along with every search for sense and a system."[68] He denies "the reality of anything beyond brute appearances."[69]

Imagine this as a divide in a conceptual road. Each path represents the tendency to head toward one of two extremes when struck by the sentiment, "many things are possible, but *this* ought not to have happened."[70] Go left, on the idealist path, and you agree with your gut and set off on a quest to see the *is* be reconciled to the *ought*. Go right, on the realist path, and you dismiss that sentiment as wishful thinking and say—"it is what it is." Admittedly, these are simplifications. In everyday life, most people live in the conflict between the two.

The terms "idealism" and "realism" are used in a variety of ways. Sometimes they are used almost synonymously with "rationalism" and "empiricism." This is not Neiman's approach. She admitted the tenacity of the historical narrative which tells how modern philosophy struggled to secure the foundations of human knowledge. But she said this "narrative is flawed, for it lacks what is central to dramatic movement anywhere: a compelling motive . . . it's a narrative of philosophers who act without intention."[71] Rather than reading eighteenth and nineteenth century philosophers as consumed in a debate about how we know what we think we know, she claimed

> the great philosophers of the canon were concerned with nothing more or less gripping than the questions that move bright seventeen-year-olds to wonder, and worry, about sense and meaning. These are the questions that unite moral and metaphysical concerns and show why each of them matters . . . Growing up makes us think more and not less often about whether history presents anything but grounds for despair, or whether hopes for progress are based on anything but wishful thinking.[72]

68. Ibid., 148.
69. Ibid., 8–11.
70. Ibid., xiv.
71. Ibid., 6.
72. Ibid., xviii.

It was not mere curiosity that motivated them, but a "demand that the world be intelligible."[73] It was a need to live with hope and therefore a demand to tell an intelligible story about the world.

Idealist. Such a story begins with declarative speech that establishes what is good as opposed to evil. This declaration gets the story going by designating the conflict in the plot. The first kind of declarative is that of an *idealist*. Among the philosophers who judged between good and evil based on a real, but hidden order, Neiman included Leibniz, Pope, Rousseau, Kant, Hegel, and Marx. She admitted that most of these thinkers "would reject each other's company." Nevertheless, "all are united by some form of hope for a better order than the one we experience."[74] In the conclusion of her chapter on these thinkers, she observed that they all wished to displace God[75]—not in the sense of claiming design rights to the universe, but in the sense of being authors of a meaningful story about the universe. As authors, they declared what was evil based on their idea of what was ultimately good. For Leibniz, this good was knowledge about the true order of things. For Kant it was the moral *ought* that stood over and against all nature and contingency. For Hegel it was the idea of historical progress toward comprehensive meaning. For Marx it was the creation of classless society. The details of their declarations were diverse. But they are unified as a form of judgment against evil by the standard of an ideal good.

Realist. The *realist* declaration is, in the first place, a critique of the idealist. The writers Neiman discussed here included Bayle, Voltaire, Hume, Sade, and Schopenhauer. She noted that grouping philosophers by these categories "overlooks many crucial differences between them. But it's no cruder than the division of thinkers into rationalists and empiricists." Generalizations always preclude precision. But they do not rule out rough knowledge, fit to the task. This generalization is appropriate here because it aligns these disparate voices into a single protest against the perceived arrogance of the first group. The realists collectively criticized the idealists for playing God by attempting to render judgment according to human standards. The realists insisted "that things are indeed what they seem." Appeals to a hidden order

---

73. Ibid., 7.
74. Ibid., 11–12.
75. Ibid., 109–10.

were either a form of escape or egotism. The world must be faced "honestly," for "experience is just what it seems."[76]

The argument between the two groups is about "what to take more seriously: the stark and painful awareness that we have for a moment when confronted with any form of evil; or the ideas and explanations that allow us to transcend it."[77] Neiman tends to classify the first group as theodicists, while the second group she describes as anti-theodicists. As I argued above regarding comedic and tragic theology, the division between theodicy and anti-theodicy does not hold. They are simply two different kinds of theodicy driven by two differing declarations about what counts as evil. For the comedic or idealist story, evil is the contrary of the ideal. For the tragic or realist story, evil is the ideal itself. Clinging to ideals obscures the real world and prevents people from facing it honestly. Each story projects a triumph over a different kind of evil. Both look to this triumph as a source of ultimate or eschatological hope. Through that expected triumph, the author that plots the story will be justified. Therefore both the idealist (comedic) and the realist (tragic) generate narrative theodicies.

Overcoming Evil

Within Neiman's division between idealists and realists, there is an additional, implicit distinction. Her organization focused on how philosophers characterized evil. But this is only the first part of the logic in a narrative theodicy. The declaration of evil sets up the conflict in the storied world. But for that story to be intelligible, the conflict must resolve. Therefore we should not only ask, "What counts as evil in this story?" but also, "How is evil overcome?" Again, I assume two possibilities: evil is overcome either *theoretically* or *pragmatically*. I treated the characterization of evil as a speech act. I do the same for the strategy to overcome evil. The *theoretic theodicy* overcomes evil by making *assertions*, that is, by a process of fitting the speaker's words to the "true" world. The *pragmatic theodicy* overcomes evil by issuing *directives* or *commissives*, that is, by a process of making the present world come to fit the speaker's word.

This implicit division between theoretic and pragmatic strategies is present through Neiman's argument. In a brief summary of the idealists, she stated the following:

---

76. Ibid., 204.
77. Ibid., 115.

> Chapter 1 examined philosophers who sought some reason or order behind the world's appearances that would explain or redeem or justify our experience. Whether they sought to show that the world could be *accepted* or that it could be *changed* can make all the difference in the world.[78]

I've italicized the key verbs which highlight the different strategies. The theoretic strategy *accepts* the world. It can do so either from an idealist or a realist characterization. An idealist would *accept* the world by trying to more precisely describe it according to its true, but hidden order. Thus, she would transcend evil. But a realist would *accept* the world by trying to more accurately describe the world according to face-value experiences. Thus, she would transcend evil by scrapping illusions and facing the world honestly. In contrast, the pragmatic strategy intends to *change* the world. It can do so either from an idealist or a realist starting point. An idealist would *change* the world by directing others and/or herself to make the world measure up to a universal ideal. A realist would *change* the world (or a small part of the world) by directing others and/or herself to make the world more useful according to local custom and convention. In both cases, evil is hoped to be overcome not through transcending it, but through transforming the conditions that enabled the experience of evil. All four accounts work to justify the author of a certain story about the world.

Neiman briefly discussed this division when mentioning the differences between the idealist Leibniz and the idealist Marx. Leibniz believed that humanity's problem consisted in blurred vision. If only we could see the world rightly, our problems would be solved. He held the "right" to "consist in an order existing behind appearances that only God—at the moment—knows how to decode." But Marx believed the problem was that we keep our heads in the clouds. The ideal was not something to be decoded in a universe designed by a supernatural being. Rather, it was to be realized in a future society designed by human beings. "Marx held the right to consist in an order that humankind could establish." Neiman summarized:

> In *practice*, the difference between them could not be greater. In *metaphysics*, they were closer than they seem, for each denied that appearances are final. Whether they placed it in heaven or in history, each believed there was another court of appeal.[79]

In terms of how they judged evil against an ideal, Marx and Leibniz were similar. But their strategies for overcoming evil and thus the narrative logic

---

78. Ibid., 203. Italics added.
79. Ibid., 203–4. Italics added.

of their theodicies were quite different. The former was theoretic. The latter was pragmatic.

Active vs. Passive. Other scholars have made Neiman's second division explicit. Sociologist Ernest Becker delineated between two forms of secular theodicy—one with a "passive" strategy and another that was "active." The first type was an effort to justify humanity's existence and status in the world by "trying to standardize and simplify life by stressing conformity to what we find" in nature and reason, which were thought to be unified. In contrast, the active type wanted to shape the world "to our own imaginative purposes." Advocates of the active type (e.g., Hume, Rousseau) criticized the former's "*naïve rationalist trust in reading nature for moral precepts.*"[80] Recall how Neiman listed Hume among the realists and Rousseau among the idealists. But Becker grouped them together in advocating an "active" or a *pragmatic*, secular theodicy. They differ in their characterizations of evil, yet they are aligned in their strategy to shape the world according to their purposes.

Contemplative vs. Active. More recently, German theologian Oswald Bayer made a similar distinction. Bayer agreed with Neiman in saying that from "the time of Leibniz, the question of theodicy has become the key problem of our modern understanding of the world . . . Now that the question of theodicy has become secularized, humanity is inescapably and totally burdened with judgment."[81] As a Christian, Bayer felt that the "dispute of justifications reaches its climax in the theodicy lawsuit about God." The lack of answers continues to press on an old wound: "Why do the just have to suffer? Why does God not restrain evil? Why does God not intervene? Why does God not seem to care? Why does God evade us? 'My God, my God, why have you forsaken me?'" Bayer suggested that at least "two answers might be given that differ from one another. The one involves contemplative thinking—let us call it 'contemplative theodicy.' The other consists of action; we call it 'active theodicy.'" Like Becker, Bayer split up the philosophers that Neiman brought together as idealists. He listed the idealist Leibniz as a contemplative theodicist and the idealist Marx as an active theodicist.[82]

Theoretical vs. Practical. Kenneth Surin also made the division. As mentioned above, his argument in *Theology and the Problem of Evil* was centered on the contrast between "theodicies with a theoretical emphasis"

---

80. Becker, *Structure of Evil*, 20.
81. Bayer, *Living by Faith*, 10.
82. Ibid., 10–18.

and "theodicies with a practical emphasis."[83] Neither Hess nor Tilley found the division useful for their projects, but for mine it is essential. Surin observed that a theoretical theodicy "has as its sole focus of investigation a range of *arguments* and *judgments* . . . which their proponents hold to be true (or false) irrespective of time, place, and persons."[84] They give reasons that can be applied universally: evil exists because "the world is a vale of soul-making;" "we are free beings;" "good is impossible without the possibility of evil."[85] In contrast, theodicies that approach the problem from an existential dimension have a "practical emphasis." Rather than giving answers that could be applied irrespective of persons, they speak to specific situations. *This* evil exists because "*I* am imprisoned *here*;" "*We* are being tortured *now*;" "*You* are indifferent to *our* hunger;" "*God* is an indifferent spectator." The tools of theoretical theodicy are critical doubt and discursive reasoning. The practical version does theodicy with cries of outrage and action to right the wrong doing.

Summary. Neiman's classification of idealists and realists is helpful because it recognizes that the notion of evil is neither static nor timeless. Good and evil can only be recognized within a storied world that has been "set up" by authoritative declaration. To say that some state of affairs is "evil" says something about the effect it has on the participants of that story. Anything that undermines trust in the author of the story is experienced as "evil." The story can either be rejected or reclaimed in the face of it, but it cannot proceed uncontested and undisturbed.

However, Neiman's account needs to be supplemented in order to derive a method for analyzing the narrative logic of these stories. The declaration gets the story moving but not resolved. Becker's distinction between active and passive theodicies says something about different *strategies* for overcoming evil. Bayer's contrast between contemplative and active does the same. But pitting "active" against "passive" or "doing" against "thinking" obscures an important point gleaned from Tilley's speech act approach. Inasmuch as theodicy is *discourse*, it is *action*. Those who sit and contemplate solutions to the problem of evil do not normally keep these thoughts to themselves. They *speak* them to others. Whether it's asserting theories or directing plans for improvement, the theodicist is *doing* something. My use of the labels "theoretic" and "pragmatic" assumes this speech act approach. The distinctive feature of the theoretic approach is not simply that it involves thinking, but that it issues *assertive declarations*. These assertions are

83. Surin, *Theology*, chap. 3 and 4.
84. Ibid., 27.
85. Ibid., 145.

part of a story about a quest for better descriptions of the world. The distinctive feature of the pragmatic approach is not that it involves action, but that it issues *directive or commissive declarations*. These are part of a story about changing the world.

SUMMARY

Wolfhart Pannenberg stated that there is "no theodicy without eschatology."[86] Michael Peterson claimed "eschatology without theodicy is implausible; theodicy without eschatology is incomplete."[87] These writers made those claims within the context of Christian theology. I aim to refigure their terms for more extensive use. Where human hope is in question, eschatology and theodicy are indispensable forms of discourse. To criticize and abandon one theodicy entails being taken by a rival eschatology. To reject a particular eschatology involves being persuaded by a competing theodicy. In order to be viable, the narrators of these rival stories must display their intelligibility. They must assume the author behind them will prove faithful in the end. But, because of the continuing threat of "evil," none of them offer certainty. Instead, they seek it. They live by hope. All of this Christian eschatology has in common with other eschatologies.

Christians ought to engage in comparative eschatology because many rivals challenge the Christian hope. To compare eschatological hopes is at the same time to compare life-organizing stories. And because every story is threatened by some peculiar problem of evil, because the implied author's reliability is contested, the story itself constitutes a theodicy. That is to say, theodicy is the author's justification which is given with the anticipated resolution of the plot. Therefore, to compare eschatological hopes is to compare narrative theodicies. In the next chapter, I will develop a typology for classifying four model narrative theodicies. The purpose of this typology will be to communicate more clearly how Christian hope is distinct from its rivals.

---

86. Pannenberg, *Systematic Theology*, 2:173.
87. Michael L. Peterson, "Eschatology and Theodicy," in Walls, *Oxford Handbook of Eschatology*, 519.

5

A Typology of Narrative Theodicies—After Ricoeur

On my smart phone, there is an app I almost never use. It has but one function: to tell me which direction I'm facing. I rarely use my compass because the same function is built into my navigational app. This app not only tells me which direction I'm facing, it also tells me how to go from point A to B. As my proxy navigator, it thinks for me. It does not encourage exploration. If I get off the preset path, my navigator chides me to turn around. But, the beauty and simplicity of a compass is that it allows for exploration.

In an age of Google Earth, exploration is optional. Geographically speaking, the map app can tell us how to get anywhere we need to go. But conceptually speaking, opportunities for exploration abound. It would take a lot of effort to never interact with someone who professes convictions and beliefs that are foreign, disorienting, and potentially threatening to me.

Further complicating the matter, living in a post-Constantinian situation entails a lack of adequate conceptual maps. Once we knew when we were entering *Catholic*, *Protestant*, *Jewish*, or *Atheist* territory. Now, religious pollsters tell us of another territory—one that is growing: the *None*. This designation does not refer to a state without any convictions. It simply means that maps from an earlier generation may not apply here. Therefore, unless we resolve to always stick close to our convictional homeland, we must venture into uncharted territory. But how do you explore without forgetting where you came from and how to get back? You need a compass.

In this chapter, I offer a typology. A typology is a conceptual compass. Hans Frei, in his posthumously published book *Types of Christian Theology*, described typologies:

> They're nothing to be particularly proud of, but they do have a limited use in projecting innocent people into the author's secret mountain retreat or underground cave, so that if they want to get out and go on from there, they'll have to use their own compass . . .[1]

The typology I offer is my attempt to more fully apprehend what it means to hope as a Christian. It is part of my conceptual lair within which I am trying to learn how to think and speak of the God of Jesus in relation to everything else. Of course, I'm not the only one seeking clarity. Most of us tend to operate with more typologies than we realize. Frei explained how typologies "help provide conceptual orientation." They keep us from getting lost in the data—whether it's the data of historical analysis or the conversations of everyday life. The trouble with typologies is that they are often "general without testing or focusing on specific topics." Second, they are often "oversimplified and not sufficiently encompassing."[2] Frei compared typologies to navigational devices. Even when we take them for granted, they help us keep from losing our bearings. For that reason, they need to be inspected, calibrated, and maintained.

Thus far I have been arguing for an alternative approach to studies in Christian eschatology. The dominant approach maintains a balanced tension reflecting the plurality of attributes internal to Christian hope. My approach does not reject this one, but supplements it. Moreover, it recalls that these attributes are abstractions drawn from the Christian story. As abstractions, they can be generally applied to many other life-organizing stories, not just the Christian one. Proleptic anticipation or inaugurated eschatology is an aspect of every story that presents itself as the *standard* one. These stories continue to be lived despite an on-going struggle with their own peculiar forms of internal conflict. Each is told in the hope that the author is reliable, giving it a now-and-not-yet character. Therefore, what the dominant approach often construes as unique to Christianity, is seen to be common when compared with rivals.

This led us to return to the Christian story and ask how it is distinct as one narrative theodicy among rivals. This is what I described as an *external use* of attributes—a use fitted for comparison rather than derivation. The

---

1. Frei, *Types of Christian Theology*, 19.
2. Ibid., 1.

two attributes or narrative features I highlighted were the conflict and resolution within the plot. I adapted Speech Act Theory as exposited by John Searle to distinguish these features. Ronald Thiemann and Terrence Tilley's work served as models for how this might be done. The speech act approach enabled to me claim that all life-organizing stories function as declarative speech acts. They attempt to disclose and establish the "real" world. They also declare what counts as evil and what counts as good. Additionally, faced with a continuing conflict between good and evil, they speak of a resolution in one of two "directions of fit"—either word-fitted-to-the-world or world-fitted-to-the-word.

Thiemann helped me describe the Christian story as a narrated *promise*, which has a world-to-word direction of fit. In this case, the speaker has the responsibility to make the world fit the word. And the speaker is the God of Abraham heard definitively in the voice of Jesus of Nazareth. Tilley helped me describe one form of Modernity's story as a narrated *assertion*, which has a word-to-world direction of fit. Leibniz's narration about how he came to see this as the best of all possible worlds was an example of this story. However, conversation with Susan Neiman led me to conclude that there are at least two competing stories of Modernity—one that characterized evil in *realist* terms (according to appearances) and one in *idealist* terms (according to an order behind appearances). Then Becker, Bayer, and Surin all suggested another dimension to the narrative logic: a strategy for overcoming evil. Putting them together, I suggested four model narrative theodicies with which the Christian story could be compared: *idealist-theoretic*, *idealist-pragmatic*, *realist-theoretic*, and *realist-pragmatic*.

To summarize my thesis: when comparing Christian hope with others, eschatology should be understood as the resolution of conflict within an all-encompassing plot. Furthermore, eschatology should be understood as theodicy and vice versa. I argued for this in the first four chapters. The following four should show how this approach yields something concrete. My purpose is inter-systematic[3] critique. I exhort fellow Christians to "stay with the story." Thus, I will give an account of our story that is distinct from its rivals. My secondary purpose is extra-systematic understanding. Such an understanding may have a three-fold impact on the Christian practice of hospitality towards outsiders: respectfulness in conversation, cooperation in doing what is good, and coherent testimony when given a hearing to account for our hope (cf. 1 Peter 3:8–15).

---

3. Cf. Lindbeck, *Nature of Doctrine*, 64, 80, "Intersystematic" concerns the "truth of coherence" within a "story" or "comprehensive interpretive medium."

A TOOL FOR UNDERSTANDING HUMAN HOPE

To show how this approach can yield something concrete, I offer a typology of four model narrative theodicies. In his 1967 book *Symbolism of Evil*, French philosopher Paul Ricoeur did something similar, but for a different purpose and with a somewhat different method.[4] I construct mine having learned much from his. The principal difference between our projects is that Ricoeur enlisted his typology in primary service to late modern culture, whereas I enlist mine in primary service to the Christian church striving to be faithful in a post-Constantinian situation.

Among his four types of "myths" about the origin and end of evil, Ricoeur did not include a "myth of Modernity." In part, this was because he, at the time, did not perceive Modernity in storied terms comparable to a "myth," that is, a "traditional narration," which has the "purpose of providing grounds for the ritual actions of men" and "establishing all the forms of action and thought by which man understands himself in his world."[5] His purpose was not to interpret modern configurations and projections of history. He wanted to reinvigorate modern culture by re-reading these older "myths."[6]

As a confessing Christian, Ricoeur acknowledged the Judeo-Christian "myth" as the place from which he viewed the others.[7] But, as a professional philosopher schooled in the Western tradition, he resolved to work according to that tradition's standards. Saying that he did this particular project on behalf of modern culture is no more an indictment of his Christian faith than saying that a Christian civil engineer designed a road for his city of residence.[8] But it does highlight a major difference between his

---

4. Ricoeur, *Symbolism of Evil*.

5. Ibid., 5. In contrast, Ricoeur's later works encourage an interpretation of Modernity as a story analogous to traditional religious myths. See Ricoeur, *Time and Narrative* and Ricoeur, *Oneself as Another*.

6. Ricoeur, *Symbolism of Evil*, 347. See also Ricoeur, *Freud and Philosophy*, 38, for his later interpretation of *Symbolism of Evil* as listening to and being nourished by the mythic symbols while continuing the "tradition of rationality" of "our western philosophy."

7. Ricoeur, *Symbolism of Evil*, 306. He said "myth" should *not* be taken as "a false explanation by means of images and fables" (5). Also, "we should not say, 'The story of the 'fall' is *only* a myth'—that is, something less than history—but, 'The story of the fall has the greatness of myth'—[it] has more meaning than a true [modern, critical] history" (236).

8. For two accounts of Ricoeur's philosophy as amenable to traditional (non-revisionist) Christian theology, see Blundell, *Paul Ricoeur* and Stiver, *Theology after Ricoeur*. More commonly, Ricoeur's work is employed by correlational (revisionist) approaches, e.g., Tracy, "Ricoeur's Philosophical Journey," in Kearney, *Paul Ricoeur: The Hermeneutics of Action*.

typology and mine. As I develop mine in light of his, it will become apparent that this difference makes the two mutually enriching, yet distinct.

Unlike Ricoeur's, my typology will scrutinize and learn from stories of Modernity and Postmodernity. I do not locate the Christian story on my chart of narrative theodicies (Figure 2, below) because my goal is to distinguish the Christian story from these. Ricoeur wanted his analysis to speak to modern people and "recharge" their language. I offer mine as an appeal to Christians to reclaim our story in the face of our particular problem of evil. In spite of this significant difference, much of Ricoeur's general approach is valid for my task. Especially instructive are his explanation of the limits and benefits of typology and his rationale for choosing stories of the origin and end of evil.

Limits and Benefits of Typology

In *The Symbolism of Evil*, Ricoeur expanded the compass metaphor for typologies. Not only are typologies good for staying on the path, they are also good for finding new ones. They are heuristic devices, tools for discovery. Ricoeur did not want his typology "to be confined to an attempt at classification," a mere drawing of borders between territories. He wanted to "go beyond the statics of a classification to a dynamics" that had "discovery" as its task.[9] A "dynamic" use of the typology would make "manifest the struggle" among the concepts being explored—how they often overlapped, opposed, subsumed, and re-invented each other.[10]

Ricoeur described in more detail how typological inquiry can be used to map and explore a field of thought. The field in front of him in *The Symbolism of Evil* was the great variety of stories ancient cultures handed down "concerning the origin and end of evil."[11] This was his problem: if ancient peoples seemed to have similar expressions of evil, defilement, sin, and guilt, but, at the same time, shared an innumerable number of stories, myths, and legends to account for those experiences, "how shall we make our way between the One and the Many?" On the one hand, he did not assume they were all expressing the same core religious consciousness.[12] On the other hand, he didn't want to get lost "in an indefinitely diversified com-

---

9. Ricoeur, *Symbolism of Evil*, 174.
10. Ibid., 309.
11. Ibid., 170.
12. Ricoeur distinguished his approach from the "phenomenologists of religion," who believed the diverse stories essentially expressed the same "pre-narrative consciousness" (ibid., 166).

parative mythology." So, to seek a "numbered multiplicity" between these two extremes, he constructed a "typology." He elaborated on this solution:

> The "types" which we propose are at the same time *a priori*, permitting us to go to the encounter with experience with a key for deciphering it in our hands and to orient ourselves in the labyrinth of the mythologies of evil, and *a posteriori*, always subject to correction and amendment through contact with experience.[13]

In asking how Christian hope compares with its twenty-first century rivals, I face a similar dilemma. How are we to make sense of the plurality of life-organizing stories that have proliferated within western culture? Like Ricoeur, I accept neither their essential sameness nor their indefinite diversification. Therefore, I adopt his dialectic between applying formal (*a priori*) distinctions with a readiness to adjust (*a posteriori*) in conversation with particular people.

The Preeminence of Stories about Overcoming Evil

Not only do I adopt Ricoeur's general typological approach, I also invoke his explanation concerning the preeminence of stories about the origin and end of evil. This explanation is important for responding to a possible critique of my general approach to eschatology. It would be fair to question the sweeping manner in which I've used the word "story." Diverse forms and uses of story abound. In the prior chapter, I noted Tilley's division between stories that set up, set in, and upset worlds.[14] Other narrative theologians have argued for the importance of everyday accounts, communal stories, and biographies.[15] Additionally, my use of the term "the Christian Story," may expose me to Ricoeur's own warning against flattening the Bible into a "linear account," thereby making it "a grandiose but frozen one-dimensional narrative in which all the varieties of discourse are leveled off."[16] I respond to this by recalling the preeminent place he gave to stories about the origin and end of evil shortly after he completed *The Symbolism of Evil*.

---

13. Ibid., 171–72. Ricoeur said he was following after Max Weber's *Idealtypen* by taking this approach (279).

14. Tilley, *Story Theology*.

15. E.g., McClendon, *Ethics*, vol. 1 of *Systematic Theology*.

16. Ricoeur, "Toward a Narrative Theology" in Wallace, *Figuring the Sacred*, 237–38. Ricoeur pronounced Hans Frei guilty of flatting the Bible into a single dimension in his *Eclipse of the Biblical Narrative*.

After publishing *The Symbolism of Evil*, Ricoeur began writing his work on Sigmund Freud.[17] In that book, he reasoned that the "correspondence between a symbolism of evil and a symbolism of salvation signifies that we must . . . reflect upon the totality formed by these symbols of the beginning and the end." He suggested that the "architectonic task of reason" is to speak on "this totality."[18] In the concluding chapter, Ricoeur returned to this point: "At the end of this journey we will discover that the great symbols [i.e., stories[19]] concerning the nature and origin of evil are not simply one set of symbols out of many, but are privileged symbols." They are privileged because even rational, systematizing discourse, in imitation of these stories, can only *project* solutions, but not solve the problem of evil. Stories about where evil came from and how it is hoped to be overcome "show in an exemplary way that there is always more in myths and symbols than in all our philosophy." These stories have an "unsurpassable character" because they organize and orient all other aspects of human life.[20] By participating in such a story, "reconciliation is looked for . . . in spite of evil. This 'in spite of,' this 'nevertheless' . . . constitutes the first category of hope, the category of confidence."[21] Thus, if there is to be Christian discourse on a hoped-for reconciliation, it must venture to speak of *the* creation-to-eschaton story given by the Christian Scriptures, in all their variety. And, if this story is to be compared, it must be set against other attempts at all-encompassing emplotment.[22]

In Ricoeur's complaint against leveling off biblical discourse, he still recognized that the Bible, especially as interpreted through the New Testament, did lend itself to be read as an "all-encompassing story." The point of his criticism was not to set aside this story, but to hear it as an "open

---

17. See Reagan, *Paul Ricoeur: His Life and Work*.

18. Paul Ricoeur, *Freud and Philosophy*, 40.

19. See Stiver, *Theology after Ricoeur*, 103–4, who noted that Ricoeur eventually came to see "how symbols and metaphors are caught up in broader narratives." But at the time of this writing, he still "tended to see the symbols as standing alone and narratives as secondary. He later saw this was a mistake; the reverse is more likely true, that is, that symbols arise in the context of larger narratives."

20. Ibid., 527. Ricoeur levied this as criticism against both Hegel and Freud who each thought their systems of discourse overcame the need for mythic or symbolic language and resolved the problem of evil.

21. Ibid., 528.

22. Ibid., xii. Ricoeur read Freud as such an attempt: "Psychoanalysis conflicts with every other global interpretation of the phenomenon of man because it is an interpretation of culture." At first, "Freud is [seen as] one combatant among many; in the end, he shall have become the privileged witness of the total combat, for all the opposition will be carried over into him" (60).

or ongoing story," and not as a closed "chronological display of intervals" by which savvy Christians can read history in advance.[23] Such a reading "tends to abolish the peripeties, dangers, failures, and horrors of history for the sake of a consoling overview."[24] Explanations about the so-called Big Picture or Divine Plan can cause Christians to forget they are still caught up in a story that remains unresolved. Ricoeur wanted to remind Christians of the contested character of their hope as much as he wanted to remind Freudian's of theirs.

PAUL RICOEUR'S TYPOLOGY

Ricoeur constructed his typology of "Myths of the Beginning and the End of Evil" in order to "recharge" modern language after a long season of "forgetfulness" of the "sacred." He believed that a critical retrieval of these ancient myths could irrigate the dry soil of Modernity. Even though modern men and women could no longer live in these myths, they could ponder them. By them, they might reconnect with the sacred and attain a "second naïveté."[25]

The Symbolism of Evil was volume two, part two of Ricoeur's larger project on a philosophy of the human will. In that larger project, he sought to understand the tension between human capability and fallibility, that is, our apparent freedom to choose what is good in contrast with our apparent bondage to evil.[26] Therefore, the organizing logic of his typology is centered on holding this tension between human freedom and bondage—a tension Ricoeur thought Modernity was losing through secularization. In the section that follows, I provide an historical narrative to frame Ricoeur's typology. Next, I describe its organizing logic, illustrate its elements of analysis, and then draw out an important distinction between two kinds of "evil." By doing so, I encounter him as a necessary "detour" on the way toward constructing my typology.[27]

---

23. Ricoeur, "Toward a Narrative Theology," 242.

24. Ibid., 238.

25. Ricoeur, *Symbolism of Evil*, 349, 351. At this time, Ricoeur was somewhat aligned with the demythologizing program of Rudolf Bultmann. However, twenty years later, in Ricoeur, "Toward a Narrative Theology," he would express his "antipathy to an *existential* theology indifferent to the historical dimension, which would be exclusively attentive to the irruption of the word in the instant of the decision of faith" (236).

26. See Blundell, *Paul Ricoeur between Philosophy and Theology*, 66.

27. Ibid., 1–12, presented the metaphor of "detour and return" to the "main road" as an appropriate way to incorporate Ricoeur's philosophy into theological discourse.

Background: A History of Human Culpability

In *Evil in Modern Thought*, Susan Neiman narrated how western philosophy passed through two world-changing crises. In her account, the names of two cities are emblematic: Lisbon and Auschwitz. The first city was destroyed by an earthquake in 1755 and the second was a center of operations for Nazi death camps: "the two events have been left to stand as symbols for the breakdown of the worldviews of their eras."[28] "In both cases, catastrophe tipped the bucket of assumptions that were already precarious. But in both cases, the events themselves created boundaries between what could and could not be thought."[29] These conceptual upheavals changed the way westerners declared evil to be "evil" and good to be "good."

Alasdair MacIntyre called this sort of upheaval an "epistemological crisis." Such a crisis is induced by a disruptive experience that makes the reigning story unintelligible. It can be resolved either by reclaiming the original story in spite of the experience or by rejecting it and telling a new one. When a new story is told, it must enable the protagonist to understand two things:

> *both* how he or she could intelligibly have held his or her original beliefs *and* how he or she could have been so drastically misled by them. The narrative in terms of which he or she first understood and ordered experiences is itself made into the subject of an enlarged narrative.[30]

The original story is not completely abandoned, but reinterpreted in light of a new plotline.

Frank Kermode's account of the literary feature "peripetiea" explains how the rejection of one plot entails the acceptance of another unexpected, but ultimately more satisfying ending. "Peripeteia . . . depends on our confidence in the end; it is a disconfirmation followed by a consonance." We thought the plot was going to resolve in a traditional happy ending, but our expectations were upended. But "in assimilating the peripeteia" we enact a "readjustment of expectations in regard to the end." And "the more daring the peripeteia, the more we may feel that the work respects our sense of reality." Having "naïve expectations" overthrown can be terrible, but in the end, we come to see we learned something we would have otherwise missed

---

28. Neiman, *Evil in Modern Thought*, 8.

29. Ibid., 239.

30. MacIntyre, "Epistemological Crises," in Hauerwas and Jones, *Why Narrative?* 140.

"on our more conventional way to the end."³¹ Experiencing a peripeteia in a life-organizing story allows an interpretive community to say: "Here's how we came to realize how misled we were." Accepting this reversal refigures the world around a new plot.

In Neiman's account, the Lisbon earthquake induced a peripeteia in the story of Modernity. Prior to that event, the distinction between natural and moral evil was not significant for how people made sense of their lives. All things came from God either as punishment, reward, or test of faith. Shaped by the Judeo-Christian belief about a personal, providential Creator, people generally assumed *all events*—both acts of human cruelty and instances of human suffering—were some form of speech act from God. Whether to pronounce curse or blessing, they heard their Creator saying something by them. Thus saith the LORD, "I make well-being and create calamity, I am the LORD, who does all these things" (Isa. 45:7). According to Neiman, pre-modern "theists were willing to give God responsibility" for human suffering and sin, while still blaming humanity for both.³² The only hope of resolution for this problem of evil would be a gratuitous act of God. Only God can reverse the curse of sin, suffering, and death. But this kind of resolution offered no consolation for the question of why some would be saved from punishment, while others would suffer eternally.³³

Neiman summarized the French encyclopedist Pierre Bayle's (1647–1706) thoughts on hell: "A Being who makes the torments of hell eternal, restricts the number of those who escape them to a tiny minority, and determines who gets what without regard to merit" makes "God appear a monster."³⁴ Even without a doctrine of predestination, "the torments of the damned" are "the block on which reason stumbles. For however bad a sin may be, it has to be finite. An infinite amount of hellfire is therefore simply

---

31. Kermode, *Sense of an Ending*, 18.

32. Neiman, *Evil in Modern Thought*, 3. Neiman cited Augustine as an example of a pre-modern theist who insisted on giving humankind the *blame* for evil, but not "responsibility" in the sense of having any power to clean up our mess (43). Neiman explained that the critical difference between blame and responsibility will always be in force as long as the notions of original sin and unmerited grace are in play. If humans cannot save themselves, they can be still be *blamed* for their damnation, but they cannot be held *responsible*, so long as responsibility implies the power to do something about it (see 36–43, 141).

33. This question was the open wound that animated the famous debate between Luther and Erasmus. See Rupp and Watson, *Luther and Erasmus: Free Will and Salvation*. Luther wrote to Erasmus: "unlike all the rest you alone have attacked the real issue ... the question on which everything hinges" (ibid., 333).

34. Neiman, *Evil in Modern Thought*, 124–25.

unjust."³⁵ As both Roman Catholic and Protestant institutions began to lose social and political power in Europe, the God portrayed in the biblical narratives seemed more and more immoral. A Christian story that included eternal punishment became an evil to be overcome through Enlightenment.

German philosopher Gottfried Leibniz (1646–1716) responded to Bayle with his essay that coined the term *Theodicy*.³⁶ He argued that the idea of a willful and capricious God was mistaken. Leibniz declared God to be rational and gentlemanly: punishments only come to those who truly deserve them and everyone has the power to avoid them. "What is modern in Leibniz's account," according to Neiman, "is the conviction that the causal links between sin and suffering will become clearer with time, as will the ways in which, despite appearances to the contrary, God has ordered all those links for the best." But, by doing so, "Leibniz . . . put reason above God Himself." It is but a small step from here to eliminate the middleman and enthrone Reason.³⁷ Whether the Christian God was pronounced evil or defended as good, in both cases, God was made subject to the declarations of humanity. "In the process of defending God, Leibniz disempowered Him . . . he gave us a God created in *our* image."³⁸

The Lisbon earthquake catalyzed the crisis that began with Leibniz's response to Bayle. Leibniz insisted God's purposes in the world were rational. The earthquake challenged this because it seemed like an unprovoked attack. Was Lisbon more sinful than any other city? To cope with the way the world dished out suffering indiscriminately, early modern thinkers like Jean-Jacques Rousseau (1712–1778) bracketed out 'natural evils' as just that—natural. "Rousseau began to demarcate a sphere of natural accident that is neutral: disaster has no moral worth whatsoever and need have no negative effects."³⁹ Earthquakes were unhappy consequences of plate tectonics. The modern deity wasn't saying anything by them because the modern deity wasn't saying anything at all. He was a one-time designer now removed from the system.

35. Ibid., 19.

36. According to Leibniz, *Theodicy*, 58, Bayle's critique was not against the Christian story, but against those who judge it by the standards of reason: "[Bayle] wishes to infer that our Reason is confounded and cannot meet her own objections, and that one should disregard them and hold fast the revealed dogmas . . . But many readers, convinced of the irrefutable nature of his objections . . . would draw dangerous conclusions." This compelled Leibniz to respond with his *Theodicy*.

37. Neiman, *Evil in Modern Thought*, 27.

38. Ibid., 24.

39. Ibid., 39. Thomas Aquinas distinguished between the "evil of penalty" and the "evil of fault," but did not disassociate the natural from the moral (*Summa Theologiae*, part Ia, question 48, article 5).

After Lisbon, "God's purposes" came to have "no public function."[40] Thus, the only problem of evil that remained rested squarely on human shoulders. A problem of evil that had caused conflict in an old plot was overcome by fiat: 'Let there be a demystified natural universe.' Human beings now bore the responsibility for evil *alone*. Any solution would have to be authored by them.

Neiman argued that Western Philosophy's second epistemological crisis and accompanying peripatetic reversal occurred after Auschwitz.[41] The evil experienced there was so overwhelming that human solutions seemed ever doomed to fail. "The more responsibility for evil was left to the human, the less worthy the species seemed to take it on."[42] Captivity to sin, suffering, and death threatened to collapse the modern separation between moral evils and natural evils. It now appeared humans had no ability to author true solutions. Thus, they could not be considered responsible, at least not in the strict sense. This made all evil "natural." People became powerless to do anything expect pick up the pieces after the dust settled. "Lisbon revealed how remote the world is from the human; Auschwitz revealed the remoteness of humans from themselves."[43]

In Neiman's account, Auschwitz was conceptually devastating because it seemed to entirely thwart "the possibility of intellectual response itself . . . for the tools of civilization seemed as helpless in coping with the event as they were in preventing it."[44] This is an important observation for understanding both Neiman's narrative and Ricoeur's typology. Both were attempting to fill a void of philosophical reflection on evil. For Neiman, Auschwitz threatened to "collapse the distinction between natural and moral evil."[45] This separation was for her an enduring demand of human reason itself. Her work is an appeal to reclaim the demystifying story of Enlightenment. Ricoeur saw the problem in similar terms, but had a different solution. The answer for him was not to reinforce Modernity's rejection of mythology, but to return to myth as the very basis of all philosophical reflection. For him, "philosophical exegesis and understanding" of myths can "create a new *peripeteia*" by which humanity might negotiate the tension between captivity to evil and responsibility to resist it.[46]

40. Neiman, *Evil in Modern Thought*, 249.
41. Ibid., 250–52.
42. Ibid., 4.
43. Ibid., 240.
44. Ibid., 256.
45. Ibid., 281.
46. Ricoeur, *Symbolism of Evil*, 162, decried a "radical demythization of all our thinking."

Ricoeur's Organizing Logic: Human Culpability

The organizing logic of Ricoeur's typology in *The Symbolism of Evil* runs on a single axis. This axis represents increasing and decreasing degrees of human responsibility or culpability for evil. There are three types of "myths" on the axis. A fourth type floats above it toward the middle, but closer to the human culpability side (Figure 1).

Figure 1. Ricoeur's "Typology of the Myths of the Beginning and the End of Evil"

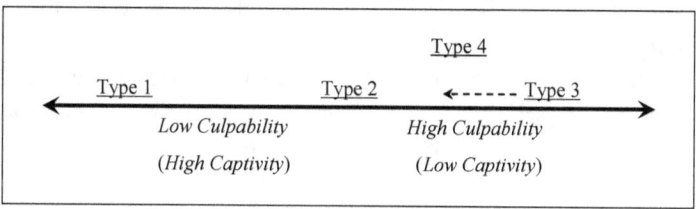

Ricoeur devoted a chapter to each "type."[47] In a summary chapter titled "The Cycle of the Myths," he illustrated the dynamic tension between them. He favored Type 3. It placed the blame for evil squarely on humanity's shoulders. And with that, it expected the most out of our kind in terms of repentance and rehabilitation. But he also argued that Type 3 needs the others as a balancing effect, so as not to demand too much of fallible men and women. The typology's conceptual payoff was to move Type 3 closer to center, hence the dashed arrow (Figure 1).

The balancing of Type 3 served as a lesson for Modernity. After 185 pages of lucid and detailed reflection, Ricoeur applied his typology to any "philosophy of the will" which "tries to remain an ethical vision of the world." An "ethical vision" is a summary of the storied world that existed between Lisbon in 1755 and Auschwitz in 1945. The power of this story was how it made human beings responsible for their actions. Its vulnerability was its limited capacity to cope with human captivity to evil without the total collapse of its ethical vision. Ricoeur spoke to this problem: a philosophy of the will must learn from the tension between the myths "so that the guilty man it denounces may also appear as the victim of a mystery of iniquity which makes him deserving of Pity as well as of Wrath."[48]

---

47. Ibid., 161–305. Ricoeur does not make his organizing logic explicit in this way, but consistently suggests it throughout. This is my interpretation and distillation of these four chapters.

48. Ibid., 346.

Ricoeur's Elements of Analysis

Ricoeur analyzed three elements in each myth: protagonist, plot, and pain of being. The importance of these storied elements issues from the typology's organizing logic. Each is a way of deciphering how the myth addresses the tension between human bondage and freedom. Each myth has a protagonist, its own "archetype," through which "man" is "manifested as a concrete universal." In "the myth the human type is recapitulated, summed up." Second, each has a plot, a "*movement* which is introduced into human experience by narration." The plot empowers the myth's participants to stave off despair and live with hope. Life happens in the history between "the perdition and the salvation of man." Third, each myth expresses the pain of being, or "the enigma of human existence." The stories convey an agonizing sense of "discordance" between what humanity is "essentially" and the present "modality" of human life.[49] Following Ricoeur, I summarize these elements within each type below.

As for naming types, Ricoeur never completely settled on a summary term, but drew from a rotary pool of words, phrases, and one-liners. He did this to reflect the nature of the types. As stories, they resist summary and distillation into discrete elements. At the same time, reading and understanding them requires some amount of second order discourse about what makes them distinct. Therefore, I selected summary terms to reflect how Ricoeur explained the *plot* of each story. I chose plot because it adequately reflects the character of the story as a whole and because this element is the focal point of my typology that follows. My terms for Ricoeur's four types are: (1) Chaos to Order; (2) Tragedy to Wisdom; (3) Rebellion to Restoration; and (4) Forgetfulness to Knowledge.

Type 1: Chaos to Order. Ricoeur called this "the drama of creation," because in it, "the origin of evil is coextensive" with the origin of all things.[50] This type is illustrated by "theogonic myths" of ancient Babylon. "These myths recount the final victory of order over chaos."[51] In the beginning, there was evil. From this chaos, the now reigning divinities emerged in struggle and violence, eventually conquering, creating order, and later making mankind as their servants. Yet even in victory, chaos (evil) remains a constitutive and unsteady part of the equilibrium between gods, man, and nature. Thus, "man is not the origin of evil; man finds evil and continues it."[52] Type 1

---

49. Ibid., 162–63.
50. Ibid., 172.
51. Ibid., 175.
52. Ibid., 178.

rests on the far left of the axis, where man is least culpable for evil and most captive to it. He is captive, but not in the sense of being bound by an alien entity. He is captive because this volatile mix of order and disorder is the nature of *all* things. The Babylonian king is the archetype within the human order. He is called to re-enact the creation drama in the cultic rituals and by waging holy war against any "resurgence of the ancient chaos."[53]

In Type 1, equilibrium is salvation. Disruption is evil. The decisive salvific event occurred *prior to* humanity's entrance on the scene. Still, salvation for human beings remains 'already-but-not-yet.' The victory has been won, but human participation in it remains uncertain. The status of the human king, the viceroy of the gods, is "revocable." The "gods have changed and can change their earthly servant. They have only to transfer the kingship to another city or another state . . . just as among themselves they grant supremacy now to one, now to another." At the same time, the hoped-for harmony is guaranteed by the salvation accomplished in the Divine King's once-and-for-all taming of the primordial disorder. By continuously re-enacting this victory, humanity endures a "pain of being," which arises from the "instability of the order."[54]

Type 2: Tragedy to Wisdom. Ricoeur called this "an intermediate type" between Types 1 and 3, reflecting its central location on the axis. It is called "tragic," because "it attains its full manifestation all at once in Greek tragedy." From this type arises a "tragic theology of the god who tempts, blinds, [and] leads astray." Here, the fault of the tragic hero is "indistinguishable" from his very existence. He "does not commit the fault," yet "he is guilty." The source of evil is the inexplicable malice of the wicked god. Salvation in this type can only be "aesthetic deliverance issuing from the tragic spectacle itself, internalized in the depths of existence and converted into pity with respect to oneself."[55] This type is centered on the axis because the tragic hero is neither responsible for the evil that befalls him nor captive to an impersonal nature. Rather, he is the personal target of the evil god(s) that choose(s) victims indiscriminately. As a result, this myth renders human will and action "impotent and irresponsible."[56]

Ricoeur thought tragic theology may be "the only theology that cannot be avowed or, at any rate, defended." An attempt to formulate such a theology "would mean self-destruction of the religious consciousness."[57] This is why Plato spoke so severely against the tragedians:

53. Ibid., 196.
54. Ibid.
55. Ibid., 173.
56. Ibid., 214.
57. Ibid., 226.

> God, since he is good, is not the cause of everything, as is commonly said; he is the cause of only part of the things that happen to men and has no responsibility for the greater part of them ... we will not allow the young to hear the words of Aeschylus: "God implants crime in men when he wishes to ruin their house completely."[58]

In spite of Aeschylus's unavowable theology, Ricoeur recognized a peculiar tragic soteriology. The plot consists in breaking the hero. His destruction is an extreme *peripeteia*. The hoped-for end of this story is the "tragic wisdom" gained for the hero and for the witnesses of the spectacle. Salvation is inaugurated by enduring suffering "for the sake of understanding."[59] Participants are transformed into new people, who, if nothing else, can exercise some freedom by refusing to give consent to the wickedness of the god(s) and looking with pity upon fellow sufferers.[60]

Type 3: Rebellion to Restoration. Ricoeur calls this the "Adamic Myth," recounted in the first three chapters of Genesis. Unlike the other two, this story locates evil in "an irrational event" within a good "creation already completed." Like Type 2, the origin of evil in Type 3 is inexplicable. But instead of locating evil in God, it locates it in the rebellious will of the creature. This moves Type 3 to the far right of the axis, placing maximum blame on humanity. The plot is marked by a "tension between two representations: that of creation brought to a close with the 'rest on the seventh day,' and that of a work of salvation still pending, until the 'Last Day.'"[61] Salvation is the "sum of the initiatives" of the Creator coupled with the believing response of a series of new Adams (Noah, Abraham, David). Salvation culminates with the "Last Adam," the "Son of Man," and the final "elimination of evil."[62]

The pain of human being in the story of Adam and Eve arises from the presence of the tragic in the form of the serpent: "he represents the aspect

---

58. Plato, *Republic*, 379c–380a, quoted in Ricoeur, *Symbolism of Evil*, 226.

59. Ricoeur, *Symbolism of Evil*, 229.

60. Ricoeur referenced Prometheus: "crucified on his rock, he does nothing; but he has the power of the word and the hardness of a will that withholds consent" (ibid., 224); also, tragedy induces *éleos*, "that merciful gaze which no longer accuses or condemns but shows pity" (ibid., 231).

61. Ibid., 172–73.

62. Ibid., 173, 237–38, 271–72 (cf. 1 Cor 15:45). Ricoeur highlighted the critical nature of *trust* as the proper response of the Second Adam by emphasizing that the critical disjuncture in the Garden was not a broken law but "the alteration of the relation of trust between man and God" (249). Compare Luther, *Lectures on Genesis*, in *Luther's Works*, 1:149, the "source of all sin truly is unbelief and doubt and abandonment of the Word."

of evil that could not be absorbed into the responsible freedom of man."[63] Man "is not the absolute evil one, but the evil one of second rank." Humans become evil "through seduction."[64] Whatever the serpent is, he is *not* a resurgence of primordial evil—"he is also a creature,"[65] under the rule of the good Creator. This threatens a "moral vision of the world," which sees all suffering as just retribution for sin, not mere collateral damage. There is an Evil in the world *above* the power of man yet *under* the rule of God. Ricoeur recalled Job, who bore "witness to the irreducibility" of the "evil of scandal" to the "evil of fault."[66] With Job, the Creator looks like the tragic god who blinds and leads astray. "Behold, he is in your hand," said the Lord to Satan (Job 2:6). "Is not God wicked? Is it not that possibility . . . the believer evokes when he prays: 'Lead us not into temptation?' Does not his request signify: 'Do not come to meet me with the face of the tragic God'?"[67]

The story of salvation in Type 3 restores the broken "trust between God and man."[68] It remarkably enfolds this tragic dimension, suppressing it, without removing it altogether. The Second Adam, who is also the Son of Man and the Suffering Servant,[69] willingly submits to "a suffering that is *outside* retribution, a senseless and scandalous suffering."[70] He embraces the pain of human being and takes upon himself the sins of the world. "Father, into your hands I commit my spirit" (Luke 23:46). Salvation is hoped for *in spite of* this spectacle. It is anticipated "beyond any ethical vision to a new dimension of faith, the dimension of *unverifiable faith*."[71] It is experienced, by hope, in "pardon" from God, which is also "participation of the individual" in the Last Adam, whom God raised from the dead.[72] The believer says all this and more in her Lord's prayer: "Lead us not into temptation, but deliver us from evil."

---

63. Ricoeur, *Symbolism of Evil*, 258.
64. Ibid., 259.
65. Ibid., 255.
66. Ibid., 314.
67. Ibid., 325–26.
68. Ibid., 249.
69. Ricoeur was awed by this: "That Jesus could be the point of convergence of all the figures . . . is an Event that exceeds the resources of our phenomenology of images . . . the event announced in the Gospel, the 'fulfillment,' is properly the content of the Christian Kerygma" (ibid., 269).
70. Ibid., 325.
71. Ibid., 319.
72. Ibid., 274.

Type 4: Forgetfulness to Knowledge. Ricoeur called this the "*myth of the exiled soul.*" It "has played a considerable part in our Western culture, because it presided, if not over the birth, at least over the growth of Greek philosophy." It differs from the other three "in that it divides man into *soul* and *body* and concentrates on the destiny of the soul, which it depicts as coming from elsewhere," straying "here below," then returning to its proper home.[73] "Divine as to his soul, earthly as to his body, man is forgetting of the difference; and the myth tells how that happened."[74] Type 4 floats above the line because it alone accounts for evil by dividing man into two parts. Like Type 3, it emphasizes human responsibility for evil and therefore it hovers on the right side (Figure 1). Since Types 3 and 4 are united in this aspect, they were often comingled.[75] Both tell of a "fall"—one, a broken trust, the other, a forgotten knowledge.

The "pain of being" in this myth is related to the "passion" of the body and contact with the perishable things of earth. Here the archetype is a fusion of two figures: the god Dionysos and the demonic Titans. As the story goes, Dionysos was captured, boiled, and eaten by the Titans. "Zeus, to punish them, blasted them with lightning and from their ashes created the present race of men. That is *why* men today participate both in the evil nature of the Titans and in the divine nature of Dionysos."[76] This is the referent behind Plato's comment about the "Titanic nature" of man.[77] The essential turmoil within the human soul is intensified by its fall into the body-prison and subsequent forgetfulness of its nature. The key to deliverance is "knowledge"—knowledge of its essence, origin, and the true order of things.[78] Philosophy "consists then in the death of the body, in order to 'behold all things themselves with the soul itself.'" The body distracts the soul: "The soul of every human being, when it is intensely pleased or pained by something, thinks that the particular object of its feeling is the clearest and truest thing in the world, although it is not so at all."[79] Therefore, the philosopher's highest duty is to speak the truth. He must fit his words to the comprehensive picture of the world, which includes both formal and mate-

---

73. Ibid., 174. Also, "there is a pact between this myth and philosophy which has no equivalent" (281).

74. Ibid., 280.

75. Also, early Christian use of a "Neo-Platonic mode of expression" and New Testament use of Hellenistic "vocabulary" makes "the myth of the exiled soul more seductive" for "Christian experience" (ibid., 330–34).

76. Ibid., 282.

77. Plato, *Laws*, 701c, quoted in Ricoeur, *Symbolism of Evil*, 298.

78. Ibid., 300.

79. Ibid., 338, quoting Plato, *Phaedo*, 66d, 83c.

rial realms. Ricoeur commented, "Platonism is throughout a justification of language."[80] Trapped on earth, humanity is tempted to speak falsely about reality. The path of salvation is paved with accurate description.

Two Kinds of Evil

To summarize Ricoeur's typology and transition to mine, I make explicit two distinct ways by which he spoke about evil. There is a *storied evil* that is addressed directly in the advance of the plot. This form of evil is the contrary of the good. There is also a *scandalous evil*, which the plot confronts indirectly. This form of evil is the contradictory of the good. It does not merely oppose the good, but threatens to unravel the storied declarations of what counts as "good" and what counts as "evil."

Storied Evil. This sort of evil can be quickly identified by the first term in each of Ricoeur's four types: *chaos, tragedy, rebellion, forgetfulness*. In Type 1, evil was the chaotic disorder that prevailed before the drama of creation. The plot dealt with this evil directly by recounting how evil was conquered and continues to be suppressed by ritual re-enactment. In Type 2, evil was the tragic spectacle visited upon the hero by the wicked god. The plot dealt with this evil directly through the suffering that produced fear, pity, and tragic wisdom. For Type 3, evil was the rebellion manifested in the serpent's seduction of Eve and Adam, followed by humanity's distrust of the Creator, which caused discord among fellow creatures. This evil was dealt with directly in the restoration wrought by God through the Second Adam. And for Type 4, the storied evil was humanity's forgetfulness of their proper place in heaven. It was overcome through education—through attaining knowledge about the true nature of things.

Scandalous Evil. Ricoeur hinted about the presence of this evil. For Type 1, he specifically noted that evil "becomes scandalous" for this myth when it becomes "historical."[81] This account cannot conceptualize an historical entry point of evil into a previously good world. The story has no fallen man or wicked god. There was only the primordial war of the gods that founded the present order. Humankind is victimized, not culpable. Even the gods cannot be held responsible. Violence goes all the way down to the essence of things. There is no truer or better order beyond this. It is what it is. The notions of sin and responsibility are scandalous because they undermine the hoped-for

---

80. Ibid., 340.
81. Ricoeur, *Symbolism of Evil*, 203.

resolution of the plot. If "sin" were assimilated into this story, it could only survive as a new *peripeteia*, an epistemological crisis that unravels the myth.

Type 2, the tragic type, is scandalized in a similar way. This story can be subverted in the direction of Type 1 or Type 3. Ricoeur spoke of the failed tragedy attempted by "the moralist." In this plot, the hero's good fortune turns to greed and pride which *then* incite the wrath of the god(s). But an "ethical moment," an "avoidable fault" scandalizes the tragic plot. Tragic wisdom requires "the mystery of iniquity of the wicked god."[82] The tragic plot can be scandalized in the opposite direction as well, toward Type 1. The victory over chaos "saves the 'tragedy' by delivering it from the 'tragic;' the 'wicked god' is reabsorbed in the suffering of the divine."[83] It is no longer tragic, because no one is to blame. It's just the way the world works.

Type 3, because of its affinity with Type 4, is vulnerable on all sides. If evil were located in the body and its earthly conditions, its way of salvation through the Second Adam would be scandalized and absorbed into the myth of the exiled soul. If evil were located in the essential nature of the creation, it would be conquered by Type 1. But Type 2, the threat of the tragic god, is perhaps most scandalous on two counts. First, a tragic element is not foreign to, but is contained *within* the plot of the Second Adam. Second, Type 3 is protected internally from Types 1 and 4. The creation and the body are declared "good" from the beginning, making the narrative logic of Types 1 and 4 foreign to Type 3. But the presence of the serpent, the undeserved suffering of Job, the spectacle of the crucifixion, and the abiding threat of eternal damnation all belong to the story proper. They all threaten the resolution. They scandalize the hope that the original trust between God and his human creatures can be restored.

Type 4 is also scandalized by the others, but in a more general way. The declarations made in the first three types would halt its hoped-for flight to the heavens. They would bring its transcendent speculation back down to earth. Type 1's declaration about the volatile order of all things would contaminate the True, the Beautiful, and the Good assumed to be at the heart of reality. Type 2's wicked god destroys its ethical vision. And Type 3's personal God, who stands over and judges human reason, threatens both its knowledge and its autonomy.

Scandalous evil brings all the stories down to the same level. All must cling to an *unverified faith*. All must wait to see if their author proves trustworthy. All must live by hope.

---

82. Ibid., 222.
83. Ibid., 228.

A TYPOLOGY OF NARRATIVE THEODICIES—AFTER RICOEUR 109

A TYPOLOGY OF NARRATIVE THEODICIES

Having taken an analytical detour though Ricoeur's typology, I now offer mine. In the remainder of this chapter, I introduce its organizing logic and elements of analysis, briefly applying them to each of the four model stories. A more detailed description will have to wait for the following two chapters. There I will engage in Christian conversation with representative authors from each type. As I noted above, the Christian story is intentionally excluded from the typology. Whereas Ricoeur wanted Moderns to learn from the "myths" of Christianity (and others), I want Christians to learn from the "myths" of Modernity (and others). In the final chapter, I will expand my summaries of Ricoeur's Type 3 to offer an account of the Christian story in distinction from the four narrative theodicies I introduce now. This will help me say more clearly how Christian hope compares and contrasts with others.

Organizing Logic: Conflict and Resolution

Ricoeur's organizing logic was centered on one horizontal axis, indicating increasing and decreasing degrees of human culpability. The logic of my typology is centered on two axes. Drawing on Neiman's distinctions,[84] I set the horizontal axis to reflect contradictory declarations about what counts as evil. The vertical axis reflects two strategies for overcoming evil (Figure 2).

Figure 2. A Typology of Narrative Theodicies

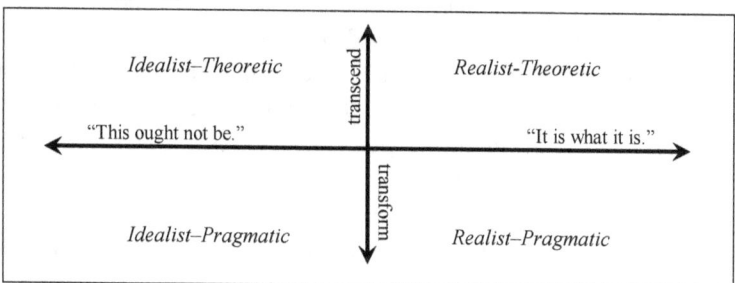

Imagine reading Elie Wiesel's report about children being thrown into the fire at Auschwitz.[85] An awful silence passes. Now imagine how we might respond. We would have at least two paths open to us. What we say will configure the conflict in our plot. If we say, "This ought not be," we turn

---

84. Neiman, *Evil in Modern Thought*. See my chapter 4, above, for an explanation of Neiman's categories.
85. Wiesel, *Night*, 32.

left, toward the *idealist* pole. If we shrug and say, "It is what it is," we turn right, toward the *realist* pole. Having made this declaration, we have another decision: What are we going to do about it now? Again, there are at least two options. We can either try to *transcend* this event or attempt to *transform* the world that made it possible. Each offers a potential strategy for resolving the conflict. These strategies could be pursued from either the left or the right side. Also, each strategy calls for us to *say* something—to utter a plan of action or to speculate as to how this fits into some bigger picture. We can either attempt to fit our words to the world or make the world come to fit our words. That is to say, we can *theorize* or we can *pragmatize*.

We now have four paths set before us. If we pick one and wish to see it through, we will begin to tell each other the story about our progress toward or regress from that goal. We will narrate our approach to the resolution of our conflict. We will *story the world* around us. This story will become our standard story. And whether we break off and narrate alone, or huddle together, or join the on-going story of some other group, our story will assume an author. To participate in this story, we must exercise an as yet *unverified faith* that our author is reliable. We must live by hope.

Elements of Analysis

Ricoeur analyzed his four model myths by protagonist, plot, and pain of being. He focused on the pain of being, the "human enigma" in each. This was fitting in light of his larger project concerned with a "philosophy of will" that could maintain an "ethical vision" after Auschwitz. He was interested in maintaining a dialectical tension between human responsibility *for* and captivity *to* evil. As Neiman observed, Lisbon revealed our alienation from the world; Auschwitz, our alienation from ourselves. Ricoeur was working to overcome this estrangement.

As a French Army Officer in World War II, Paul Ricoeur spent five years in a German concentration camp. Since the French and Germans both had signed the Geneva Accords, Ricoeur and his countrymen were treated humanely. This was not the case with the Russian prisoners, who were housed about 500 meters from the French camp, close enough for one to see what was happening in the other. Ricoeur's biographer reported:

> [The] Germans visited humiliation, cruelty, and frequently death on the Russian POWs. The French could see the horrible physical condition of the Russian prisoners and could see them daily burying their dead in a trench-like grave at the back of

their camp . . . only 1,400 Russian prisoners remained alive out of the 4,000 who were initially imprisoned there.[86]

The overriding interest behind Ricoeur's typology written 15 years after his release was still immersed in the on-going project of the Enlightenment—what Ernest Becker summarized as an "anthropodicy"[87]—a justification (and rehabilitation) of the ways of Man to humanity. His typology appropriately bore the problems of its time. I do not wish to resolve the Enlightenment's problems, but to return to their source—to re-read the stories of Enlightenment and understand how they seek to justify their authors. I employ Ricoeur's elements of analysis to do so, focusing especially on the dynamics of *plot*. I ask: how does this story declare conflict and speak toward resolution? In other words, how is *storied evil* supposed to be overcome? I address the other elements—the protagonist and the pain of being human—in relation to the status of the author. The hope and pain of being human is theodicy. Can the story render its author trustworthy in face of *scandalous evil*?

I briefly explore these elements within the four types, sketching the narrative logic of each. In the next two chapters, I will add detail and texture by conversing with representatives of the four types.

Idealist-Theoretic. Within his discussion on the story of the exiled soul, Ricoeur stated, "[T]here is a pact between this myth and philosophy which has no equivalent."[88] He returned to this point at the end of that chapter. He explained how Greek philosophy demythologized the stories about the Titanic nature of man and the soul's fall into the body. The philosophers interpreted these narrative events as "principles," thus making "Good" and "Evil" into universal concepts. Ricoeur called this shift "a new peripeteia."[89] Greek philosophy moved the battle between Good and Evil from the world into the mind. The plot no longer comprised a sequence of primordial, dramatic, or historical events. Instead it was formed by a series of speculations.

Put abstractly, the conflict in the Idealist-Theoretic plot advances by *assertive declaration*. The central strategy is for the protagonist to fit his or her mind and words to a more encompassing picture of the world. It begins with a declaration: there is more to the world than meets the eye—there is genuine truth and beauty and goodness that cannot be empirically measured, but

---

86. Reagan, *Paul Ricoeur*, 12.
87. Becker, "Science of Man as Anthropodicy," in *Structure of Evil*, 18–19.
88. Ricoeur, *Symbolism of Evil*, 281.
89. Ibid., 305.

only perceived by rational minds. This *declaration* immediately overcomes one class of negative experiences, so-called "natural evils." Reality is divided between a natural order and a rational order. The natural order contains events proper to its transient nature: growth and decay, pleasure and pain, calm and storm, life and death. The rational order contains what is proper to it: the True, the Good, the Sublime.

With one set of evils overcome by fiat, the Idealist-Theoretic plot faces its *storied evil*: immorality. It challenges human behavior that doesn't conform to the rational order. In the face of human crime, it responds, "This ought not be." The protagonist recognizes a rift in the order of things. Humans, as rational beings, must act in accord with the rational order, not the violence of the natural order. The conduct is condemned, but the person is presumed innocent. He or she is truly a lost soul, who has forgotten or has not been properly educated concerning the truth. Therefore, the strategy is to overcome storied evil by *assertion*. It is to more clearly and comprehensively describe the world, thereby conforming human minds to the truth. And because the organizing principles of the world are already set, the movement of the story depends on the emplotment driven by the discourse of enlightened humanity. They are its authors.

Idealist-Pragmatic. Similarly, the resolution of this plot is also guided by the authority of enlightened humanity. But instead of overcoming the conflict by assertion, this story overcomes by *directive declaration*. The key strategy here is for the protagonist to make the world come to fit his or her words. Having also turned left toward the idealist pole, this form of pragmatism has already overcome so-called "natural evil." The material world was *declared* inert and amoral. It must now be governed by another reality.

Unlike the theoretic idealist, the pragmatic idealist locates the principle of governance in the human mind. The human mind is not dependent on or reflective of some imagined, transcendent reality. The universe doesn't issue commands. Humanity does. We must put the natural world in order. Whatever does not fit should be corrected: "This ought not be . . . and we must transform it." The storied evil in this plot is whatever doesn't match the enlightened ideal. Humans don't transcend into the ideal. The ideal must be directed down to earth to become historical reality. And every completed project is a proleptic sign of this author's reliability.

Realist-Theoretic. This story also starts with a *declaration*. But it begins by declaring the first two options, "Wrong." The problem with the world is not the world. It is the false ideals projected on it. The world "is what it is." To put it in the shadow of some transcendent world or manipulate it according to some passing human dream is wrong-headed at best, evil at worst. This powerful, authoritative utterance has instantly overcome the storied evils of the prior two plots. This new author has subsumed the first two into a new storied world—the *real* world.

In doing so, he or she has created a different form of *storied evil* to overcome: the perceived need for ideals. Like the idealist, the realist theoretician answers the conflict by *assertion*, by outlining an education to reality. The challenge to this program is false thinking. Immature attempts to cope with reality must be exposed and excised from human thought. Both pleasures and pains are to be transcended by a better description of the world. By fitting one's mind to the world as it really is, false hope is dispelled and true hope becomes possible, assuming this author can be trusted.

Realist-Pragmatic. This fourth plot also turned right. By denying the declarations of the idealists, the realist authors have collapsed the division between moral and natural evils. The idealist hope that arose from this division was continually dashed to pieces. Arrogantly, they acted as if they lived in a world created in their image. Again and again, speculations and plans failed. Isn't it time to grow up? And so the realist story begins by *declaring* ideals to be infantile illusions. Moral evil is overcome by fiat. There is nothing better hidden in heaven or the human psyche. There is just reality. It is what it is.

But contrary to the theoretician, the pragmatic realist faces a challenge of human behavior, not of human thought. The key to overcoming the evil of immaturity is habituation and socialization. The strategy taken in this type is *directive* discourse. Make the world fit the word. Unlike the idealist, these words are not to be heard as universal demands. They are simply cultural conventions and agreed-upon practices. Humans don't stand above their biology, they are products of it. We should use our limited endowments to make life more tolerable. The human race must travail through many peripeties, many falsified expectations, and naïve hopes. But this is the way into adulthood, into authentic enlightenment. It is truly the best hope we have.

The Scandal of Evil. In those brief introductions to the four stories, the explicit challenge was evil in its *storied* form. But as Ricoeur hinted, *scandalous evil* always threatens to undermine each plot. In my typology (Figure 2), colonizing advances made across either axis represent the scandal of evil. The vertical division between idealist and realist reflects the rival stories of Modernity suggested by Neiman. Each declaration about what counts as evil intends to overrule the other. One projects an order behind appearances. One says appearance is all we have. The horizontal division between theoretic and pragmatic approaches is similar. Of course, theory does not rule out practice; nor does practice rule out theory. Both assume constant collaboration between human thought and action. But when it comes to theodicy, one must lead. The theodical question is, "Which form of discourse is our best hope for overcoming evil: *assertive* or *directive*?" Where is the problem of evil ultimately located, in thought or behavior? In the terms set by the stories of Modernity, one approach must overrule the other.

To borrow yet one more phrase from Ricoeur, scandalous evil results in an irreducible "conflict of interpretations."[90] For the time being, no story can claim absolute supremacy over the others. They can only persuade. They can only attempt to out-narrate their opponents. In doing so, they all exercise the hope that their author will prove trustworthy.

SUMMARY

This side-trip into Ricoeur's work helped us calibrate our compass. We needed to get our bearings before setting out on a longer expedition. The most important gain from the detour was his implicit distinction between *storied evil* and *scandalous evil*. But Ricoeur can only take us so far. We are not searching for a fountain of youth to revive languishing Modern culture. We are trying to map paths for engaging the myths of Modernity and Postmodernity.

In this chapter, I introduced my typology of life-organizing stories. For general use, I recommend it as a conceptual compass for understanding how human hope begins and where it leads. In particular, I offer this compass to help Christians give a more contextualized account of the hope arising from the Christian story. I want my interpretive community to become more aware of the colonizing advances of these other stories. I want us to tell and live the Christian story, especially when we face our particular *scandal* of evil: the awful hiddenness of the God whom we have come to know in Jesus.

Unlike Ricoeur, my goal is not to find the golden mean or achieve the proper dialectic tension between the types. My intent is to hear and understand the distinct voices of the competition. In the next chapters, we will listen to some of those voices and converse with them.

90. Ricoeur, *Conflict of Interpretations*.

6

Idealist Types

On July 6, 2015, the seventy-five-year-old Kingshighway Bridge, near the Missouri Botanical Garden in Saint Louis, closed for reconstruction. Kingshighway is an arterial route for traffic circulation within the limbs and torso of St Louis. The resultant detour around Kingshighway has, in our more rushed moments, raised the blood pressure of countless Saint Louisans, myself included. At the same time, being forced to follow less frequented avenues, I've become better acquainted with the Shaw and Tower Grove neighborhoods near the Botanical Garden, plus the Hill—an historic Italian immigrant community. This goes for most detours: initially experienced as a disorienting inconvenience, we can let them deepen our appreciation of unfamiliar places. However, once the King's-highway is reconstructed, I have every intention of returning to the main road.

These next two chapters are a detour. This book is about Christian hope. My goal is to say something clear and distinct about it—something that would have been less obvious without the detour. In preparation for this detour, we (re)discovered that Christian hope is distinct because Christians participate in a peculiar story of the world. Like others, Christians organize and interpret life within an all-encompassing plot. Unlike others, the plotline—the main road given in the Christian Story—follows the way of Jesus, Israel's King and the world's Lord.

The Christian Scriptures narrate a life-organizing story. Moreover, they project it prophetically, learn wisdom within it, express it in poetry, and assume it in argumentation. The conflict driving its plot is fundamentally *not* a matter of missing knowledge, improper conduct, or inauthentic consciousness, but of Israel's and all nations' broken trust with the God of

Jesus.[1] As in other stories, the strategy for overcoming this conflict centers on issuing speech acts. But resolution in the Christian story is not realized in assertions made to match the world or directives given to modify it. Its hope is realized only when its storied world comes to match the promise God has made and still makes in and through Jesus and his church. The full realization has been summarized in the Nicene Creed: "And he will come again to judge both the living and the dead. And his kingdom will have no end." The Christian hope is for this promised state of affairs to attain. Until it is so, the story is contested and threatened by rivals. Therefore, as with all other life-organizing stories, the trustworthiness of its author is in question. Its theodicy still awaits vindication.

When comparing Christian hope with others, eschatology should be understood as discourse on the resolution of conflict within a narrated theodicy. The Christian theodicy is distinct because its conflict resolves in the appearing of Jesus to "judge the world in righteousness" (Acts 17:31). The advent of Jesus to judge will be the vindication of God's faithfulness to his promise to bless all the families of the earth in and through Abraham's family (Gen 12:1–3). Prior to this event, the Christian story remains threatened by its peculiar forms of *storied* evil and *scandalous* evil.[2]

Storied evil for Christians is humanity's broken trust with and subsequent rebellion against their Creator. Scandalous evil for Christians is the hiddenness of their God who works all-in-all to include suffering, death, and condemnation. The scandal threatens to render the story unintelligible and its author unreliable. That God in his hiddenness seems to contradict God's promise in Jesus is the unresolved scandal of the Christian story. This challenges its participants' hope of overcoming storied evil. As long as the God of Jesus strikes them as unreliable, their trust in him will be contested and attacked. When faced with this peculiar problem of evil, the Christian narrative theodicy is distinguished by its strategy to overcome the conflict resident in its plot. Rather than overcoming it theoretically by issuing more accurate assertions or pragmatically by giving successful directives, its participants seek to overcome by narrating the promised advent of the crucified and risen Jesus to judge and save. The Christian hope is unique because it

---

1. There is a difference between the unfaithfulness of Israel and that of the nations. Israel broke faith with Yahweh by transgressing the covenant made with Abraham and its development at Sinai and again with David (2 Sam 7, cf. also, Jer 2–3, 11). But the nations are also judged for their idolatry. They too have broken faith with their Creator (e.g., Exod 12:12, Deut 9:5, Isa 23–24, especially Isa 24:5, Jer 46–51, especially Jer 46:25, 48:7, 49:4; also Ps 9:15–20).

2. See chap. 5, "A Typology of Narrative Theodicies—After Ricoeur," for a description of this distinction.

is elicited by this *commissive* speech act performed in the Spirit and by the authority of Jesus.

Eschatological hope arises from a life-organizing story, that is to say, a narrative theodicy. Theses hopes are both realized and unrealized because their supporting stories are unresolved. As on-going stories, they do not enjoy resolution, but project it. They cling to signs and proleptic fulfillments along the way. Slogans such as "realized" or "inaugurated" eschatology are appropriate for discussions internal to Christianity. But they obscure the matter when Christian hope is compared with others.

I propose a better way to distinguish Christian hope in a post-Constantinian setting. This involves not only returning to the Christian story, but also concretely saying what *staying with the story* sounds like. In short, it sounds like the church making promises for God by the Spirit and under the authority of Jesus. Christian hope arises from this narrated promise. Competing hopes arise from other narrated speech acts.

To say more clearly how these narrated speech acts differ from the Christian narrated promise, I offered a typology of narrative theodicies. In the first place, the typology says what Christian hope is *not*. To put it more technically, it furthers an exercise in *apophatic* theology along the *via negativa*. It's a detour. Once these other eschatological hopes are seen to arise from rival stories, the typology can also serve an *analogic* or constructive theology along the *via positiva*—the main road. It can help say what Christian hope *is* by hearing echoes of its story even in its rivals. Given that the Christian story enfolds the entire creation as its setting and claims to be the common ending of all stories, it is appropriate for Christians to identify traces of their hope in competing plotlines. Thus, the typology both highlights the differences and reveals a common ground as a potential source of cooperation with other story-formed communities.

In this chapter, I engage the two forms of idealist narrative theodicy, the *theoretic* and the *pragmatic*. In the next chapter I will consider the realists. The focus of this chapter is the difference between the theoretic (assertive) and pragmatic (directive) strategy, neither of which is the mode of resolution in the Christian plot. The focus of the next chapter will be the difference between the idealist and the realist declarations, both of which contest the creative declarations of God in Jesus. Then, in the final chapter, I will give my constructive account of the Christian story and highlight some areas of overlap that it shares with each of the four types. To summarize, chapters six and seven take a detour to say what Christian hope is *not*. Chapter 8 returns to the *King's* highway and says what Christian hope *is*.

Seeking to say what Christian hope is not, I will converse with actual expositors of each type. The two main expositors included in this chapter are Gottfried Leibniz and Karl Marx. In chapter 7, I will converse with two "realists," Friedrich Nietzsche and Sigmund Freud.[3] Along the way, I will bring in other authors to provide context for their work and suggest ongoing impact. I do this to illustrate the themes of each type, not to argue for an authoritative interpretation of any given author. I do, however, intend to offer a plausible reading of the works examined. There may be dimensions of each that do not fit the formal constraints of the typology. I would welcome discussion about better representatives. The content of these two chapters is illustrative, not constitutive for my thesis. The authors discussed are important insofar as each can help say what Christian hope is not. Additionally, their conflict with each other can help identify a common ground with Christianity, even if that commonality is expressed only in mutual opposition to a shared rival.

DETOUR: IDEALISTS

As announced earlier, I do not seek an objective or neutral perspective. I meet these writers as a Christian and read them from within the contested hope of that story. At the same time, I recognize how their accounts truly anticipate intelligibility for their own storied worlds. This position is neither "fideist" nor "relativist." It is, to borrow a term from Kermode and Ricoeur, *peripatetic*. It pursues resolution, expects to be judged, and hopes for vindication. On the way, it endures a conflict of interpretations.

The conflict of interpretations is both external and internal to the Christian church. The typology I now employ is fitted for offering criticism and building consensus within my own divided interpretive community. What is our story? Where does its conflict reside? What is our strategy to overcome? For what do we hope? And how is this hope distinct from others? To offers answers to these questions, I start with the last one. I account for the hope that arises from other life-organizing stories. The fundamental distinction of the Christian story is that it looks for evil to be overcome in the promised *parousia* of Jesus to judge and save. Others look elsewhere.

Idealist-Theoretic

The story that enacts an idealist-theoretic theodicy is perhaps the closest rival to the narrative theodicy Christians have received, re-told, and

---

3. Cf. Neiman, *Evil in Modern Thought*. I am building upon Neiman's *idealist* and *realist* categories.

interpreted over the last two millennia. Recalling Ricoeur's study, the myth of lost and re-learned knowledge "played a considerable part in our Western culture, because it presided, if not over the birth, at least over the growth of Greek philosophy."[4] This resulted in an unparalleled pact between Greek philosophy and the myth of the exiled soul. It was into this conceptual soil that some of the first seeds of the Christian gospel were sown.

Ricoeur argued that early Christian use of a "Neo-Platonic mode of expression" and the New Testament's use of Hellenistic "vocabulary" makes the myth of the exiled soul especially "seductive" for "Christian experience."[5] Even more powerful than shared vocabulary was a conviction common to both the Christian and Platonic traditions. It is the conviction that the world's ultimate source is reliable in spite of experience that seems to say otherwise. As Irenaeus of Lyons (circa 120–202) wrote, "Plato is shown to be more religious" than other pagans because "he shows the Creator and Maker of this world to be good."[6] These historical and conceptual links have made a Platonic version of the idealist-theoretic story sound plausible to Christians scandalized by evil. Notable among them was Gottfried Leibniz (1646–1716).

Leibniz is an important example for at least three reasons. First, having coined the word "theodicy," he recognized that the reliability of God was a most crucial problem for human thought and action. Second, he was a confessing Christian who identified himself as an Evangelical (Lutheran) and aligned himself with the theologians of the Augsburg Confession.[7] Framing him as a narrator of a rival story illustrates how Christians are liable to be co-opted by competitors, especially when straining under scandalous evil. Third, his *Theodicy* can be read in two ways—either as direct competition with the Christian story or as a Christian defense gone astray.[8] Therefore, he offers a link between extra-systematic observation (detour) and intra-systematic critique and reconstruction (main road). For now, he will stand as the former. I read him as an exponent of a rival hope, an idealist-theoretic narrative theodicy.

---

4. Ricoeur, *Symbolism of Evil*, 174.

5. Ibid., 330–34.

6. Irenaeus, *Against Heresies*, III.25.5.

7. Leibniz, *Theodicy*, 67, 70, 167. However, the people of his hometown thought he was an atheist because he never went to church. See Ross, *Leibniz*, 27.

8. See Hinlicky, *Paths Not Taken*, chap. 6, who presented "Two Versions of Leibniz's Failure"—Leibniz the "Platonic Rationalist" and Leibniz the "Augustinian in Denial." Hinlicky argued for version two.

Leibniz was a "universal genius."[9] He was a mathematician, inventor, alchemist, statesman, librarian, lawyer, historian, and philosopher. His "life was dominated by an unachievable ambition to excel in every sphere of intellectual and political activity."[10] His many projects fit within a larger effort to unify Christendom "in the face of a Europe devastated by the Thirty Years' War." His work should be understood in the context of "an Empire in decline and impotent against the rise of new independent states, and a Christian church torn apart by radical reforms and captured by the new 'national' political units."[11]

Like Plato, "his great philosophical hero,"[12] Leibniz believed that good theology was the key to good politics. The body politic must see God as powerful, wise, and praiseworthy if these virtues are to have a fighting chance among us mortals. Theology should be placed in service to civil life. Theology could serve civility because Leibniz believed that "God's benevolence is known by pure reason, and apart from Christian revelation."[13] This belief was directly opposed by Pierre Bayle, who claimed that the God revealed in the Bible could only be trusted if Reason were "compelled to lay down its arms, and to subjugate itself to the obedience of the faith."[14] It was to Bayle that Leibniz addressed his *Theodicy*, first published in 1710.[15]

Bayle was only the catalyst. At stake was theology's power to form European culture. A lawful, orderly society must be grounded in good principles. For public and private virtues to be secure, they must be "reasonable," that is, "related to God, who is the supreme reason of things." Therefore, the "purpose of religion should be to imprint these principles upon our souls." Without them, one cannot love God. To love God is to know and reflect his perfections in "true piety."[16] Misguided people may "ill understand the goodness and the justice of the Sovereign of the universe" and thus "imagine a God who deserves neither to be imitated nor to be loved." Leibniz warned of the dangers of false knowledge: the "source of piety should be preserved

---

9. Ross, *Leibniz*, 2.

10. Ibid., 26.

11. Loemker, *Struggle for Synthesis*, 4. Cf. 18.

12. Ibid., 74.

13. Farrer, "Editor's Introduction," in Leibniz, *Theodicy*, 10. Hinlicky, *Paths Not Taken*, chap. 6, contested a strict, rationalist reading of Leibniz. At the same time, he conceded that if we take Leibniz at his word, reading him as a "Platonic Rationalist" is plausible.

14. Bayle, *Historical and Critical Dictionary*, quoted in Leibniz, *Theodicy*, 120.

15. Farrer, "Introduction," in Leibniz, *Theodicy*, 47. Having died in 1706, Bayle was unable to respond.

16. Leibniz, *Theodicy*, 52.

from infection." Bayle's arguments and others like them were a threat to civilization. And so they demanded a response. Leibniz explained, "I have been compelled to gather up my thoughts on all these connected questions, and to impart them to the public."[17]

When Leibniz set out to justify God's ways to men, he started with a general Christian framework. He assumed God to be the author of all things. He assumed human beings bore the image of God and were created for communion with Him. He also assumed the basic Christian plotline. God had sent various prophets to reveal himself, culminating in his Divine Son, Jesus Christ. Leibniz cast Jesus' mission as serving the propagation of true knowledge of God:

> It is clear that Jesus Christ, completing what Moses had begun, wished that the Divinity should be the object not only of our fear and veneration but also of our love and devotion . . . Love is that mental state which makes us take pleasure in the perfections of the object of our love, and there is nothing more perfect than God . . . To love him it suffices to contemplate his perfections, a thing easy indeed, because we find the ideas of these within ourselves. The perfections of God are those of our souls, but he possesses them in boundless measure; he is an Ocean, whereof to us only drops have been granted.[18]

Leibniz used elements and themes from the Christian story, but he refigured them within the plotline of Platonic philosophy. In this life-organizing story, the conflict is resolved in the movement from forgetfulness to knowledge. Here, the strategy for overcoming evil is to issue accurate assertions that will cause minds to be fit to the world as it truly is, despite appearances.

When Leibniz gave his account of the problem of evil, he began with a Christian perspective. He assumed God's omnipotent governance of the universe. When disease, disaster, and death strike, we must receive them from God's providential hand. Additionally, God's rational creatures (angels and humans) are no less dependent on Him. Granted, these creatures, in their freedom, have the capacity to choose moral evil. But, Leibniz acknowledged, "an action is not, for being evil, the less dependent on God."[19] This makes it difficult to understand how God can threaten to punish moral evil. Is not God somehow an accomplice to moral evil since he sovereignly permits it?

---

17. Ibid., 53.
18. Leibniz, *Theodicy*, 51.
19. Ibid., 124.

This difficulty is not relieved, but multiplied in light of God's plan of salvation. Leibniz admitted that "it is much worse when one considers the life to come, since but a small number of men will be saved and since all the rest will perish eternally."[20] Just as appeals to creaturely freedom did not seem to solve the problem of temporal suffering, neither do they help when faced with eternal suffering. God has promised only to save those with faith. And "this lively faith is a gift from God," because "we are dead to all good works," including faith. We must conclude that "God is the final reason of salvation, of grace, of faith and of election in Jesus Christ."[21] Leibniz, goaded on by Bayle, did not shrink from the stunning implication:

> So it is a terrible judgment that God, giving his only Son for the whole human race and being the sole author and master of the salvation of men, yet saves so few of them and abandons all others to the devil . . . And this outcome inspires all the more horror, as the sole cause why all these men are wretched to all eternity is God's having exposed their parents to a temptation that he knew they would not resist . . . These men too are condemned to be for ever rebellious against God and plunged in the most horrible miseries . . . though in essence they have not been more wicked than others, and several among them have perchance been less guilty than some of that little number of elect, who were saved by grace without reason, and who thereby enjoy an eternal felicity which they had not deserved.[22]

The only thing more stunning was Leibniz's proposal: "I hope to remove all these difficulties."[23]

The main challenge Leibniz faced was the problem of *moral* evil, or sin. Since men and women were made in the image of God, morality, which is rational behavior, is most natural for their kind. To be morally evil is irrational. Leibniz's standard for judging between good and evil was God's own moral perfection, which is the organizing principle behind the natural world, despite its chaotic and unruly appearance. But if the moral order is the true nature of all things, how do we explain sin?

Leibniz's answer: the source of human sin can only be ignorance or misunderstanding. If misconceptions about God and the world are present, sin will result. When God is conceived as "an absolute prince employing despotic power, unfitted to be loved," humans will likewise act without

20. Ibid., 125.
21. Ibid., 125–26.
22. Ibid., 126.
23. Ibid., 61.

wisdom and love. They will become unworthy of love. Following this diagnosis, Leibniz stated his strategy to overcome moral evil: "Our end is to banish from men the false ideas that present God to them as ... unworthy of being loved."[24] Sin is caused by misinformation. It is dispelled by knowledge of the pre-established harmony of the universe.

Leibniz issued assertions to make the minds of his readers conform to this hidden reality:

> I offer a vindication of [God's] perfections ... I explain how evil has a source other than the will of God ... I show that it has been possible for God to permit sin and misery, and even to co-operate therein and promote it, without detriment to his holiness and his supreme goodness.[25]

This is the critical point: the conflict that drove Leibniz's life-organizing story was not *that people suffer* in their mistrust and rebellion against their Creator. Rather, his conflict was our *ignorance* as to how this misery was nevertheless part of an ultimate harmony.

To dispel our ignorance, Leibniz sub-divided evil into three kinds: "*Metaphysical evil* consists in mere imperfection, *physical evil* in suffering, and *moral evil* in sin."[26] To say something has metaphysical evil is simply to say that it is not God. To wish for metaphysical evil not to exist would be to wish for there to be no creation. As one Leibniz commentator put it, the world was "as perfect as it could be without collapsing back into God himself. Consequently, to blame God for creating this universe as he did would be tantamount to saying that he should not have created anything at all."[27] Creaturely imperfection is what makes physical and moral evil possible. Moral evil, or sin, becomes a reality only when a rational creature ignorantly chooses it. God accepted moral evil as the cost of having virtuous creatures who freely love Him. And as a righteous consequence of moral evil, God responds with physical evil, or suffering.[28] Thus, all evils are accounted for. *Metaphysical* evil is simply "not-God-ness." *Moral* evil is what non-divine rational beings have the potential to do. *Physical evil* is the just reward for moral evil.

Leibniz's theoretic theodicy turns on two points: first, God's freedom is perfect, but not absolute; second, God's freedom is compatible with human

24. Ibid., 127.
25. Ibid., 61.
26. Ibid., 136.
27. Ross, *Leibniz*, 103.
28. This includes eternal damnation, for God will not condemn those "without the necessary light" (Leibniz, *Theodicy*, 300).

freedom. Human freedom is exercised within God's lawful order and has real consequences, for good or for ill. Armed with this defense, Leibniz sought to vindicate his Divine client. In Neiman's words, Leibniz explained "that the accused could not have done otherwise." Like any other agent, God "was constrained by the possibilities available to Him." Furthermore, he asserted "that all the Creator's actions in fact happen for the best."[29]

It may be objected here that Leibniz has taken salvation out of God's hands and made it depend on human choice. Leibniz's counter claim was to show how God's choices and human choices harmoniously correlate. As Hinlicky summarized, "Leibniz's over-arching argument is that God, as cause of all causes, though not maker of all choices, is justified in His judgments since divine determination is compatible with human freedom, given certain clarifications."[30] The divine defendant is vindicated to the degree the judge accepts that God wanted "to produce as much good as possible." Thus, when God "permits sin, it is wisdom, it is virtue."[31]

Leibniz is typically criticized in one of two ways: either he makes evil less evil or he makes God less God. His critics often say his argument collapses into a form of fatalism. Ross concluded, "Leibniz is therefore committed to the Stoic position that all is predestined by Providence." He thought we should acquiesce and apply our reason "to the task of aligning our perspectives on the world with the optimal perspective that God has."[32] Hinlicky, however, has criticized this position. He claimed that determinist presentations of Leibniz are typically "parasitic upon the parody Voltaire rendered with the figure of Dr. Pangloss in *Candide*," and do not reflect Leibniz's actual arguments.[33]

From Hinlicky's perspective, "Leibniz in the end retreated to the semi-Pelagianism of the later Melanchthonian tradition, defending half-heartedly free will on a priori ground, in order to maintain his posture as an independent, rational, or natural theologian."[34] In other words, Leibniz used free will as a concept to keep us from thinking of God as an irrational, unprincipled force. He wanted to save us from Spinoza, the modern Stoic and philosophical hero of Friedrich Nietzsche.[35] Above all, he wanted to

---

29. Neiman, *Evil in Modern Thought*, 21. Cf. Bayer, *Living by Faith*, 11.
30. Hinlicky, *Paths Not Taken*, 267.
31. Leibniz, *Theodicy*, 138.
32. Ross, *Leibniz*, 112.
33. Hinlicky, *Paths Not Taken*, 18.
34. Ibid., 258.
35. Ibid., 32, "Leibniz's famous formulation about God's choice of the best of all possible worlds originated as an alternative to Spinoza's view . . .." For Spinoza's influence on Nietzsche, see chapter 7, below.

maintain an ethical vision of the world. Whether seen as a determinist or a voluntarist, Leibniz, from either perspective, was scandalized by an evil that remained absurd or inexplicable. He authored a story that would resolve when it successfully explained why all evil is necessary for the greater good.

Leibniz's theodicy is not merely theoretical. It is for him a life-organizing story. His essays on the Goodness of God, the Freedom of Man, and the Origin of Evil are the culmination of a life-long *conceptual* quest to align his view of the world with the optimal view that is God's. He had meditated on this problem "since his youth"[36] and narrated his progression:

> Indeed, there are perhaps few persons who have toiled more than I in this matter . . . I flitted from book to book . . . I was charmed by the work . . . of Luther against Erasmus . . . I had opportunity on my journeys to confer with some excellent men of different parties . . . I have also since read many and various good authors on these subjects, and I have endeavored to make progress in the knowledge that seems to me proper for banishing all that could have obscured the idea of supreme perfection which must be acknowledged in God.[37]

The *Theodicy* was a major achievement toward transcending evil by means of knowledge.

Here Christians might be tempted to call this "over-realized" eschatology. The problem with this assessment is that Leibniz was the first to admit that he had not arrived at the final goal. He had not achieved, but anticipated comprehensive knowledge. He had only proleptically resolved the conflict. The final resolution would only come with the "*light of glory*."[38] Leibniz used the term Luther employed in his argument with Erasmus, but in a different sense from Luther.[39] The hoped-for light, in Leibniz's story, was not dependent on the promised *parousia* of Jesus to end this present evil age. Instead, it was divine insight God dispensed to individuals upon a sainted death or perhaps, in special cases, before.[40]

---

36. Leibniz, *Theodicy*, 62.

37. Ibid., 67.

38. Ibid., 120, "Hitherto we have been illumined by the *light of Nature* and by that of *grace*, but not yet by that of *glory*. Here on earth we see apparent injustice, and we believe and even know the truth of the hidden justice of God; but we shall see that justice when at last the Sun of Justice shall show himself as he is" (ibid.).

39. Rupp and Watson, *Luther and Erasmus*, 329–32.

40. Leibniz, *Theodicy*, 122, assumed that Bayle, who died in 1706, was now in "the academy of heaven" and "surrounded by that light [of glory]." But, it was perhaps possible to be illumined earlier "by a peculiar grace."

Leibniz recognized he had not yet arrived. What sets apart his eschatological hope is not its degree of realization. It is distinct because it arises from a life-organizing story that judged evil with respect to a hidden moral principle and sought to overcome it by assertive discourse. His conflict is resolved by re-interpreting the experienced world so that it fits with the declared morally-principled world. This is not Christian hope because it has the potential to resolve independent of the Christian story, which will only resolve with the coming of Jesus to judge the world in righteousness. Leibniz began with but did not stay in the Christian story. In this way, he offered an exemplary idealist-theoretic narrative theodicy.

Idealist-Pragmatic

Like the first type, narrators of idealist-pragmatic stories judge the world according to a hidden ideal. Unlike the former, this type does not look for the ideal in a pre-established harmony reflected in the natural world, but in the moral vision of humanity. This difference dictates a change in strategy for overcoming the declared gap between *is* and *ought*. Since the ideal is not already present, waiting to be described, it must be prescribed. The goal is not to uncover the Good but to actualize it, to fit the world to the word. Whereas storied evil for the theorist was ignorance, storied evil for the pragmatist is an unjust world that allows for concrete injustices. And so the ideal must be brought into historical reality as directed by the voice of authority. The pragmatic idealist does not wish to transcend evil but to transform the conditions that have made evil possible.

Karl Marx (1818–83) wrote, "The philosophers have only *interpreted* the world differently, the point is, to *change it*."[41] This eleventh thesis on Feuerbach is perhaps "Marx's most frequently quoted saying."[42] With this criticism, Marx set himself apart not only from Feuerbach, but also from Hegel, who introduced his lectures on world history by saying that "our method is a theodicy, a justification of God, which Leibniz attempted . . ."[43]

Like Leibniz, Hegel tried to justify God and the world by transcending evil—by coming to see everything within a harmonious whole. Both of these giants of German Idealism assumed humans could discern this harmony because our Reason participates in God's. Then Feuerbach came

---

41. Marx, "Appendix: Theses on Feuerbach," in Marx and Engels, *German Ideology*, 199.

42. Lash, *A Matter of Hope*, 36.

43. Hegel, *Reason in History*, 18.

along and asserted that God was merely a human projection.[44] As Marx said, Feuerbach's "work consists in resolving the religious world into its secular basis." But Feuerbach went wrong by raising this secular basis into "an independent realm in the clouds."[45] Like the others, he was merely offering a different interpretation of the world. For all their differences, Leibniz, Hegel, and Feuerbach are agreed that evil is primarily a problem of having an insufficient mental picture of the world. Their strategy to overcome it was *theoretic*—to better fit their minds and words to the world as it "actually" is. Marx's difference is his rejection of this strategy. He was not content to assert the truth, but directed "Man" to "prove the truth . . . in practice."[46]

Marx's Idealist-Pragmatic Story. Why study Marx as a rival? Weren't his communitarian hopes utterly dashed by the failures of the twentieth century? Even if Marx's revolutionary vision included predictions that now seem doubtful, his basic story of taking pragmatic action to create the best possible world continues to be persuasive. Compared to abstract theories that explain evil and silence its victims, Marx's call to unite as a community and take concrete steps to eradicate specific evils comes as a relief. The Marxist story is important because it opposes the theoretic strategy of coping with evil. It is still an *idealist* story, for it continues to denounce evil by measuring it against a declared, universal, human good. But, it is a new kind of story because it directs how the world should be reformed to bring this good into being. Marx's plot is worth studying, keeping in mind it is only one form of the idealist-pragmatic type. Abolishing private property and overcoming class differences are not essential to the general type. This kind of story begins when someone declares that theorizing conceals our real task, which is "to take responsibility for the world rather than explain it, to transform rather than to endure."[47]

One year after Marx was born, a steamship crossed the Atlantic for the first time. Six years later the first railway was opened for business. Ten years later electric telegraph wires went live. "Within a few decades, the frontiers of the world had been marvelously expanded. The fables of antiquity had been realized. The productivity of human labor had been increased to an

---

44. Feuerbach, *Essence of Christianity*, 185, "The essential standpoint of religion is . . . subjective."

45. Marx, "Theses on Feuerbach," in *German Ideology*, 198.

46. Ibid., 197. Cf. Becker, *Structure of Evil*, 313, "Marx . . . saw that *action* was inseparable from any *explanation* of evil . . . He could not accept any kind of explanation which did not put power into man's hands."

47. Neiman, *Evil in Modern Thought*, 105–6.

incredible extent."[48] But these advances were not without cost. According to one Marxist historian, the factory workers paid the price, and reaped little reward:

> The proletarian had himself become a commodity... He was a beast of burden... an instrument, a wheel in the machinery of exploitation, a dead thing. Impotent... he must accept his lot, under pain of starvation should he refuse.[49]

Neither Marx nor his associate Friedrich Engels were of proletarian origin. Marx's father was a Jewish lawyer who had converted to Protestant Christianity when Karl was six. Engels's father was an industrious Calvinist, part-owner of a textile firm with factories in Germany and England. As young men, the two became disillusioned with their bourgeois Judeo-Christian heritage. They first met when Marx was the editor of *Rheinische Zeitung*, a socialist newspaper with revolutionary leanings. They became close friends when working together in Paris after the paper was shut down due to conflict with government censors.[50] By 1846, they had co-authored *The German Ideology*, which Roy Pascal called the "first full statement of Marxism."[51]

In the preface to a later work, Marx said that in 1845 he and Engels "resolved to work out in common the opposition of our view to the ideological view of German philosophy, in fact, to settle accounts with our erstwhile philosophical conscience." This "resolve was carried out" in the *The German Ideology*.[52] Marxist historian Otto Rühle explained how the book was the product of a year-long labor to move "beyond the criticism of philosophy, of politics, and of economics, to the criticism of the interpretation of history." It contains "an elementary formulation of the materialist interpretation of history, which was subsequently to be worked out as a complete method."[53] Therefore, Marx's thought can be viewed "as a continuing meditation on central themes first explored in 1844."[54] In light of this, Nicholas Lash, in his study on Marx, used *The German Ideology* as a gateway into Marx's work.[55]

---

48. Rühle, *Karl Marx: His Life and Work*, 4.
49. Ibid., 7.
50. Ibid., 11–86.
51. Pascal, "Introduction," in Marx and Engels, *German Ideology*, ix.
52. Marx, "Preface," in *Essential Marx*, 166.
53. Rühle, *Marx*, 93, 98.
54. McLellan, *Karl Marx*, 303, quoted in Lash, *A Matter of Hope*, 22.
55. Lash, *A Matter of Hope*, 36–47.

I follow Lash's approach and take this early statement as a rough outline of the narrative theodicy authored by Marx (and Engels).

The German Ideology tells a powerful story about human liberation culminating in the development of "complete individuals," united in community and "the casting-off of all natural limitations."[56] In the preface, Marx offered a brief parable to introduce the work: "Once upon a time an honest fellow had the idea that men were drowned in water only because they were possessed with the idea of gravity." Eager to save lives, "he fought against the illusion of gravity." By knocking this idea "out of their heads," he hoped to remove the danger of water. "This honest fellow was the type of the new revolutionary philosophers in Germany."[57] The dig was against the Young Hegelians, represented by Feuerbach. They thought they could fix society simply by fixing human ideas. These "ideologists, in spite of their allegedly 'world-shattering' statements," are in fact "the staunchest conservatives."[58] They relocated the foundation of society from the mind of God to the mind of men, but in the process they changed nothing. They only re-asserted the "ideas of the ruling class" as the "ruling ideas."[59]

For Marx and Engels, the real engine of history was not concepts but material conditions. Hegelianism excluded "the relation of man to nature" and created a false "antithesis between nature and history."[60] Actual history is made by living human beings interdependent on each other and on their natural environment. "The writing of history must always set out from these natural bases and their modification in the course of history through the action of men."[61] Morality, religion, metaphysics, consciousness, and all forms of ideology are dependent on the material conditions. These conditions determine modes of human production and provide for basic human needs.[62] The conflict in this story, then, arises not from religious and philosophical illusions, but from the reality that great masses of human beings are limited, controlled, and dehumanized by their insufficient material conditions. The conceptual illusions "are nothing more than the ideal expression of the dominant material relations . . . the relationships which make one class the ruling one."[63]

56. Marx and Engels, *German Ideology*, 69.
57. Ibid., 2.
58. Ibid., 6.
59. Ibid., 39.
60. Ibid., 30.
61. Ibid., 7.
62. Ibid., 7, 14, 16.
63. Ibid., 39.

"Marxism," in general, narrates "the collective struggle to wrest a realm of Freedom from a realm of Necessity."[64] Humanity, in the state of nature, experiences a tension that must be resolved. People by nature are mutually interdependent. At the same time, nature has placed them in conflict with each other, due to their differing needs, dispositions, and fortunes. This creates a cleavage "between the particular and the common interest." Where do we most clearly see the conflict between the individual and the community? The involuntary division of labor. It makes a man's productivity "an alien power opposed to him." It "enslaves him instead of being controlled by him." When labor is thus distributed in the interest of the common good, the individual is estranged and alienated from his work. He is assigned an "exclusive sphere of activity, which is forced upon him and from which he cannot escape." Human production becomes a "power above us, growing out of our control, thwarting our expectations, bringing to naught our calculations."[65] This aggravates the estrangement among individuals, classes, and the greater community.

Eventually, only revolution will relieve the pressure. But these revolutions will remain penultimate so long as they continue to produce new ruling classes. The division of labor, the possession of property and capital may shift hands, but the estrangement remains. Thus Marx and Engels held out the prophetic hope of a time when new modes of mass production would enable a final Revolution. Up till now, "a mass of individuals remained subservient to a single mode of production." But in the anticipated proletarian revolution, "a mass of instruments of production must be made subject to each individual and property to all."[66] This classless people without private property would finally rid themselves "of all the muck of the ages and become fitted to found society anew."[67] In a "communist society," forced labor divisions will be replaced by self-creating activity. Contingency and fortune will be removed. General production will be so precisely regulated as to liberate humanity. Marx delighted in this hope: It will be possible for me "to hunt in the morning, fish in the afternoon, rear cattle in the evening, criticize after dinner, just as I have a mind, without ever becoming a hunter, fisherman, shepherd, or critic."[68]

Marx "threw his whole being into a powerful protest against all the current foibles of his century, understanding their utter inadequacy to

---

64. Jameson, *Political Unconscious*, 19.
65. Marx and Engels, *German Ideology*, 22–23.
66. Ibid., 67.
67. Ibid., 69.
68. Ibid., 22.

the problems and needs of the time." He aimed to "shock his age out of its complacency."[69] This attack was a means to a greater end—to realize hope not by transcending theoretic evil, but by transforming the material conditions that produce actual evils. Like other narrative theodicies, the story Marx told made sense of suffering by showing how it could be overcome. "In one respect, however, he broke with every preceding form of theodicy. What others left implicit, half-thought or half-dared, was for Marx as serene as an axiom. Theodicies had hitherto defended God; the point was to replace Him."[70]

Marx's life-organizing story is criticized in a variety of ways. Neiman thought all his talk of common good reduced to petty interest-group politics. His blasphemous demand to replace God made him sound like Plato's tyrant Thrasymachus, for whom justice was "doing good to your (class) comrades and evil to your (class) enemies." Everything else was condemned as "bourgeois ideology."[71] Becker took a slightly different perspective. He complained that Marx's vision was an insufficient call to action because it ultimately collapsed into determinism. Becker noted how other interpreters had pointed out this contradiction between Marx's "urge to activism and his faith in historical inevitability." On the one hand, he calls man to "make himself," but on the other, he "shares the futuristic optimism" of thinkers like "Leibniz." Becker thought one must finally choose: either faith or works, but not both. In his reckoning, Marx opted for faith. He threw "the whole burden of perfectibility and progress into an automatic law of history, aided by the continual class struggle."[72]

Fredric Jameson defended Marx and Marxism against both of these criticisms. Jameson noted that local revolutions must be understood "as vital episodes in a single vast unfinished plot."[73] Universal in scope, the "ultimate Marxian presupposition" is that the "socialist revolution can only be a total and worldwide process." Jameson also responded to the accusations that Marx naively thought this process would happen automatically. Historical "Necessity" is "presented in the form of the inexorable logic involved in the determinate failure of all the revolutions that have taken place in human history."[74] These local revolutions are restricted by their objective limitations. *The* Revolution must be brought about by liberated humanity

---

69. Ernest Becker, *Structure of Evil*, 63–64.
70. Neiman, *Evil in Modern Thought*, 109.
71. Neiman, *Moral Clarity*, 70.
72. Becker, *Structure of Evil*, 66.
73. Jameson, *Political Unconscious*, 20.
74. Ibid., 102.

on a global scale. And it will be free human beings who give this inexorable *form* of development its material *content*.

Whether Marx is judged as insufficiently activist or overly tyrannical, his story generated hope that the declared gap between *is* and *ought* would be overcome only when the world came to fit his words. Whether or not his perceived *ought* reflected true justice is irrelevant to classifying his response to evil as *idealist*. However, if we choose not to take his demand to "change the world" at face value, but hear it as a deterministic prediction, then his narrated discourse would no longer be a *directive*, but an *assertive*. His story would simply be a re-telling of Hegel's Leibniz-inspired idealist-*theoretic* theodicy.

So if Marx resorts to predictive assertions in the end, do we have a better example of an idealist-pragmatic theodicy? When Becker accused Marx of determinism, he did so in the interest of correcting and completing Marx's directive to restructure human society and thereby overcome the conflict in Marx's plot. If Marx's theodicy fails to be fully pragmatic, then Becker aims to finish the job. This would make Becker's narrative of sociology a more fitting representative of the ideal pragmatic type.[75]

Modern Democracy's Idealist-Pragmatic Story. In order to add to the illustration of this type, let me take in hand a narrated theodicy that, to some at least, might seem to be the opposite of Marxism, namely, the standard story of modern democracy. In this next sub-section, I portray the triumphal quest of democracy as another form of an idealist-pragmatic narrative theodicy—a story that resolves its own declared problem of evil by making the present world conform to its directive word.

William Cavanaugh offered support for this portrayal of modern democracy in his 1995 article on the so-called "Myth of Religious Violence."[76] As the story goes, "the modern, secularized State arose to keep peace among the warring religious factions."[77] Having saved Europe from the Post-Reformation wars of religion, it created the possibility of a perpetual peace through religious tolerance, free markets, and strong national defense. Next, liberal democracies banded together in an international coalition to spread this practical hope of peace around the world, fighting wars only as a means to this most noble end. As Francis Fukuyama argued, history has, in fact, come to an end with the arrival of liberal democracy. The "end of history"

---

75. See Becker, *Structure of Evil*, especially chap. 13, "Vision of the Science of Man."

76. Cavanaugh, "A Fire Strong Enough to Consume the House," 397–420. He expanded this thesis in his recent book, William Cavanaugh, *Myth of Religious Violence: Secular Ideology and the Roots of Modern Conflict*.

77. Cavanaugh, "A Fire Strong Enough," 398.

does "not mean that the natural cycle of birth, life, and death would end," but that "there would be no further progress in the development of underlying principles and institutions, because all of the really big questions had been settled." Fukuyama clarified that this ending was proleptic in that "the greater part of humanity" still needed to be led "to liberal democracy."[78]

Cavanaugh called this story a "myth" because it is generally accepted as unquestionably true.[79] He offered a counter-narrative to challenge the normative status of the "Myth of Religious Violence." Cavanaugh argued that what was at stake in the so-called wars of religion was not church doctrine but conflicting intentions to "consolidate Imperial power," "control the monarchy," or stop "the nobility's challenge to royal pretensions to absolute power."[80] Cavanaugh explained how the very phrase "wars of religion" is anachronistic:

> what was at issue in these wars was the very creation of religion as a set of privately held beliefs without direct political relevance. The creation of religion was necessitated by the new State's need to secure absolute sovereignty over its subjects.[81]

The "religion" created by the formation of the modern State was molded after the "Platonic scheme." It was a "universal human impulse common to all" and was based on "common, universal truths which underlie all particular expressions of 'religious belief.'"[82]

With religious expression internalized and removed for the material world, the liberal State could exercise its role as the eschatological bringer of the "end of history." Cavanaugh called this the "soteriology of the State." Because it presents itself as the best solution to keeping the "war of all against all" at bay, the State's "sovereign authority" must be "without rival."[83] Once the State became the guarantor of freedom and peace its ultimate goal was to "maintain itself perpetually."[84] A soteriology of the State implies an "idolatry of the State."[85]

In a similar fashion, Richard Bauckham spoke of a more general myth, or eschatology of progress, which continues to take an

---

78. Fukuyama, *End of History*, xii.
79. Cavanaugh, *Myth of Religious Violence*, 6.
80. Cavanaugh, "A Fire Strong Enough," 400, 401, 402.
81. Ibid., 398.
82. Ibid., 404.
83. Ibid., 406.
84. Ibid., 408, quoting Immanuel Kant, *Metaphysics of Morals*.
85. Ibid., 416.

> idealistic, even messianic, form ... in the United States, [where] it retains the quasi-religious aspects ... the conviction of historical inevitability and the aura of salvation that attends the freedom it proffers. In its American version, the old idea of the United States as a messianic nation still justifies an imperialistic role that is portrayed as a mission to bring freedom to the rest of the world.[86]

According to Cavanaugh, the modern idolatry of the State was made possible in part by inventing a form of Christianity separable from the church. In order for Christianity to become a sub-species of a more general class of religious longing and expression, it must be removed from the life-organizing story of Jesus' church, whose public gathering, proclamation, and worship is a proleptic fulfillment of God's intention to bring the entire creation to fit his word of promise. Without the narrated promise, Christian hope is reduced to a vague hopefulness or elation that can comfortably fit within any number of rival stories.

In terms of tactics, the hope of Marx's classless society and the hope of modern democracy's perpetual peace are opposites. But in terms of general strategy for overcoming storied evil, they both speak of resolving their conflict by issuing successful *directives*—by making the world fit their word. Likewise, they are both scandalized by failed directives. With the large-scale collapse of socialism in the late twentieth century, would-be Marxists were faced with an epistemological crisis. Would-be participants in the life-organizing story of modern democracy have a similar problem. When faced with continuing wars, identity politics, self-inflicted environmental disasters, economic catastrophes, they must continue to recount their proleptic triumphs. They must assume their authorities can be trusted. They must live by hope.

Summary. I grouped these idealist stories because they all begin by invoking a universal standard of goodness to condemn some aspect of experience as evil. This condemnation should be taken as a declarative speech act. It does what is says and says what is does. It simultaneously fits the world to the word and the word to the newly declared world. But, what is the status of that storied world? Is it complete or is it deficient? The answer to that question sets the narrative strategy for overcoming the *storied evil*. If the storied world was deemed complete, then the participants just need to struggle to get their assertions in line. For them, the strategy is to fit their *words to the world* as it is was already declared to be. This is the *theoretic*

---

86. Richard Bauckham, "Conclusion," in Walls, *Oxford Handbook of Eschatology*, 677.

strategy. If the storied world was deemed deficient, then the strategy is to fit the *world to the word*. The declared standard must be brought into being by issuing fulfilled directives. This is the *pragmatic* strategy.

Within each type, the successes of the strategy are chronicled in a narrative past. For the *theoretic* type, success might be the construction of a more full and balanced body of doctrine. For the *pragmatic* type, success might include the implementation of social or political sanctions. However, in spite of these successes, each story continues to be threatened by a *scandalous evil*. This evil does not merely undermine the strategy, but attacks the very declaration that created the storied world. Therefore, they are all contested and unfinished stories. If they are to remain life-organizing stories, they must project their ultimate triumph into the future.

The Possibility of a Dual Strategy to Overcome Evil

In the prior chapter, we saw how Ricoeur used his typology of myths not merely to classify and draw static borders between types. The typology was also a heuristic device given for the task of discovery. Ricoeur said a "dynamic use" would reveal how the types often overlapped and created hybrid versions.[87] In this chapter, I chose Leibniz and Marx as the ideal types because the discourse in their respective works—*Theodicy* and *The German Ideology*—roughly follow my formal definitions of idealist-*theoretic* and idealist-*pragmatic* narrative theodicies. But, as we saw in the discussion, Leibniz's narration incorporated elements of both the Christian and Platonic plotlines. Also, Marx made Hegel's story his point of departure and it remains unclear how Marx's strategy is different from that of his forebear. As idealists (in Neiman's sense of the word), they all condemned evil by some allegedly universal standard of goodness—be it knowledge of the pre-established harmony, the future realization of the Absolute Spirit, or the creation of a harmonious, classless society. After the declaration was made, two formal strategies were open to them: either re-describe the world or change it. In my classification, I assumed that only one strategy can be taken: you can either transcend or transform, but not both. However, given Leibniz's worldly activism and Marx's determinist prophecies, we should ask whether or not a story can work *both* strategies.

In *Evil in Modern Thought*, Neiman presented Kant as the model for how to work both strategies in tandem. He aimed to transcend evil by appeal to a higher order and at the same time demanded we transform the world to fit the ideals of reason. Kant can be heard as telling either a

87. Ricoeur, *Symbolism of Evil*, 309.

theoretic or pragmatic narrative theodicy. Bayer listed Kant as the model of an "active theodicy." He explained how Kant argued that we cannot *think* out, but can only *act* out solutions for evil.[88] Recall Kant's vision of a moral kingdom of heaven on earth, which we "*have a glimpse of* in the continuous advance and approximation toward the highest possible good on earth."[89] In a contrasting assessment, Becker expressed dissatisfaction with Kant. He thought Kant was *too* theoretic and did not offer a more definite plan for enacting social progress. He complained that although "Kant had opted for man as a . . . moral agent, his inability to carry through critically on any but a philosophical level had its expected issue."[90] That issue for Becker was Kant's failure to provide concrete directions on how to transform human society and remove moral evils.

Neiman explained these conflicting accounts of Kant. She argued that Kant believed the empirical world should in fact match the rational mind. "Kant thought all moral action has one goal: to realize a world in which happiness and virtue are systematically connected. Every time we act rightly, we are acting to bring the world closer to this ideal." But in everyday experience, we often fail and the world fails to bend to our demands. So as not to despair, Kant posited the need for a rational faith. We must "believe that all our efforts to be virtuous will be completed by a Being who controls the natural world in ways we do not."[91] Without this belief, and without some signs of progress, the modern distinction between moral evil and natural (or physical) evil would eventually collapse, and with it, the notion of human responsibility.

Neiman admired a brilliant tension inherent in Kant's thought. On the one hand, if we had certain knowledge that Providence ordered all things for the best—justly paying out happiness to those who deserve it—we would instrumentalize God and render virtue void. On the other hand, without the hidden work of Providence blessing our efforts with signs of progress, we would give up. God's hiddenness in the face of human failure and suffering is a necessary part of Kant's (and Neiman's) system.[92] Evil is justified like we might justify a father teaching his son to ride a bike—wisely giving the right blend of unnoticed help while still letting him fall occasionally. It is an attempt at a double strategy for telling an intelligible story of the world.

88. Bayer, *Living by Faith*, 12–13.
89. Kant, *Religion and Rational Theology*, 162–63 (italics original).
90. Becker, *Structure of Evil*, 59–60.
91. Neiman, *Evil in Modern Thought*, 66. Cf. Kant, *Religion and Rational Theology*, 58
92. Ibid., 257. Inspired by Kant, Neiman took the "third avenue" open for theodicy after Auschwitz.

If we were certain there were a just God with his hand guiding history, we wouldn't struggle to practice justice. But without the practical hope of a just God, we would eventually grow cynical and give in to despair.

In spite of an impressive attempt at a dual strategy, I read this as a final retreat into theory. When faced with scandalous evil, Kant and Neiman return to the *assertion* that the natural world *must* appear random, senseless, and amoral in order for humanity to be free and virtuous. God's hiddenness surprisingly makes this the best world after all. "Einstein said the Creator was subtle; Kant's thought showed Him brilliant. Our very skepticism is a providential gift."[93]

Nevertheless, I find Kant's attempted dual strategy distinct enough to give him a special place in the typology. I mentioned I would not portray Christianity as maintaining the ideal balance between theory and practice; or, anticipating the next chapter, between the idealist and realist response to evil. If anyone deserves this tragic and torn middle ground, it is Kant.

Kant's almost-successful dual strategy for overcoming evil gives his story a unique capacity to co-opt others. Cavanaugh identified Kant as "the intellectual forebear to many of today's liberal political theorists."[94] Kant's private sphere was the realm of faith and religion. It was for him the last stronghold against despair in the face of scandalous evil. It provided space for individuals to transcend personal guilt and suffering in a private quest for meaning. In contrast, the public realm provided space for modern nation states to transform the conditions that allow for the suffering caused by moral and, to some extent, natural evil. In this division between private and public realms, Kant's story attempted to subsume every other life-organizing story. Other stories could survive as private beliefs which must remain subservient to the ends and means dictated by the public story—the story of the triumphal, modern nation state.

When Christians practice their faith submitting to these constraints, it "is no longer a matter of certain bodily practices within the Body of Christ, but is limited to the realm of the 'soul,' and the body is handed over to the State."[95] In a recent essay, Pannenberg explained how Kant's story of moral and political progress provided a place for Christian hope, so long as it limited itself to hope for the soul in the afterlife.[96] In this way, it would become essentially the same as all other private stories. It would function

---

93. Ibid., 327.

94. Cavanaugh, "A Fire Strong Enough," 408.

95. Ibid., 405.

96. Wolfhart Pannenberg, "Modernity, History and Eschatology," in *Oxford Handbook of Eschatology*, 495.

as a bulwark against despair when troubled by evil as defined by the story of Enlightenment. The Enlightenment's original scandal of evil was that a just God would reveal himself via external discourse and make this-worldly promises to some particular group of people. Once a group of people believed they had received and now speak the definitive word from God, society would soon collapse into the religious intolerance and wars of the past. Kant's arrangement kept God safely hidden and known only by a private faith. It allowed for individuals to arrive at their own theoretic resolutions to evil while the State issued and, if necessary, lethally enforced its directives to ensure society never returned to the hopeless warfare caused by superstitions and irrational beliefs.

Most of the prior paragraph is a restatement of Cavanaugh's argument warning against the idolatry of the modern democratic State. Cavanaugh, a Roman Catholic scholar, was *not* calling for the church to take up her medieval sword once more. "Contesting the State's monopoly on violence does not mean that the church should again get a piece of the action, yet another form of Constantinianism." He only argued that pulling the sword from the church "did nothing to stanch the flow of blood on the West's troubled pilgrimage. The pitch of war has grown more shrill, and the recreation of the church as a voluntary association of practitioners of religion has only sapped our ability to resist."[97] Cavanaugh made a "plea for the social and political nature of the Christian faith . . . a plea for a Christian practice which escapes the thrall of the State."[98]

Hearing this plea from a Confessional Lutheran position means taking Article XVI of the Augsburg Confession seriously: "Christians, therefore, are obliged to be subject to political authority and to obey its commands and laws in all that may be done *without sin*."[99] Escaping the thrall of the modern democratic state and developing the means to resist its idolatry begins by subsuming its narrative into the Christian narrative. To do so would be to take a cue from Marx and narrate it as a mere temporary stage on the way, not to a communitarian utopia, but to the new creation in Christ.

SUMMARY

The eschatological hopes discussed in this chapter are not Christian because they do not depend on the Christian story. They do not follow the King's highway—the main road given with the story of Jesus. They are rivals to

---

97. Cavanaugh, "A Fire Strong Enough," 414.
98. Ibid., 409.
99. Kolb and Wengert, *Book of Concord*, 50. Italics added.

Christian eschatology because they tell a different story. Representing the idealist response, they issue a definitive judgment on what counts as good and what counts as evil. They either displace or replace the God of Israel, who has appointed one person to judge—the man he raised from the dead (Acts 17:31). Moreover, they take up a different strategy to overcome their own forms of storied evil. Their plots resolve by fitting assertions to a hidden, impersonal reality; or by making the world match their directives.

This detour through rival storylines has begun to highlight the unique features of the Christian story. The Christian strategy to overcome evil is to speak by the Spirit of Jesus and make threats and promises for God. This "deputized discourse"[100] happens in the context of the on-going story of Jesus-in-Israel-and-the-church. In the era between the resurrection and return of Jesus, the Holy Spirit is at work through the church's public, embodied speech acts to bring the plot to final resolution.

Like other life-organizing stories, the Christian one is threatened by its own particular form of scandalous evil. This scandal threatens to undermine the seven-fold declaration that got the story going: "And God saw that it was good" (Gen 1:4, 10, 12, 18, 21, 25, 31). God's promise, as announced by the church, is that in the crucified and risen Jesus, God has and will finally deliver his creation from evil. God has promised to defend and vindicate its goodness. But the terror of present and eternal suffering—which is also part of the story—is the scandal that threatens to undermine this narrated promise. If God's promise implies his unilateral commitment to deliver his creatures from evil, then why are some delivered, but not others? When Christians are confronted with this scandalous evil, they are often tempted to seek solutions in other narrative strategies—in theory, practice, or both. But by doing so, they unintentionally promote rival stories, other forms of hope. They may also be tempted to redefine evil according to the idealist scheme, that is, to place even their God under some self-projected standard of goodness. If this temptation is resisted, and we "let God be God,"[101] then another temptation, to be discussed in the next chapter, arises. It is the temptation to reject the notions of *good* and *evil* altogether. This is the response that gets realist stories going.

---

100. Wolterstorff, *Divine Discourse*, 42–51.
101. Luther, *Career of the Reformer I*, in *Luther's Works*, 31: 10.

7

Realist Types

THIS CHAPTER IS A continuation of the detour, the *via negativa*, we began in the prior chapter. The authors considered on this *apophatic* path help express what Christian hope is not. In chapter 6, I discussed the idealist response to the experience of sin and suffering. The idealists said, "This ought not be." By doing so, they presumed to judge the experience against some universal standard of the Good. For them, the Good was presently hidden. It was hidden in either a pre-existing rational harmony or in an as yet unrealized future. Their strategies to approach the Good divided them into separate types. They either re-described the world with more accurate assertions, or attempted to re-make the world by issuing successful directives. The focus of that chapter was on the difference between the theoretic (assertion-making) and the pragmatic (directive-giving) strategies. This chapter incorporates and develops that distinction while focusing on the difference between the declarations that get a life-organizing story going. The idealist declared, "This ought not be." But the realist replies, "It is what it is."[1]

DETOUR: REALISTS

The two exemplary realists I discuss here are Friedrich Nietzsche and Sigmund Freud. Others will be included to provide context or to suggest contemporary manifestations of their form of life-organizing story. Again, I

---

1. Cf. Neiman, *Evil in Modern Thought*. I have been following Neiman's categories throughout the book.

do not seek an objective or neutral perspective. Nor do I intend to offer an authoritative interpretation of their works, only a plausible one. I read them in the interest of saying how Christian hope is distinct both from the idealist hopes they disdain and from the tragic and mature hopes they offer.

Narrators of a realist story begin by rejecting the idealistic appeal to a better reality, hidden behind appearances. For the idealists, the hidden Good served as a standard by which to judge human thought and behavior. It served as a moral *ought*. As long as this ideal was in place, the distinction between physical evil (suffering) and moral evil (sin) held. Physical or natural evil could be managed and mitigated. With the advent of modern science, it was completely demystified. The designer of the universe wasn't saying anything by "natural" disasters or death by "natural" causes. These evils were overcome by fiat. Only moral evil remained a problem, since it was caused by human beings and was therefore within human power to prevent. But the realist story, by condemning this ideal as a personal projection, collapsed the distinction between what *ought* to be and what *is*. All the nasty things people are inclined to call "evil" are part of a single natural reality that is indifferent to our projections. To condemn something as "evil" because it fails to meet your personal ideals becomes a sign of immaturity. In both the theoretic and pragmatic versions of the realist story, immaturity is part of the conflict to be overcome.

Realist-Theoretic

Friedrich Nietzsche (1844–1900) claimed he was the first to formulate the following insight: "*there are absolutely no moral facts.*"[2] He thought that we "rob reality of its meaning, value, and truthfulness" to the extent that we "*make up* an ideal world."[3] It is for axioms like these that he has been hailed the "godfather of contemporary 'postmodernism.'"[4] Not only is there continuing philosophical interest in his life and work, he is also increasingly discussed within Christian theology, especially in postliberal and radical orthodox schools of thought.[5] Besides his present popularity, he is important

2. Nietzsche, *Twilight of the Idols*, 182–83.

3. Nietzsche, *Ecce Homo*, 71.

4. Young, *Friedrich Nietzsche*, 4. Young qualified Nietzsche's position "plural realism" versus "postmodernism." The second says no single view is either true or false. The first "thinks of reality as multi-aspected, so that different perspectives reveal . . . different aspects of it" (338).

5. For recent theological studies, see Hovey, *Nietzsche and Theology* and Deane, *Nietzsche and Theology*. For a seminal "radical orthodox" treatment, see Milbank, *Theology and Social Theory*, who made Nietzsche and "Nietzschean postmodernism" a central target of his critique of secular reason.

for my project because, according to Julian Young, Nietzsche's "most famous book, *Thus Spoke Zarathustra*," should be read as a *"religious* work"[6] that "challenges all existing religions,"[7] and aims to narrate a "great theodicy."[8]

In 1888, just prior to, or perhaps on the cusp of his descent into madness, Nietzsche, the once pious son of a Lutheran pastor, completed his autobiographical account titled "Ecce Homo." He took the title from the words Pontius Pilate spoke to present Jesus to the riotous crowed: "Behold, the man" (John 19:5).[9] In "Ecce Homo," Nietzsche narrated how he became the author of *Zarathustra*, which he asserted to be the "greatest gift" humanity "has ever received."[10] To become the giver of such a gift, he had to pass through at least two significant epistemological crises: the first occurring shortly before publishing *Human, All Too Human* (1878), the second beginning in 1881, when *"the thought of the eternal return"* came to him while hiking in Switzerland.[11] Young used these two turning points to index Nietzsche's work in three stages: romanticist, positivist, and mature. His romanticist stage consisted in his acceptance of Schopenhauer's version of Kant's metaphysical idealism. The positivist stage involved his rejection of idealism, concluding that *"Nothing* exists 'behind' nature, nothing exists *but* nature." His mature stage was not a rejection, but a synthesis "of the romantic and positivist horizons into a third."[12]

An important influence in this mature stage was the pantheistic philosophy of Baruch Spinoza (1632–77),[13] who was one of the great opponents Leibniz discussed in his *Theodicy*. After reading of Spinoza in 1881 near the beginning of his mature period, Nietzsche wrote to a friend, "I have a forerunner. And what a forerunner! . . . I discover myself in [Spinoza's] teaching: he denies freedom of the will, purpose, a moral order of the world, the unegoistic, evil . . . In sum, my aloneness . . . is now at least a two-ness."[14] Nietzsche's doctrine of the "eternal return" meant that Spinoza's "realist" world could be conceived as sacred on its own. It could be affirmed, without modi-

---

6. Young, *Nietzsche*, 358, 366.

7. Ibid., 366. This is Nietzsche's own claim in a letter he wrote describing the book.

8. Ibid., 381. See also 351.

9. Ibid., 518–19. On the young Nietzsche's Lutheran piety, see ibid., chaps. 1–2.

10. Nietzsche, *Ecce Homo*, 72.

11. Referring to the first, he said *"Human, All Too Human*, is the monument to a crisis" (ibid., 115). For the second, he said the idea of eternal return was conceived in 1881 and gestated until "the sudden birth that took place in February of 1883" (ibid., 123–24). He began drafting *Zarathustra* in January of 1883 (Young, *Nietzsche*, 358).

12. Young, *Nietzsche*, 242–43, 351.

13. Ibid., 319–20.

14. Ibid.

fication or further re-description. Even Schopenhauer's "*worst* of all possible worlds"[15] could be seen as good, without appeal to a higher harmony, blessed future, or personal immortality. The conflict in this budding story of salvation was in how to bring oneself to affirm life, as a whole, without exception—even the "devastated battlefield" through which Nietzsche once walked as a medic during the Franco-Prussian War; even the images of the "indescribably sad human body parts and stinking corpses" that haunted him.[16] This too must be celebrated.

Nietzsche's eschatological hope was to move beyond the false ideals that condemn the real world. In his 1888 book *Twilight of the Idols*, he summarized how the "true world" (the ideal) "finally became a fable." It began with the proposition that the "true world" is "attainable for a man who is wise, pious, virtuous." The philosopher who had proleptically completed his journey to speak truthfully about the world embodied the ideal: "I, Plato, *am* the truth." Next, said Nietzsche, the "true world" became "unattainable for now, but promised" to those who continue to make conceptual progress. This hope held for a while, but eventually Kant made it "unattainable, unprovable, unpromisable." Nevertheless, "the very thought of it" could still be "a consolation, an obligation, an imperative." Finally, the "true world" became an "idea that is of no further use, not even as an obligation." The realists demanded, "let's get rid of it!" At this, "Plato blushes in shame" because of the "pandemonium of all free spirits." The ideal has vanished. The "longest error" has ended.[17] All that remains is the *real* world.

The real world, thus declared, is the setting of Nietzsche's life-organizing story. It is an account of coming not only to accept all that is, but to will it, to celebrate it. The conflict in his story can be resolved only by coming to desire the "eternal return" of life and death "throughout infinite time—not an expurgated version with the bad bits left out, but *exactly* the same life, down to the last detail, however painful or shameful."[18] Nietzsche's hope of salvation resembles that of the "tragic myth" explored by Ricoeur. There, suffering is endured "for the sake of understanding." Salvation is aesthetic deliverance, the bestowal of "tragic wisdom."[19] Tragedy, said Nietzsche, is

---

15. Schopenhauer, *World as Will and Representation*, 2:583.

16. Ibid., 137. See also 139. This description comes from Nietzsche's letter to his mother.

17. Nietzsche, *Twilight of the Idols*, 171. See also Nietzsche, *Beyond Good and Evil*, 4.

18. Young, *Nietzsche*, 3.

19. Ricoeur, *Symbolism of Evil*, 229.

"the highest art of saying yes to life."²⁰ "What doesn't kill me makes me stronger."²¹

Seeking tragic wisdom, the "mature Nietzsche's prime aim" was "world-affirmation."²² *Thus Spoke Zarathustra*, written between 1883 and 1885, was among the first of his mature works. Nietzsche called it "a fifth Gospel." According to Young, it was to be "the central, sacred text of the new religion" supposed to "replace the now-'dead' Christianity." It would be a religion "of life," rather than of "after-life."²³ It chronicled the protagonist's journey toward world-affirming wisdom and his efforts to make disciples along the way: "To lure many away from the herd, for that I have come . . . Fellow creators, Zarathustra seeks, fellow harvesters, fellow celebrants."²⁴ Zarathustra, a Christ-like figure, in a sense "*is* Nietzsche," the "ideal Nietzsche," the person he wanted to be.²⁵

When he was thirty years old, Zarathustra left his home to live alone in the mountains. After ten years of solitude, he emerged full of wisdom, "like a bee that has gathered too much honey." He needs "hands outstretched to receive it."²⁶ He goes to a city, which represents the sickly culture of the modern west.²⁷ Upon seeing the crowd gathered to watch a tightrope walker in the town square, Zarathustra shares his message: "Man is a rope, tied between beast and overman [*Übermensch*]—a rope over an abyss. A dangerous across, a dangerous on-the-way."²⁸ The *Übermensch* is the icon of humanity overcoming their need to protect themselves from reality by appealing to conventional ideals. He was a signpost of the hope that some would come to will the eternal return and so attain salvation.²⁹ But first, they must go over (*über*). Zarathustra urged his hearers to "*remain faithful to the earth.*" Do "not believe those who speak to you of otherworldly hopes!"³⁰

With the crowd rejecting him, Zarathustra leaves town to call disciples and deliver his speeches. He tells his fellow celebrants of the earth they

---

20. Nietzsche, *Ecce Homo*, 110.
21. Nietzsche, *Twilight of the Idols*, 157.
22. Young, *Nietzsche*, 408.
23. Ibid., 366. See also Nietzsche, *Ecce Homo*, 72.
24. Nietzsche, *Thus Spoke Zarathustra*, in *Portable Nietzsche*, 135–36.
25. Young, *Nietzsche*, 367.
26. Nietzsche, *Thus Spoke Zarathustra*, in *Portable Nietzsche*, 122.
27. Young, *Nietzsche*, 368.
28. Nietzsche, *Thus Spoke Zarathustra*, in *Portable Nietzsche*, 126; Nietzsche, *Werke*, 2:281.
29. In *Ecce Homo*, 123, Nietzsche explained, "The basic idea of [*Zarathustra*]" is "*the thought of eternal return*, the highest possible formula of affirmation."
30. Nietzsche, *Thus Spoke Zarathustra*, in *Portable Nietzsche*, 125.

must learn to conquer every "thou shalt" with a resolute "I will."³¹ They must become the creators of their own values. The evils they must overcome are the "afterworlds," the heavenly mansions, rational pre-established harmonies, moral universes, and utopias dreamt by a weariness "that wants to reach the ultimate with one leap." Zarathustra explains how "suffering and incapacity" led people to abandon the real world and invent "gods and afterworlds."³² When people speak of "highest good" and "great evil," they are simply sounding "the voice of their will to power."³³ Zarathustra, the great educator, teaches his disciples "to speak ever more honestly" about the world.³⁴ To become as the *Übermensch*, they must learn to fit their words, minds, and wills to the world created by the realist declaration.

But Zarathustra still struggles with this doctrine and so he often removes himself from his disciples and returns to solitude. He recognized that he continues to be a man "on-the-way." He knows the only salvation possible in a realist story of the world must begin by sacrificing every moral *ought*. He must not only accept, but must *will* the world *as it is* and so transcend it. To recreate all "it was" into a "thus I willed it"—"that alone should I call redemption [*Erlösung*]."³⁵ But he knew he had not yet arrived. Zarathustra chided himself: has "the will yet spoken thus?" Has "the will yet become his own redeemer and joy-bringer?" That "will," is "the will to power." It must be taught to will "backwards." But, "Who could teach him also to will backwards?"³⁶ Who could muster the courage to say "once more" to life?³⁷—to return eternally "*not* to a new life or better life," but to this "same, selfsame life"?³⁸

Zarathustra believed that it was his "destiny" to be "the teacher of the eternal recurrence."³⁹ He must create a storied world in which "time itself is a circle." There, time does not fly forward as an arrow toward a target, but forward as a giant wheel endlessly rotating toward what has gone before. From the perspective of those entangled in time and causality, the path appears to go on eternally in opposite directions, never to meet. But in fact,

---

31. Ibid., 138–39.
32. Ibid., 143.
33. Ibid., 170.
34. Ibid., 144.
35. Ibid., 251. Nietzsche, *Werke*, 2:394. See also, Young, *Nietzsche*, 379.
36. Nietzsche, *Thus Spoke Zarathustra*, in *Portable Nietzsche*, 253.
37. Ibid., 269.
38. Ibid., 333.
39. Ibid., 332.

the paths *do* come together where each individual stands—"here at this gateway" called "moment"...

> From this gateway, Moment, a long, eternal lane leads *backward:* behind us lies an eternity. Must not whatever *can* walk have walked on this lane before? Must not whatever *can* have happened, have been done, have passed by before? ... Must not this gateway too have been there before? And are not all things knotted together so firmly that this moment draws after it *all* that is to come? Therefore—itself too? For whatever *can* walk ... it *must* walk once more.[40]

Nietzsche's life-organizing story begins by saying of the world, "It is what it is." As a creative declaration, it discloses a storied world filled with purposeless pain and fleeting pleasure. The plot moves forward like a man moving precariously across a high-wire strung out over an abyss.[41] It is a struggle of an evolving perspective: to move from a false (idealistic) perspective, through an honest (realistic) yet despairing perspective, eventually to arrive at an empowered, joyous perspective. It's a story about growing up, not to change the world, but to affirm it as it is. The conflict resolves only when the protagonist can honestly match his words to this world and say, "Thus I willed it."

It is not until the conclusion of Part Four that Zarathustra enjoys a proleptic experience of salvation. Otherwise, the thought of the "eternal return" nauseates him.[42] It finally overtakes him during his "drunken song"—drunk on life, that is, and maybe buzzing on wine. Surrounded by his celebrating higher men, he exclaims, "Joy . . . wants recurrence, wants everything the same . . . You higher men, do learn this, joy wants eternity. Joy wants the eternity of *all* things."[43] The next morning, Zarathustra awakes and leaves his higher men. For a moment, he almost pities them and regrets the loss of their company. But then hardens his face like flint: "Well then, *that* has had its time!" he says. "My suffering and my pity for suffering—what does it

---

40. Ibid., 270.

41. The emblematic tight-rope walker at the beginning of the book consequently fell to his death. The dead man ironically becomes Zarathustra's first disciple. See ibid., 131–35.

42. In ibid., Part Three, "The Convalescent," 327–28, Zarathustra tries to summon awake his "abysmal thought," that is, the eternal recurrence of the same events. He says, "I, Zarathustra, the advocate of life, the advocate of suffering, the advocate of the circle; I summon you, my most abysmal thought!" But when it awakes and takes his hand he shouts, "Huh! Let go! Huhhuh! Nausea, nausea, nausea—woe unto me!"

43. Ibid., 434, 436.

matter?" Then he sets off to continue his journey, "glowing and strong as a morning sun that comes out of dark mountains."[44]

Zarathustra's story, especially his speech on *Erlösung*, "salvation," reveals what Young called "Nietzsche's basic strategy: theodicy—showing that problematic phenomena are really just blessings in disguise." Young continued: "In narrating one's life in this way one is, of course, giving it unity, 'composing into one' all that was previously meaningless 'accident'. Apparent accidents become parts of 'personal providence'. To authentic 'selves' accidents never happen."[45] For the mature Nietzsche, "Redemption, salvation, finding the world perfect, *amor fati*, embracing the eternal return, are one and all simply different expression of the same thing."[46] They speak to the resolution of the plot's conflict, which intends to justify both story and author. "Nietzsche's work tried to overcome theodicy by offering a bolder version of it."[47]

Nietzsche and Leibniz shared a similar strategy.[48] They both aimed to match their assertive discourse to their storied worlds. Granted, they inhabit two radically different narrative settings. Leibniz's world came into being by the declaration that there be a universal, impersonal ideal in which God, humanity, and nature participate. In this world, divine and human freedoms are compatible. Leibniz's storied evil was human immorality, which must remain distinct from "natural evil" (e.g., the Lisbon earthquake). In some respect, natural or physical evil is part of how the world works, but is aggravated by moral evil, or sin. And at the root of all moral evil is always human ignorance. It is overcome by education. But Nietzsche (and Spinoza before him) declared the world *all* natural. This collapsed the distinction between moral evil (sin) and physical evil (suffering). By doing so, he brought an entirely new storied world into existence. Here, human beings are irretrievably entangled in the natural, causal order just like everything else. This world has no end goal or final purpose. It just *is*.

Nietzsche's story opens up a way of salvation that offers hope *against* nihilistic despair. The storied evils in this plot are the false ideals that condemn the world or seek to modify it. They are evil because they weaken the will. They delay the coming of the Overman. In his place, they created the "last man," the "most despicable man," who "lives longest" and "invented

---

44. Ibid., 439.
45. Young, *Nietzsche*, 379.
46. Ibid., 380.
47. Neiman, *Evil in Modern Thought*, 222.
48. Cf. Milbank, *Theology and Social Theory*, 281.

happiness."[49] And so, as with Leibniz, salvation must be delivered through education, through making more honest assertions. Nietzsche saw himself as a doctor of culture. His aim was to rightly diagnose and heal the idealist disease.[50] He believed this was both his will and his causally determined destiny, making him evermore resolute in his calling. Though his methods appeared harsh, he was working for the salvation of others—to teach them even as he continued to teach himself to say "Once more!" to life—and mean it.

Nietzsche's life organizing story has ties to Eastern religious thought in general, and Buddhism in particular. In *The Anti-Christ*, Nietzsche said that "Christianity promises everything and delivers nothing," whereas "Buddhism does not promise," but "delivers."[51] Not that Nietzsche recommended Buddhism—he thought it belonged with Christianity as a "nihilistic" religion. At the same time, he said "Buddhism is a hundred times more realistic [*realistischer*] than Christianity."[52] In sharp contrast to Christianity, which he had called "Platonism for the 'people,'"[53] Nietzsche thought Buddhism "has left the self-deception of moral concepts,—it stands, as I put it, *beyond good and evil*."[54] Buddhism delivers, because it does right by reality [*der Wirklicheit*].[55]

Like Nietzsche's story, "Buddhist Eschatology" narrates an individual journey through perspectives: from delusional, to honest, to enlightened. Buddhist scholar Jan Nattier explained:

> To speak of Buddhist eschatology is, in a sense, a misnomer. If eschatology is understood to refer to "final things"—that is, the idea that the world will one day come to a definitive end—there is simply no parallel in the Buddhist tradition. On the contrary, Buddhist scriptures regularly refer to "beginningless *saṁsāra*," a cycle of birth and death of the universe (as well as of the individual) for which no starting point can be discerned. Nor is there an end . . . It is only on the level of the individual living being . . . that Buddhist texts do speak of an ultimate and final end. Indeed, the entire purpose of the Buddha's teachings . . . was to provide his followers with the means to escape from

---

49. Nietzsche, *Thus Spoke Zarathustra*, in *Portable Nietzsche*, 129–30.
50. Young, *Nietzsche*, 483.
51. Nietzsche, *Anti-Christ*, 38.
52. Nietzsche, *Der Antichrist*, in *Werke*, 2:1179.
53. Nietzsche, *Beyond Good and Evil*, 4
54. Nietzsche, *Anti-Christ*, 16.
55. Nietzsche, *Der Antichrist*, in *Werke*, 2:1179.

the treadmill of *saṁsāra* once and for all. This could be accomplished by carrying out a process of self-cultivation . . . that would ultimately lead to a complete and definitive awakening to the understanding of reality as it is, the experience known as *nirvāṇa*.[56]

Nietzschean and Buddhist eschatologies appear to be different in that the Buddhist hopes to escape the treadmill, while Nietzsche hopes to say "Once more!" eternally. But they are similar in the way they declare conflict and seek resolution in their respective plots. Storied evil in both accounts is a false picture that imagines life were something other than a pendulum between unsatisfied desires and post-satisfaction boredom.[57] The Buddhist strategy can be stated negatively or positively, either as extinguishing one's will or as awakening one's understanding. Likewise, Nietzsche's strategy can be stated negatively or positively, either "willing backwards," or replacing every "it was" with a "thus I willed it." In both cases, storied evil is transcended by authentically matching one's words, mind, and will to the declared world. Thus, they both serve as fitting examples of a realist-theoretic narrative theodicy.

Realist-Pragmatic

The pragmatic realist, like the theoretic, begins by declaring ideals to be infantile illusions. There is no better world hidden in the heavens or reflected in the human psyche. There is just reality. It is what it is. The pragmatist hope is distinctive because it pursues a different strategy to overcome the conflict that remains in its plot. This type is not ultimately concerned with speaking honest assertions about its storied world. Instead, it aims to issue successful directives that will manipulate human and non-human nature to match local or personal preference. Sigmund Freud (1856–1939), the Austrian-born father of psychoanalysis, will be our main expositor of a realist-pragmatic narrative theodicy.

Ernest Becker called him a "true Enlightenment figure," who "crowned" that tradition.[58] Paul Ricoeur thought he was *the* Master of the modern mas-

---

56. Jan Nattier, "Buddhist Eschatology," in Walls, *Oxford Handbook of Eschatology*, 151–52.

57. Cf. Young, *Nietzsche*, 83. Also, Schopenhauer, *World as Will and Representation*, vol. 1, 312, "Life swings like a pendulum to and fro between pain and boredom, and these two are in fact its ultimate constituents . . . after man had placed all pains and torments in hell, there was nothing left for heaven but boredom."

58. Becker, *Structure of Evil*, 151.

ters of suspicion.[59] Philip Rieff portrayed him as "*the* transitional figure" for understanding our present day culture.[60] Susan Neiman said he was responsible for "the most widespread assumptions that determine contemporary thought" on the so-called problem of evil.[61] Compared to the others, portraying Freud as a theodicist may seem strange. Leibniz and his intellectual heir, Hegel, were expressly attempting a theodicy. Many recognize Marx and Nietzsche as implicitly striving after some form of secular or post-secular theodicy. But most scholars agree that Freud refused to offer any form of consolation. So in what sense can we say he offers a rival hope?

I answer by returning to my formal definitions. I argue that Freud, in spite of his irreligious convictions, nonetheless has a life-organizing story. As with others, his story develops a conflict and strains after a resolution. Final resolution has not yet occurred, but he can point to signs of its coming. Although his storied evil still needs to be managed, the movement of the plot elicits hope and effectively defends against despair.

We might be tempted to say that Freud's eschatology is not hopeful because it doesn't offer Heaven, Utopia, or even a resolute will to say to life, "Once more!" But, as experienced from within Freud's story, those are all infantile illusions. They offer no genuine hope. His account differs from others because it aims to offer real hope—a mature hope stripped of delusion. By removing the projected wishes of those false hopes, he also avoids the antisocial neuroses caused by their counterparts: the fear of Hell, the anxieties of Revolution, or the nausea of trying to will the Eternal Return. Freud offers *eschatological* hope, not because he speaks of "end times," but because he speaks to the *resolution* of a story that discloses the "real" world. "Not in any beyond," said Freud, "but here on earth most men live in a hell: Schopenhauer has seen this very well. My knowledge, my theories and my methods have the goal of making men conscious of this hell so that they can free themselves from it."[62] The intelligibility of this story of liberation depends on whether or not its author proves trustworthy. Freud's hope, like all the others, is elicited by the telling of a narrative theodicy.

To depict Freud as a narrative theodicist, I make an analogy between his account and the chaos-creation myth Ricoeur described in *The Symbolism of Evil*. We've seen similar analogies with the others. Like the Platonic philosophers, Leibniz re-told a version of the myth that resolved by moving from ignorance to knowledge. Marx's progressive, communitarian hope has

---

59. Ricoeur, *Freud and Philosophy*, 32–36, 60, and 64.
60. See Rieff, *Triumph of the Therapeutic*, xi.
61. Neiman, *Evil in Modern Thought*, 227.
62. Freud, quoted in Jacoby, *Social Amnesia*, 119, 177n1.

been interpreted as a kind of biblical drama dressed up in secular garb.[63] Nietzsche's quest for tragic wisdom is completed through suffering an education to reality. Now Freud's account brings us back to the far left side of Ricoeur's typology,[64] to ancient Babylon.

Paul Ricoeur gestured toward this reading of Freud in his *Freud and Philosophy*. Ricoeur connected Nietzsche and Freud with the life-organizing story of Spinoza, the early modern pantheistic determinist, whom Leibniz had credited with "destroying freedom," by divesting "God of intelligence and choice, leaving him a blind power, whence all emanates of necessity."[65] Spinoza, Nietzsche, and Freud all tell a similar story, a *realist* story. It is an account of passing through stages of maturity. First, being confronted with "bare reality," one "finds himself a slave" of necessity, captive to the primordial impulses and causal connections that determine the universe. Next, "he understands his slavery." Finally, "he rediscovers himself free within understood necessity."[66]

Ricoeur noted how "the final development" of Freud's theory "marks the return of psychoanalysis to a sort of mythological philosophy, the emblems of which are the figures of Eros [urge toward sexual union], Thanatos [urge toward death], and Ananke [necessity]."[67] Freud's interest in a global interpretation of culture was brought to light in his 1920 essay, *Beyond the Pleasure Principle*. There Freud argued for the hypothesis that all reality was governed by two conflicting primordial forces: the life instinct (Eros) and the death instinct (Thanatos). The first "seeks to force together and hold together the portions of living substance." The second is a kind of inertia that struggles against the first. It "was brought into being by the coming to life of inorganic substance."[68] In 1930, Freud developed these reality-governing principles in *Civilization and Its Discontents*. There he claimed that the development of civilizations presents

> a struggle between Eros and Death [Thanatos], between the instinct of life and the instinct of destruction, as it works itself out in the human species. This struggle is what all life essentially consists of . . . And it is this battle of the giants that our nursemaids try to appease with their lullaby about Heaven.[69]

63. See Löwith, *Meaning in History* and Moltmann, *Coming of God*, 184–92.
64. See my chap. 5, figure 2.
65. Leibniz, *Theodicy*, 348.
66. Ricoeur, *Freud and Philosophy*, 35.
67. Ibid., 63.
68. Freud, *Beyond the Pleasure Principle*, in *Works of Freud*, 18:60–61n1.
69. Freud, *Civilization and Its Discontents*, in *Works of Freud*, 21:122.

Ricoeur commented on this passage: "In placing the task of culture in the field of the struggle between Eros and Thanatos, Freud raises his interpretation to the rank of a single and strong idea," a "global and sovereign" worldview.[70]

Like Spinoza and Nietzsche, Freud declared into existence a world dominated by natural, impersonal forces. In one powerful move, this declaration solved the various problems of evil created by the idealist versions of the world. It did so by removing the distinctions between moral, physical, and metaphysical evils and judged them all to be "natural." In one sense it created a new, more mature, late-modern world. In another sense, it re-created the old world arising from the "theogonic myths" of ancient Babylon.[71] In this story, salvation was already granted with the equilibrium forged in the violent struggle of life out of lifelessness. Violence is inscribed "in the origin of things, in the principle that establishes while it destroys."[72] Since salvation was given proleptically with the original life-equilibrium, the remaining storied evil can only be a "resurgence of the ancient chaos."[73] The conflict that drives the plot is located in the problem of individuals and communities falling prey to disruptions of the equilibrium. In order to participate in salvation, they must ritually re-enact the ancient victory. Eschatological hope is realized in the proper management of the chaos and maintenance of the order.

In Freud's version of the realist story, one of the great obstacles to realizing this hope is traditional religion itself. In his 1927 essay, *The Future of an Illusion*, he argued that religion was "the universal obsessional neurosis of humanity."[74] All religious doctrines have developed out of the human urge to seek pleasure and avoid pain. Civilization invented religion to restrict antisocial behavior and to offer consolation when life gets too hard. Freud admitted these doctrines have had some benefit for culture, but have since exhausted their usefulness. They console and restrict people only by coddling their infantile wishes. And the "pitiful rearguard actions" of modern philosophers are no better. They think "they can rescue the God of religion by replacing him by an impersonal, shadowy and abstract principle."[75] What civilization needs now is an "*education to reality.*"[76]

---

70. Ricoeur, *Freud and Philosophy*, 258.
71. Ricoeur, *Symbolism of Evil*, 175–210.
72. Ibid., 183.
73. Ibid., 196.
74. Freud, *Future of an Illusion*, in *Works of Freud*, 21:43.
75. Freud, *Civilization and Its Discontents*, in *Works of Freud*, 21:74.
76. Freud, *Future of an Illusion*, in *Works of Freud*, 21:49.

The new reality of which Freud speaks is the world governed by Eros, Thanatos, and Ananke—by life, death, and necessity. In *Civilization and Its Discontents*, he offered a strategy for effectively dealing with reality. He recognized that we are threatened by a threefold suffering: a decaying body, a harsh external world, and a malicious humankind. The best hope for mitigating this suffering is to become "a member of the human community." Then, "with the help of a technique guided by science," we should continue "the attack against nature" and subject "her to human will."[77]

The attack against nature comes in two forms: one directed toward the non-human and the other toward the human. Some scientists exercise their craft upon the external, non-human world. They apply their technique directly by physically manipulating objects and natural forces. Other scientists exercise their craft upon human nature. They manipulate the human psyche and the cultural arrangements within which the psyche is formed and managed. They must apply their technique indirectly by working through human consciousness to manipulate the determinative natural forces at work in the unconscious. Like the royal priesthood of ancient Babylon, they must master and enact the various rituals of renewal and "rites of elimination"[78] and so maintain the social equilibrium.

Unlike Nietzsche, Freud's strategy for overcoming storied evil is ultimately *pragmatic*. Though both could speak of an "education to reality," Freud did not think that bringing oneself to celebrate the world as-is would help society at-large. Since the "clamor of life proceeds for the most part from Eros,"[79]—from that swirling reservoir of desire stored in every individual—human life is fundamentally "a problem of the economics of the individual's libido."[80] Unconscious desires can be relieved, displaced, transferred, or sublimated. The point is, they need to be channeled somewhere. If they are mismanaged or repressed, a resurgence of the ancient chaos is bound to recur.

Freud's life-organizing story offers both individual and communal hope. For the individual, he described a journey that each person must take to learn the right technique for managing the supply-and-demand of their personal desires. Therapists can serve as guides or life coaches in this endeavor. This technically savvy priesthood knows there "is no golden rule which applies to everyone: every man must find out for himself in what

---

77. Freud, *Civilization and Its Discontents*, in *Works of Freud*, 21:77.
78. Ricoeur, *Symbolism of Evil*, 196.
79. Freud, *Ego and the Id*, in *Works of Freud*, 19:46.
80. Freud, *Civilization and Its Discontents*, in *Works of Freud*, 21:83.

particular fashion he can be saved."[81] All sorts of factors will play into developing the right technique for living: ability to modify the external world, psychical constitution, external circumstances. In order to develop a mature Ego, a customized set of activities, stimulants, and discharges will need to be assembled and prescribed for every individual.

The best hope for communities is to keep these individual Eros-economies in mind. The problem with forming culture via religion is that it "restricts this play of choice and adaptation." Traditional religion "imposes equally on everyone its own path to the acquisition of happiness and protection from suffering. Its technique consists in depressing the value of life and distorting the picture of the real world."[82] But a properly structured civilization will learn to "lower its demands" on the individual. The "id cannot be controlled beyond certain limits. If more is demanded of a man, a revolt will be produced in him or a neurosis, or he will be made unhappy." A principal example of an over-demanding religious imposition is the commandment, "Love thy neighbor as thyself," which is "impossible to fulfill."[83] Nothing else "runs so strongly counter to the original nature of man" and is, in the end, counterproductive to the aims of civilization.[84]

According to Rieff, Freud's goal was simply to "soften the collar" of civilization around the neck of humanity.[85] Stated even more modestly, Freud wanted "to transform hysterical misery into common unhappiness."[86] This might not sound like much for hope, but compared to the unreasonable demands and the undeliverable promises made by religionists and revolutionaries alike, it wasn't half bad. Having declared humanity to be a volatile mix of aggressiveness, self-love, and inclination toward death, Freud thought that "mastering the disturbance of the communal life" was a challenging but attainable goal.[87] He cast his hope upon the endeavors of "scientific work," through which "we can increase our power" and "arrange our life." The modest hope of science is "no illusion. But an illusion it would be to suppose that what science cannot give us we can get elsewhere."[88] Freud ended the 1930 version of *Civilization and Its Discontents* on a hopeful note. He

---

81. Ibid.
82. Ibid., 84.
83. Ibid., 143.
84. Ibid., 112.
85. Rieff, *Triumph of the Therapeutic*, 6. Rieff called this the "gospel of freer impulse" (ibid., 24).
86. Roth, *Psycho-Analysis as History*, 15.
87. Freud, *Civilization and Its Discontents*, in *Works of Freud*, 21:145.
88. Freud, *Future of an Illusion*, in *Works of Freud*, 21:56.

looked for Eros, the urge toward life and unity, to "make an effort to assert himself in the struggle with his equally immortal adversary"—Thanatos, the urge toward death and destruction. In the 1931 edition, after Adolf Hitler's intentions were becoming more apparent, Freud added the following: "But who can foresee with what success and with what result?"[89]

Becker called Freud's *"scientific theory of ego development"* a *"critical anthropodicy."*[90] It sought to justify the human being to humanity not simply by absolving our guilt and relaxing our demands. More critically, Freud offered a story within which to organize life. His account explained why some people never fully grew up and, at the same time, offered a plan of action for those who were willing to learn the technique and follow its prescriptions. Evil, in his storied world, was disruption and disturbance within "the eternal struggle between Eros and the instinct of destruction or death."[91] His strategy for overcoming evil was to issue successful directives to redirect and reconfigure the natural forces that govern the universe, as far as we are able.

In the prior chapter, I mentioned Fukuyama's *The End of History and the Last Man* as a possible example of an idealist-active narrative theodicy. However, it is possible the problem he addressed makes better sense within Freud's story. Fukuyama struggled with the problem of "the last man" at the "end of history." Here he was referring to Nietzsche's "last man," that most despicable man who invented happiness. Liberal democracy was destined to produce such creatures—"men without chests"—because it replaced human strife with self-preservation and prosperity. Fukuyama's fear was that the "last man" was an inherently unstable creature because he lacked an outlet for his aggression. He had no way to win for himself recognition from others. Liberal democracy might have made life too easy for humanity. Might "the fear of becoming contemptible 'last men' not lead men to assert themselves in new and unforeseen ways, even to the point of becoming once again bestial 'first men' engaged in bloody prestige battles, this time with modern weapons?"[92]

Though he never cited Freud, Fukuyama's solution sounded rather Freudian. The internal inconsistency of liberal democracy is that it grants equal recognition, rights, and dignity to unequal people. But if everybody's a winner, then nobody's a winner. So how does a liberal nation state prevent its own undoing from its citizens' desires to exalt themselves over others?

89. Freud, *Civilization and Its Discontents*, in *Works of Freud*, 21:145n1.
90. Becker, *Structure of Evil*, 148.
91. Freud, *Civilization and Its Discontents*, in *Works of Freud*, 2:132.
92. Fukuyama, *End of History*, xxii–xxiii.

It needs to create positive outlets to release this aggression and "grounding wires that bleed off excess energy that would otherwise tear the community apart."[93] It needs to help its citizens develop their own customized techniques for managing their reservoirs of desire. Some might find an outlet in entrepreneurship. Others will find it in climbing K-2, developing new technologies, or by excelling in "perfectly contentless formal arts."[94] And if none of these work, the people might need to let off some steam by fighting "a short and decisive war every generation or so to defend its own liberty and independence."[95]

Fukuyama spoke of a struggle between "rational desire" (self-preservation) and "rational recognition" (self-exaltation). He argued "that modern liberal democracy" ushered in the end of history because it "best satisfies" these two giants "in some kind of balance."[96] That is to say, it "constitutes the best possible solution to the human problem."[97] Was it the final solution because it best reflected the universal standard of the Good? Or because it discovered an effective technique for managing the most base natural forces? In the end, it sounds like democracy wins by quelling our infantile urges with the right mix of upper-middle class lifestyle, extreme sports, and wartime heroics. If his solution to the problem of the "last man" at the "end of history" failed to be fully idealistic, then his book is a testament to the influence of the story told by Freud.

Whether or not we judge him as succeeding, Fukuyama, like the other idealists, wanted to maintain a notion of human freedom that could rise above our biology. In stark contrast to this is contemporary philosopher Daniel Dennett, who explicitly embraced the realist-pragmatic plotline. Theologian Paul Hinlicky, in his "critical retrieval of Leibniz," confessed that Dennett's book *Darwin's Dangerous Idea* "awoke me from my proverbial 'dogmatic slumbers.'" He said that Dennett's so-called secular fundamentalism showed him "in plain print how the Kantian walls of the past two centuries [i.e., the distinction between *is* and *ought*] . . . have indeed come crashing down like those of old Jericho."[98] In *Darwin's Dangerous Idea*, Dennett argued that "We need to grow up."[99] We must come to grips with the fact that there is no divine parent or intelligent designer or moral meaning

---

93. Ibid., 315.
94. Ibid., 320.
95. Ibid., 329.
96. Ibid., 337.
97. Ibid., 338.
98. Hinlicky, *Paths Not Taken*, 259–65.
99. Dennett, *Darwin's Dangerous Idea*, 514.

behind the world. Accepting this reality is a small, but hopeful step toward maturity.

In a more recent article, Dennett argued that Charles Darwin is "by far the scientist who has made the greatest contribution to philosophy." "If I could give a prize for the single best idea anybody ever had," said Dennett, "I'd give it to Darwin. In a single stroke Darwin's theory" united "the realm of physics" with "the realm of meaning." For Dennett, this was cause to celebrate. The chains of idealistic tradition had been broken. Now we can receive all things as gifts—"as fruits on the tree of life."[100] Dennett told a Darwinian story of how our "'godlike' powers of comprehension and imagination" arose from "naturalistic forces" alone. Remarkably, the tree of life has granted us power to change our situation and navigate from "sub-optimal" peaks, through set-backs, on to what might be a "global summit." Though we "are not perfect truth-trackers," we can "evaluate our own shortcomings by using the methods we have so far devised, so we can be confident that we are justified in trusting our methods in the foreseeable future."[101] With the right technique in play, Dennett's pragmatic story proffers both personal and corporate hope. It provides a personal eschatology in terms of growing up and overcoming our childish beliefs. It also provides a corporate eschatology with the hope that the "tree of life" will ultimately lead us to the global summit.

The Possibility of a Dual Declaration

In the last chapter I discussed the possibility of a dual strategy for overcoming evil—one that would attempt to both transcend it by assertion and transform it by issuing directives to modify the social structures that produce evil. I gave Kant the pride of place for an attempt to hold his footing on this tortuous middle ground. In this chapter, I will consider whether or not it's possible to hold the tension across the vertical division in the typology, that is, the line between the realist and idealist responses to experience. I take James Edward's book *The Plain Sense of Things* as an attempt to issue this paradoxical dual declaration: the world "is what it is" *and* "ought not be this way."

Edwards's stated problem was how to restore the power of a sacred reality in a culture of "normal nihilism."[102] In this setting, it seems we can only appeal to personal values or local customs and not to "truth." So, can

---

100. Dennett, "Darwin's 'strange inversion of reasoning,'" 10061.

101. Ibid., 10065.

102. Edwards, *Plain Sense of Things*.

Western intellectuals still be shaped by a powerful, transcendent norm? Does there remain any moral "ought" that does not reduce to mere personal preference? Edwards, an atheist philosopher trained in the post-Nietzschean school of Martin Heidegger, wanted an affirmative answer to these questions. He sought to imagine a set of religious practices that could "contain, concentrate, and transmit the sacramental energies—energies for limitation in the face of hubris and for transformation in the face of complacency—that used to be bound up in the stories of the gods."[103]

Edwards began by telling a version of the Enlightenment's story about growing up. Like Freud, Edwards believed that the human problem was with how to cope with the vicissitudes of life in the body abused not only by the external world but also our fellow man. "We are, as we somehow all know at some level of consciousness, *coping*, trying to make sense of things."[104] By his count, Westerners passed through at least four stages or four kinds of coping mechanisms. First they told the stories of the gods, who exercised their inscrutable will over humanity. The benefit of this stage was that it curbed human pride and kept people in line. The downside was that it offended their sense of justice and personal autonomy. During the second stage, humanity domesticated their gods and subdued them under the impersonal ideals of Goodness, Truth, and Justice. This addressed the deficiency of the first stage. But, after working for about 2,000 years, it began to falter because few agreed on what exactly this "ideal" was. It seemed there were as many ideals as there were authorities who taught them. In an effort to ground the ideal in something certain, people scrapped the traditional authorities and looked for solid ground in the individual human mind. But this third stage only multiplied the number of authorities. By seeking an impersonal standard of judgment, they had made every person the final judge. This moved Western culture into its fourth and present stage, which Edwards called the "Age of Transvalued Values." This mode of coping created our present "mood" of "normal nihilism."[105]

The theme of this story was the "gradual but inexorable loss of the sacred's power."[106] What started as a way to cope with reality by privileging human autonomy led to a flaccid humanism. Edwards's example of what this looks like was the local shopping mall, where life is transformed into "lifestyle."

103. Ibid., ix.

104. Edwards, *Plain Sense of Things*, 54.

105. Ibid., 41. This paragraph was a summary of Edwards's first chapter. See also Joel Meyer, "Christian Justification After Nihilism," for a helpful engagement with Edwards's argument.

106. Edwards, *Plain Sense of Things*, 41.

> The tools, garments, and attitudes specific to particular times and places become commodities to be marketed to anonymous and rootless consumers ... An outfit, an electronic toy for bored adult males, a book detailing an aerobic exercise program for Christians—these are, in Nietzsche's sense, *values*.[107]

Now that humanity has become the creators and masters of their own values, Western culture is vulnerable to both "runaway humanism" and "triumphant normality."[108] The first threat is a "quasi-religious demand" that we "continually create new and better forms of human life;" where "life for the sake of life ... becomes change for the sake of change."[109] The second threat is the fearful response to the ever-multiplying options of the first. Here, we sink into well-defined social roles. Our desire to hold on to "normality" is threatened by anything that appears "abnormal." Edwards admitted, "I am afraid these powerful forces will beset us in vicious alternation, leaving us (and our fellow travelers on the planet, and finally the planet itself) spoiled and exhausted."[110] It seems our current coping mechanism—the Freudian story about acquiring a custom-fit technique for living—has undermined our hope for a better future.

So far, Edwards appears to be working squarely within the scheme of a realist-pragmatic narrative theodicy. Life is hard. Over the years humanity has prescribed different ways to cope. Some offered sacrifices. Others went shopping. But Edwards thought this pick-and-choose religiosity had proved self-defeating. What we lack is that old-time religious *Pathos*. Back in the day, before the gods were domesticated, people believed things because they were *true*, not because they were valuable. Edwards wanted to discover a form of religious practice that could not be cherished or discarded as personal therapy. He wanted a normative *Thou shalt* that could stand over and judge a human *I prefer*. He wanted to embrace this aspect of religious life without surrendering the hard-fought intellectual battles that led to Enlightenment maturity.

> While traditional supernatural religion is no longer possible for us, we still need something: something to bound our temptation to eat up the earth and ourselves in pursuit of ever new, and ever more reckless, forms of self-fashioning;

---

107. Ibid., 50.
108. Ibid., 56.
109. Ibid., 52.
110. Ibid., 54–56.

and—simultaneously—something to loosen our captivity to whatever particular form of life is commonsensically dominant here and now.[111]

For what is Edwards asking? He did not want (in the manner of Nietzsche) to transcend the pain of being human by turning every "it was" into a "thus I willed it." He did not want (after the method of Freud) to develop more effective techniques for managing libidinal urges. Rather, he wanted to come under the scrutiny of something truthful that would make human life "transparent to itself." He wanted religious practices that could critique and shape our values and not merely express them.[112] Edwards approached the human problem not at the level of strategy, but at the moment of the declaration that characterized the conflict in the plot. He wanted human life to be judged and vindicated by something more than human. At the same time, he could not bring himself to unconditionally trust any external judgment, especially if it claimed to be divine. He wanted to be judged. And he wanted to retain his right to negate the judgment.

Edwards summarized his proposed religious practice as "poetic dwelling on earth as a mortal," an approach drawn from four of Heidegger's essays written in the 1950s.[113] Heidegger's later works turn on theological-sounding phrases like "the realm of revealing," "the turning of the age," and measuring oneself "against the godhead."[114] Edwards noted that these should not be heard as referring to the "personified supernatural presences of vulgar religious belief."[115] Instead, they are expressions of that paradoxical hope to be judged without finally coming under authoritative, external judgment.

What was Edwards was trying to do? He was not advocating one strategy over another, as Marx rivaled Leibniz or as Freud rivaled Nietzsche. He was looking for a trustworthy authority to declare what counts as good and what counts as evil. On the one hand, he did not trust an individual's capacity to reflect infallible Reason. According to his Nietzschean argument, reflection is always projection of the will to value. He did not want to make personal subjectivity the uncontested guide of life because this is precisely what led us to the crisis of normal nihilism, to the shopping mall. On the other hand, he did not advocate becoming a faithful disciple of

---

111. Ibid., 197.
112. Ibid., 198.
113. Ibid., 153.
114. Ibid., 156, 172, and 177.
115. Ibid., 172.

some religious tradition, for this would demand "intellectual and spiritual suicide"[116]—a surrender of Enlightened maturity.

On what basis could Edwards judge these rival stories if he couldn't trust his own internal moral compass to direct him? In place of a sacred person or an innate sense of the Good, Edwards looked for sacramental practices that could guide him. But in the very process of assembling these secular sacraments and interpreting their meaning, he would still be either crafting or participating in a story of how he got there and where he's going. To fulfill his desire to be formed by an authority that stands over every human value, he must come under judgment and follow as disciple. To exercise unchecked, critical judgment, he must become a shopper at the mall. When faced with the conflict that drives our stories, when faced with the problem of evil, we must finally either judge, or be judged. A declaration must be made if our stories are to have a world and our worlds are to have a story.

SUMMARY

Edwards was a good case study for the realists because his desire to be judged while rejecting external judgment reveals the similarity between the realists and the idealists. At first it seemed as though the realists were different because they refused to judge humanity and the world by some self-devised ideal. They rejected the idealist "ought" and said, "It is what it is." But now we have come to hear the realist response also as a form of judgment. In the case of Nietzsche, it was more obvious. He condemned those who would condemn life and declared that the eternal recurrence of all things must be desired and celebrated. Freud also began his story by rendering judgment on the infantile ideals of those who refused to grow up. Edwards hesitated. He wanted the formative power of the idealist declaration as well as the liberating power of the realist declaration. But as long as he wished to maintain hope against the despair of normal nihilism, he must either judge or be judged. He must become the author of his own customized story. Or he must be storied within some other author's world.

This concludes our detour to say what Christian hope is not. As we return to the main road, toward an effort to say what Christian hope is, we must ask: Why are these various kinds of hope not Christian? It would be a mistake for Christians to evaluate these narrative theodicies by some abstract standard. I do not criticize the theorists as being socially unproductive or too willing to accept the status quo. I do not criticize the pragmatists as being conceptually unsatisfying or too optimistic. I do not judge either

116. Ibid., 55.

group on their ability to maintain the proper balance between presumption and despair. Each story has the potential to meet all these standards in their own way because each intends to render its narrative world intelligible. Each story has the power to speak to some human longing, depending on the person's present disposition and life setting. None of them have a special advantage over the others in this regard. They all point to signs and experiences of fulfilled hope. They are all equally plagued by some sort of scandalous evil. And so my aim was not to evaluate them in terms of their potential to form culture or assuage existential angst. My aim was only to say how they are not Christian.

Furthermore, these standards of judgment (e.g., optimistic, soberminded, socially productive, conceptually satisfying, properly balanced), as Edwards helped us see, are all values. And values always proceed from *personal* judgment. Christians are people who have come under the judgment of a person: Jesus, Israel's King and the world's Lord. They are people who participate in the story that will resolve only in his advent for final judgment.

8

Staying in the Story

THIS MORNING I LEFT my house with an important letter. I saw a white minivan parked across the street with the words "Postal Service" painted on the back. Without thinking twice, I walked to the van and waved to the driver. "Good morning, ma'am, may I give you this letter?" "Sure." Walking away, I was struck by the degree of trust I had instinctively placed in this person and the two-hundred-and-forty-year-old institution she represented.

Trust is basic to human life. From conception through childhood we were dependent on parents and guardians. As adolescents, we listened to other people telling us who we are and what we might become. As adults, the words and actions of others continue to shape and direct us. We live a tension between trust and suspicion. We think twice about relying on some people. Others, we take at their word. Much of human life is a struggle to find out whom we can and cannot trust.[1]

There are many ways to identify someone as trustworthy. We may simply observe their behavior over time and draw this conclusion. Often, it comes from personal interaction. Promise-making is a common practice for building trust. In chapter 3, I drew on the work of Searle to describe promises as commissive speech acts. They announce the speaker's intention to do something that the hearer perceives as good.[2] In Wolterstorff's terms, a promiser takes up a "normative stance" toward the hearer.[3] Such a

---

1. Kolb, *Christian Faith*, 8, who borrowed from Erikson to describe *"Faith"* as "the trust that provides the core orientation for our lives," which "largely determines the way in which individuals view the world."

2. Searle, *Mind, Language, and Society*, 149.

3. Wolterstorff, *Divine Discourse*, 93.

stance offers the hearer the right to hold the speaker to his or her word. He or she takes up duties and obligations toward the recipient of the promise. Why would a speaker do this? The intended effect is trust. The speaker aims to evoke or maintain a bond of trust with the hearer. A mail courier says, "Neither snow nor rain nor heat nor gloom of night" will keep me from completing my appointed route. A husband promises his bride, "I will be faithful." A mother promises her son, "I will never stop loving you." The trust evoked depends on the identity of the speaker established through past performance—promises kept or broken. It can be threatened or confirmed, depending on the outcome of outstanding promises.

THE TRUSTWORTHINESS OF THE GOD OF JESUS

Christian hope is distinct because it depends on the trustworthiness of the God of Jesus, who has vowed to make the world fit to his word of promise to Abraham. Christian hope arises from the life-organizing story centered on this promise. As Paul confessed before King Agrippa's court: "I stand here on trial because of my hope in the promise made by God to our fathers" (Acts 26:6). In the New Testament, the particular man Jesus of Nazareth, who is called Christ, the Son of God, is depicted as the paradigmatic recipient of this promise, and, paradoxically, its authoritative maker and keeper.

To help make Christian hope's distinctive features more obvious, we took a detour through four other life-organizing stories that held out eschatological hope for their participants. Our comparative exercise was guided by the assumption that human beings, inasmuch as they struggle to maintain hope against despair, face some peculiar problem of evil. This problem undermines the trustworthiness of the author that narrates the story and therefore becomes the central source of conflict. Because the story anticipates a resolution to the conflict, it elicits *eschatological* hope that the author is trustworthy. A participant in the story might assume the mantle of authorship and attain a form of personal providence. Or, he or she could look to an institution or individual to fill that role. In both cases, the participant takes it on faith that the story will resolve and the author will prove trustworthy. Therefore, a life-organizing story offers a narrative *theodicy*, with *theos* conceived as the author or agent of emplotment.

This is precisely what Christian hope holds in common with other life-organizing hopes. All imply an eschatology—a logic of resolution that offers a narrated theodicy. They elicit a hope that "evil" will not prevail. This thesis has at least two important implications. On the one hand, Christians should not distinguish their hope by claiming a cognitive certainty, a religious consolation, an existential meaningfulness, or an ethical productivity that rises above others. Their problem of evil is as acute and unresolved as in all other life-organizing stories. On the other hand, Christians, when pressured by this problem, should remember that other prospective stories of the world are plagued by a residual conflict that is no less scandalous and corrosive.

If Christians wish to distinguish and maintain their peculiar hope, they should bear witness to what is most *appropriate* for their corporate struggle against evil, not what is most *effective*.[4] The appropriate place of struggle for Christians to maintain hope against despair is within the Christian story as narrated in the Bible, summarized in the ecumenical creeds, assumed in the dogma of the church, and reflected in the biographies of the baptized. This story has a characteristic mode of resolution to its continuing conflict with evil. In the Christian plot, evil will be overcome by the action of God in his Son and Spirit to fulfill his promise to Abraham: "I will make of you a great nation, and I will bless you and make your name great, so that you will be a blessing. I will bless those who bless you, and him who dishonors you I will curse, and in you all the families of the earth shall be blessed" (Gen 12:2-3).

Ever since Yahweh made his pledge to Abraham, God's people have been tempted to find a more effective solution to their problem of evil. In search for more satisfying modes of resolution, they have made declarations and pursued strategies that are inappropriate. That is to say, they have participated in rival life-organizing stories. Or, in more traditional terms, they have broken the First Commandment. They have committed idolatry by trusting a rival agent of emplotment. As we observed in the last two chapters, these stories—whether conceived as personal, communal, or cosmic—offered effective and empowering hopes. But they were not Christian. To be a Christian, to hope as a Christian, is to participate in the Christian story. In this concluding chapter, I entreat fellow Christians to identify and embrace their unique hope. When confronted with both *storied* and *scandalous* evil, Christians should stay in the story.

In the first part of this chapter, I will account for *storied* evil as it is encountered in the Christian drama of salvation. In general terms, this is the conflict dealt with directly in the unfolding of the plot. In the second part, I will address the problem of *scandalous* evil. Also in general terms, this is the conflict that threatens the intelligibility of the story as a whole. It cannot be addressed directly from within the story. It can be resolved in one of two ways. On the one hand, the plot and author can be rejected in favor of a different story. This constitutes an epistemological crisis or peripatetic reversal. On the other hand, the scandal can be endured from within the original story. If the first option is taken, and one becomes apostate with

---

4. Cf. Yoder, *Politics of Jesus*, 232, "The triumph of the right . . . is sure because of the power of the resurrection and not because of any calculation of causes and effects."

respect to the prior story, the original scandal will be removed. But, a new one will take its place. I illustrated this phenomenon in chapters five, six, and seven. However, if the second option is taken, if one opts to remain in the story, the scandal of evil can only be lamented with an as-yet unverified hope it will be overcome in the plot's final resolution, that is, in the *eschaton*. These problems are common to all stories that propose to organize life for their participants. Christians, as participants in the story of Jesus-in-Israel-and-the-church, resist and lament evil in their peculiar, Christian way.

By recounting the life-organizing stories modeled by Leibniz, Marx, Nietzsche, and Freud, I have said much about what Christian hope is not. Now I aim to say what Christian hope *is*. I identify it as one narrative theodicy among rivals. Returning to the main road, I draw upon the understanding gained from the detour. More importantly, I return to what Richard Bauckham called the "Christological foundation and criterion of Christian hope," which is "contested by few who write intentionally Christian eschatology."[5] The Christian hope is most properly distinguished by a specific man: Jesus of Nazareth, crucified under Pontius Pilate, buried, raised from the dead on the third day, who "will come in glory as Savior of those who are saved and as Judge of those who are judged."[6]

Christian hope arises within a narrative *theodicy*. It is an account of the righteousness of the God who made a promise to Abraham and raised Jesus from the dead. The righteousness of God means that God does right and makes right. It also means that God displays the characteristic of righteousness (trustworthiness). As the creator and sustainer of all things, God alone justifies the initial and continuing existence of his creation. He decides whether or not his creatures do right by him. If and when his creation goes awry, God assumes full responsibility, as N. T. Wright likes to say, "to set the world to rights."[7] Thus, the question of justification (setting right) does not arise first with regard to sin and redemption, but already with creation.[8] God is the justifier because God is the creator.

But this raises questions about the righteousness God displays. How can God be relied upon in the face of evil? How can God be trusted if we are sinners under his wrath, who experience suffering as his disfavor or indifference? The story of Jesus-in-Israel-and-the-church is an answer to these questions. It is a narrative theodicy because it testifies that this God does right and makes right, thereby displaying his trustworthiness. Of course, the

---

5. Richard Bauckham, "Conclusion," in Walls, *Oxford Handbook of Eschatology*, 672.

6. Irenaeus, *Against Heresies*, III.4.2.

7. Wright, "Letter to the Romans," in *New Interpreter's Bible*, vol. 10, 424.

8. See Bayer, *Living by Faith*, xiv.

on-going experience of evil contests this answer on all sides. The Christian hope is that evil will not prevail, that the conflict in the plot will resolve.

It should go without saying that this is not a definitive or exhaustive account of Christian hope. I have narrowed my witness within the confines of this project. I'm attempting to say what it means to stay in the story and to hope as a Christian among the four rival narrative theodicies. In purely negative terms, the Christian hope is set in contrast to an idealist or realist declaration of what counts as evil. Furthermore, Christian hope will neither be realized with more accurate descriptions of God and the world, nor in successful prescriptions to change the world. Instead, it will be realized when the God of Jesus brings his world to match his word of promise, which he extended to Abraham's family.

The Christian confession is that Jesus of Nazareth is both the paradigmatic recipient and authoritative fulfiller of this promise. The Christian hope will be realized only when God acts in Jesus to keep his promise to Abraham. The pattern of fulfillment has already been given in God's act to vindicate Abraham's true heir by raising him from the dead. God will finally fulfill his promise when he fits the world to the image of his crucified and resurrected Son. In so doing, God will vindicate his trustworthiness.

In this chapter, I account for Jesus as both *speaker* and *recipient* of God's promise to Abraham. As the definitive speaker of the promise, Jesus assumed the authority, power, and responsibility to make the world fit to his word. I argue that confessing Jesus as the speaker and fulfiller of God's promise is an appropriate way to proclaim and participate in the Christian story, especially when faced with the problem of storied evil. Thus, Jesus' role as *speaker-fulfiller* will be the focus of the first part of the chapter. In the second part, I focus on Jesus' role as the paradigmatic *recipient* of God's promise. He is Abraham's heir, the anointed son of David, the King of Israel, to whom God promised to give the nations, the ends of the earth, even the whole cosmos as his inheritance (Ps 2:8, Rom 4:13). As the recipient of God's promise, he waited, lamented, and ultimately trusted his Father to deliver him from evil. Thus, Jesus' life in the Spirit, crucifixion, and resurrection are the paradigm of participation in the Christian story. Accounting for Jesus in this way is most appropriate for enduring the on-going scandal of evil.

CHRISTIAN HOPE AGAINST STORIED EVIL

Earlier, I characterized the plot of the biblical narrative to be driven by the problem of false trust, or idolatry. This is not the only way to speak of the conflict in the Bible's plot. Christians have characterized the conflict in other ways. For example, the story can be understood in anthropological terms as the endeavor to overcome human corruptibility and culpability. Or, it can be understood theologically as the removing of all that tarnishes God's glory and opposes God's will. It could even be understood in broad ecological terms as God's project to forge a proper home for him to dwell peaceably with his creatures, having delivered them from all enemies. I do not deny the viability of these or other accounts. However, I will not focus on them here because they do not correspond as well with the account of the Christian story as a narrated promise, a notion which I began developing in chapter 3. This is the drama of a promise given, proleptically fulfilled, but now contested in the interim between proleptic and final fulfillment. The conflict centers on the trustworthiness of the promiser in the hearts and minds of the hearers.

Storied Evil as False Trust

Why tell the story this way and not some other way? From the beginning of this book I have been pursuing an *external use* of attributes. This was a use fitted for comparing one storied system with another. It is distinct from an *internal use* of attributes, which is fitted for deriving and attaining a greater understanding of a single storied system. If we were interested in appreciating the plurality and complexity of features that cohere within the biblical narrative, then reflection on the plot in all its anthropological, theological, or ecological dimensions would be appropriate. However, since we are comparing the Christian story with other life-organizing stories, these themes are less helpful. Recall how many of the rival narrative theodicies examined in chapters five through seven had no place for human guilt, an offended God, or an eternal dwelling place. They did, however, all begin with a *declaration* of what counts as good and evil. Furthermore, they continued with a strategy for overcoming evil that involved issuing *assertive* or *directive* speech acts. Having made a declaration and set a strategy, they experienced a sense of conflict and trusted an agent of emplotment whose reliability was still contested. To formulate the Christian story in comparable terms would be an external use of attributes. This requirement was met by an account of Christian hope as it arises from the on-going story about a *commissive* speech act: the narrated promise the God of Jesus made to Abraham.

In chapter 2, I anticipated that this focus on the external features of Christian hope would yield significant insights for those on the inside of the story. Characterizing the Christian conflict as a singular problem of trust may be one such insight. Conceptually, the problem of mistrust or false trust dialectically incorporates anthropological, theological, and ecological elements. The biblical narrative is not exclusively about human guilt, divine glory, or creator-creature communion. It is about the creator who promises to establish himself as trustworthy to sinners who have traded out trust in him for trust in his creatures. This, of course, is not a novel insight. This point is a hallmark of Reformation teaching, which is especially noticeable in the works of Martin Luther and in the Confessional documents authored by his colleagues and students.

Admittedly, having been formed in a Lutheran tradition, I have been trying to think like a Lutheran all along. But this requires two clarifications. First, what it means to be "Lutheran" today is by no means a settled matter. Second, a foundational point of the historic Lutheran Confessions is that Luther is dispensable, Jesus is not. Lutherans are disciples of Jesus who participate in the on-going conversation about what constitutes the Christian tradition.[9] In my reckoning, the main contribution Lutherans bring to the one, holy, catholic, apostolic table is still the Reformation dogma of justification by grace through faith (or trust) in the promise on account of (*propter*) Christ.[10] This formula expressed something foundational to the tradition, something upon which it stands or falls. Or, as Lutheran theologian Oswald Bayer said, something upon which the whole world stands or falls.[11] During the detour of chapters six and seven, we heard how the proponents of other life-organizing stories also struggle with the singular problem of whom to trust. Which author will finally resolve the conflict and so prove trustworthy? Every storied world stands or falls on this question.

In the interest of this question, I have used the notion of "narrated promise"[12] to compare the Christian story with other narrated speech acts. This approach formed the basis of the typology of narrative theodicies. The Christian story is a narrated promise with the corollary conflict of a false trust. This articulation facilitates an external use of Christian hope's attributes. Such a use is a pressing matter for Christian discipleship and mission in a post-Constantinian context. Where Christianity is surrounded by many rival ways of storying the world, it is, perhaps, easier to see that our central dilemma is not simply between faith and reason or between religious trust and critical doubt. Rather, it is between one trust and another. Broken trust with respect to the Christian God implies a rival trust in another authority and participation in another story. To the degree that humans hold fast to

---

9. For a similar definition of theology, cf. McClendon, *Ethics*, vol. 1 of *Systematic Theology*, 17–46.

10. Bente, "Confessio Augustana," art. IV, in *Concordia Triglotta*, 44.

11. Bayer, *Living by Faith*, xiii–xiv.

12. Cf. Thiemann, *Revelation and Theology: Gospel as Narrated Promise*.

hope against despair, they inhabit a story. There is no neutral, un-storied realm for uncommitted, critical thinkers. Doubt toward one authority is enabled by trust in another. This makes the conflict in the Christian story reside between trust in God or idols, not merely between belief and unbelief.

Jesus as Speaker and Fulfiller of God's Promise

In the Genesis narrative, Yahweh repeated a promise to Abra[ha]m: "Fear not, Abram, I am your shield; your reward shall be very great." We are told that the promise "took." Abram believed Yahweh, and Yahweh "counted it to him as righteousness" (Gen 15:1-6). The entire biblical narrative is a drama about this bond of trust built upon this promise made to Abraham and to all who "walk in the footsteps" of his faith (Rom 4:1-12).

The New Testament writings, especially the Gospels and Acts, ascribe to Jesus of Nazareth the ultimate authority to make, renew, and keep God's promise to Abraham's family.[13] In his sermon at Pentecost, Peter proclaimed "Jesus of Nazareth" as "a man attested to you by God with mighty works and wonders and signs that God did through him in your midst" (Acts 2:22). Among the mighty words and deeds of Jesus, Luke reported how Jesus came "in the power of the Spirit" (Luke 4:14) and taught in the synagogues, preaching "the good news of the kingdom of God" (4:43). He commanded the unclean spirits "with authority and power" (4:36), declared a leper clean and it was so (5:13), forgave sins and they were forgiven (5:20-26), spoke to a dead man and he arose (7:14-15), and silenced a storm with a word (8:24). According to Luke, these words and works are what led to Jesus' arrest, trial, condemnation, and death. Israel's own authorities accused him of blasphemy for daring to forgive sins (5:21). They were "filled with fury" when he healed on the Sabbath (6:11). They planned to destroy him after he condemned their appropriation of the temple, God's house (19:45-47, 20:9-19). Finally, they condemned him for claiming to be "the Son of God" (22:70).

Ironically, the title that God himself had ascribed to Jesus is what finally got him killed. In Luke's account, God, the Father, speaks verbally only two times. First, the Father declared directly to Jesus, "You are my beloved Son, with you I am well pleased" (2:22). Second, he spoke directly about Jesus to Peter, James, and John, with Moses and Elijah present on the mountain: "This is my Son, my Chosen One, listen to him!" (9:35). Finally, after Jesus prayed his dying words from the cross—"Father, into your hand

---

13. The following account of Jesus as God's personal Word is indebted to Nafzger, *These Are Written*.

I commit my spirit!" (23:46)—God spoke non-verbally by raising by him from the dead. He vindicated Jesus as his Son, the Chosen One, Israel's King and the world's Lord.

Shortly after Pentecost, Peter stood in the temple and bore witness to the crucified and risen Jesus. First, Peter made his own people responsible for Jesus' death: "you killed the Author of Life, whom God raised from the dead" (Acts 3:15). God reversed this great evil so Jesus could go on doing what the Father had sent him in the power of the Holy Spirit to do: "God, having raised up his servant, sent him to you first, to bless you by turning every one of you from your wickedness" (3:26). Through these ambassadors, Jesus was continuing to speak with God's own authority to declare blessing and favor so that through Abraham's offspring "all the families of the earth" shall "be blessed" (3:25).

This meant, among other things, that Jesus is the fulfillment of God's promise to raise up for Israel a prophet like Moses from among their brothers: "You shall listen to him in whatever he tells you." Anyone that "does not listen to that prophet shall be destroyed from among the people" (3:23). Luke ascribed to Jesus the authority and power to speak and fulfill God's promise to Abraham for the blessing of all nations. The conflict, that is, the storied evil, in this account is the singular problem of trust. Having once rejected and killed him, will Israel now listen to and trust their God-given King? And will the nations turn from their idols and toward their Lord who will come from heaven at "the time for restoring all the things about which God spoke by the mouth of his holy prophets long ago" (3:21)?

Appropriately, Luke left these questions unresolved at the end of Acts. Along the way, many of the Lord's witnesses have been murdered, persecuted, and imprisoned because of their testimony. Paul has been put under house arrest while he awaits trial before the Roman Emperor. In spite of these afflictions, Luke tells us Paul continued welcoming all who came to him. The narrative ends like it began. First there was Jesus "speaking about the Kingdom of God" (Acts 1:3); then Paul, "proclaiming the kingdom of God and teaching about the Lord Jesus Christ with all boldness and without hindrance" (Acts 28:31). Those who hold to the Christian hope today continue to "story the world" as the setting for the coming rule and reign of God. Their hope is distinctive because they look for God's reign to be uncontestably established "on earth as it is in heaven," at the coming of Jesus.

As Luke and the other evangelists have told the story, this awaited reign of God is not ultimately ushered in by brute force. There is, without doubt, a terrifying threat of force against all God's enemies. Jesus compared himself to a coming king who would say, "But as for these enemies of mine, who did not want me to reign over them, bring them here and slaughter them before me" (Luke 19:27). But the intended effect of this threat is not despair or resignation but repentance. It is given to turn all people away from their false faith in idols toward true faith in Jesus, God's Son. He promises forgiveness and life to all who turn and hear him. One day his kingdom will come and crush all rivals. Now it is established and built up by God's Word and Spirit. It is received by listening to him, by taking him at his word.

Storied evil is mistrust in the God of Jesus supported by a false trust in some other authority, whether religious, philosophical, cultural, or personal.[14] The strategy for overcoming evil is listening[15] to the man accredited by God through mighty works and wonders and signs. This is why the church has traditionally retold a portion of one of the four Gospels in her weekly gatherings to celebrate the Lord's Supper and so "proclaim the Lord's death until he comes" (1 Cor 11:26). This was and is a primary time to listen to her Lord, to heed his warning to turn from evil, and to hear his promise of forgiveness and blessing.

Note that this is a *pragmatic* strategy for overcoming evil. But, it does not seek a resolution to the story's conflict by issuing successful *directives*. Instead, it resolves only when the promise is finally fulfilled. Like the pragmatists of chapters six and seven, Christians look for the world to conform to the word, not vice versa. They share this quality against the theorists who hoped to transcend evil by coming to see how it necessarily fit into a greater harmony or by coming to accept or celebrate the world as it is. Christians, similar to the pragmatists, expect this world to be transformed, not transcended. The difference between these two kinds of pragmatic solutions is not the direction of fit, but the responsibility of fit. God, as he has spoken definitively in Jesus, bears the full burden of demonstrating himself to be trustworthy by fulfilling his promise.

Jesus, as the story's commanding character, is the final actor. He will bring all these things to pass. God, having announced and pledged his intentions in advance, is re-creating a relationship of trust between himself and his people. His kingdom comes by the Word. It calls for a faithful, active response from those who hear from this God "who gives life to the dead and calls into existence the things that do not exist" (Rom 4:17). Thus, storied evil, or false trust, is overcome by listening to Jesus, turning from idols, and keeping his commands while waiting for him to make good on his promise.

---

14. I have focused on Luke–Acts. Something similar could be said of John's gospel. See Koester, *Word of Life*, 65, "Sin, in John's gospel, is first a relational concept. It is unbelief or alienation from God, and it is therefore the antithesis of faith . . . people relate rightly to God by believing in Jesus, the one whom God sent."

15. Kolb, *Christian Faith*, 91, "Sin is, at its root, being deaf to the Word of God, not trusting the Lord."

Along the way toward final fulfillment, God has given Abraham's family advances, signs, and guarantees of his faithfulness: a deliverer in Moses, the Exodus, the Promised Land, the Davidic kingship, the Temple, the word of the prophets, the return from exile. These testify of God's faithfulness to his people. This is why it is not only the Gospels that are re-told and proclaimed in the church, but the entire narrative and counsel of Holy Scripture. Together, they attest to the trustworthiness of the God of Israel, the God of Jesus. The church is the community that listens, remembers, and retells God's story. This is the story about the promise God made to Abraham. Within this storied world, the God of Abraham continues to speak that promise through his Son.

The Church's Role in Overcoming Storied Evil

Christian faith and hope is directed toward Jesus. It is not directed toward an idealist explanation of the universe. It is not directed toward a pragmatic plan of action, but to a specific man. Like the realists, the Christian story privileges a concrete experience over all ideals. But it is unique because it privileges the particular experience of being confronted with the on-going, verbal, apostolic witness to the crucified and risen Jesus. This specific experience is privileged above all other experiences. It also contradicts the realist who has claimed to transcend the idealist's distinction between what *is* and what *ought to be*. Christians live by the hope that Jesus will act with universal authority to vindicate all that is good and to condemn all that is evil.

Christian hope is elicited by this narrated promise now proclaimed by the church. The story establishes the real world as the world pledged to Abraham's family and under the impending judgment of Jesus. The creation has been declared "good," but corrupted by trust in authorities other than the Creator as he has revealed himself definitively and finally in Jesus. While evil comes in many manifestations, its root and source is condemned by the First Commandment: "You shall have no other gods before me" (Exod 20:3). Having been distorted by idolatry, God's good creation has come under condemnation. As it stands, it is deficient and needs to be transformed.

The strategy is not to transcend evil by re-description and speculation about an unseen, higher harmony. The Christian story anticipates a pragmatic solution rather than a theoretic one. But its practice differs from those seeking to resolve the conflict by issuing successful directives. The direction of fit is the same for a directive and a commissive, but with a commissive, the responsibility of fit is carried by the speaker rather than the hearer. The Christian plot, having been characterized by a promise, will resolve only when the Promiser transforms the world to match his word. Jesus assured his apostles that these conditions will attain at the "close of the age" when he sends his angels to gather out of his reign all causes of stumbling (*skándala*) and workers of lawlessness and to throw them into the "fiery furnace." Then, the righteous will shine like the sun in the reign of their Father (Matt 13:41–43).[16]

As the speaker and fulfiller of God's promise, Jesus is the commanding character of the Christian story. After his resurrection, he gave his apostles the promise of his Father, pledging they would be "clothed with power from on high" and so become his witnesses (Luke 24:48–49). Even though all of the initial apostles have died, the church throughout all times and places has been deputized[17] and empowered to perform the same authoritative, commissive speech acts that were recorded in the book of Acts. At the end of Luke's Gospel, Jesus' explanation to the apostles serves as a charter: "Thus it is written that the Christ should suffer and on the third day rise from the dead, and that repentance and forgiveness of sins should be proclaimed in his name to all nations, beginning in Jerusalem" (Luke 24:46–47).

The church has received the sermons and speeches in Acts as a canonical standard for what qualifies as discourse deputized by the crucified and risen Christ. This discourse can be summarized as a narrated threat and promise, with the understanding that the threat, while real and to be taken seriously, is not an end in itself. It always serves the promise. As the risen Lord told Paul on the road to Damascus, the threat is made so that both Jews and Gentiles "may turn from darkness to light and from the power of Satan to God, that they may receive forgiveness of sins and a place among those who are sanctified by faith in me" (Acts 26:18).

The Acts' speeches made to Gentile audiences are especially suited to help distinguish Christian hope from others. The pre-Constantinian setting in Acts resembles the post-Constantinian situation of the church today.[18] There the Gospel of Jesus as Lord and Christ was preached amid rivals. In the following analysis of Paul's speech in the Areopagus at Athens (Acts 17:16–34), note how Paul both engages and criticizes the existing life-organizing stories of his hearers. Though Paul did not have our typology in mind, his brief (and interrupted) confession can help us reflect on how the Christian story both overlaps and scandalizes the four model narrative theodicies. By hearing Paul's speech in this way, we can continue to mark how storied evil will be overcome according to the Christian account.

---

16. Cf. Gibbs, *Matthew 11:2—20:34*, 690–711.
17. Cf. Woltersdorff, *Divine Discourse*, 42–51.
18. Yoder, *Priestly Kingdom*, 80–85.

This vignette in Acts begins with Paul waiting in Athens for his missionary partners. Luke tells us that Paul got angry when he saw the city filled with idols. As was his custom, he entered the synagogue and reasoned from the Jewish Scriptures that Jesus was the Messiah (see 17:2–3). He also conversed "in the marketplace every day with those who happened to be there," including some of the "Epicurean and Stoic philosophers" (vv. 17–18). There, Paul's witness to "Jesus and the resurrection" is met with both confusion and derision. This prompted an invitation for Paul to speak to a larger audience, presumably to other philosophers and perhaps even "an official body that has responsibility for the city, including its religious facilities and rites."[19]

Robert Tannehill argued that this setting posed a "rhetorical problem" that appears to have guided Paul's strategy in the speech. Paul had already spoken of Jesus and the resurrection, but this seemed to be a conversation-stopper with the Greeks. He likely recognized that this new audience was "already prejudiced against him and not disposed to listen to anything he may say." In this situation, it behooves a speaker to lay an ad hoc "foundation for understanding on the part of the audience before bringing up the central issue."[20] And this is just what Paul did. Before the speech was over, he had quoted a Greek poet and expressed resonance with themes in Greek philosophy, such as divine transcendence and the universal importance of theology.[21]

Paul began by noting that the people in Athens were "very religious." They even had an altar "to the unknown god" (vv. 22–23). He then proceeded to make this unknown God known to them. This God is the maker and sustainer of all things. Paul depicted "God's role in creating and giving as irreversible. God gives and creates for humanity; humanity may give and create, but not for God."[22] As the One who creates and gives unilaterally, the Creator has the right to address his creatures from a privileged position. They are responsible to him. God's present demand upon "all people everywhere" is that they "repent" and turn to him in faith. Paul's ground for making this claim was that God has "fixed a day on which he will judge the world in righteousness by a man whom he has appointed," that is, the man he raised from the dead (v. 31). At the mention of "the resurrection of the dead," he was interrupted and mocked as he was in the marketplace after preaching "Jesus and the resurrection." Luke reported how the conversa-

---

19. Tannehill, *Narrative Unity of Luke-Acts*, 2:216.
20. Ibid., 36.
21. Dibelius, *Studies in the Acts of the Apostles*, 54.
22. Ibid., 215.

tion continued elsewhere, leading some of the Athenians to convert to the Christian faith (vv. 32–43).

In a similar analysis of this speech, Joel Okamoto borrowed from Paul Griffiths to argue that Paul was "giving an account" of the world that was for him "comprehensive, unsurpassable, and central." Paul was telling a life-and-world-organizing story that made claims on and contested every other such story. Paul's account not only defined and identified the one true God, but also declared his will. According to Paul's account, God is defined not merely as the authority that backed one's personal life-organizing story, but as the author of all things. God is the one who "gives all things their being and stands over and against all things as creatures." This God is identified "ultimately and definitively with the man Jesus, whom he had raised from the dead." And this God calls everyone to repent "and finally receive God's promises of forgiveness, life, and salvation."[23]

By defining God, identifying him, and declaring his will in this way, the Christian account critically engages each of the four model narrative theodicies. Here we note both overlap and contradiction. Like the realist accounts, the Christian story scandalizes the idealists. Christians can affirm realist criticism of the idealist response to evil. Seen from within the Christian story, the idealist appeal to a disembodied, dehistoricized, universally accessible moral *ought* is exposed. Such appeals to impersonal standards of judgment are always projections and impositions of a veiled personal or communal judgment.[24] Like the realist, the Christian account agrees that judgments are always rendered by persons.

But the Christians and the realists diverge over the matter of universality. Here the Christian response to evil scandalizes the realist and joins sides with the idealist by declaring that all people everywhere are accountable to a universal judgment. But in the Christian story, evil will be condemned and overcome by the authority and power vested in a single, specific person. God the Father has placed all matters of judgment into the hands of the Son. "The Father judges no one, but has given all judgment to the Son, that all may honor the Son, just as they honor the Father" (John 5:22–23).

CHRISTIAN HOPE IN SPITE OF SCANDALOUS EVIL

Paul Ricoeur thought that hope is always exercised in spite of evil.[25] Every life-organizing story, whether it hopes to finally explain the world or

23. Okamoto, "Christian Mission," 167–68. Cf. Griffiths, "Response to Religious Plurality," 3–11.

24. Cf. Bayer, *Gott als Autor*, 163.

25. Ricoeur, *Freud and Philosophy*, 528.

change it, will eventually run up against some scandalous evil that cannot be resolved within that particular plot. Against this scandal, the story can either be reclaimed or rejected. If it is rejected, the participant in that story will experience a peripeteia, a reversal of expectations, a discordance followed by concordance within a refigured plot. This plot will eventually collide with other stories, other authorities, and another scandal of evil. However, if the story is reclaimed, the scandal can only be endured. Its agent of emplotment must be trusted in spite of evil.

The Christian hope shares this plight with hopes arising from other life-organizing stories. It is distinguished not by its degree of epistemological certainty, social productivity, or psychological consolation. Instead, the external character of Christian eschatology is discerned by how it characterizes conflict and anticipates a resolution. The conflict, or storied evil, in the Christian plot can be characterized as trust in authorities other than the God who has identified himself in Jesus of Nazareth, whom he raised from the dead. The Christian strategy for overcoming storied evil is listening to and proclaiming God's narrated promise and turning away from all idols to actively follow the Lord Jesus, keep his commands, and look for his appearing. False trust is overcome by listening to and participating in the story. This strategy is supported by an account of Jesus as the speaker of God's promises, having the authority and power to fulfill them at his coming to judge the living and the dead.

The Scandal at the Center of the Story

The Christian story scandalizes the others at the level of the declaration made about what counts as good and evil. Storied evil in this account is not simply infantile ideals or immoral behavior, but trust in authorities other than God as he has identified himself in his crucified Son and his lowly deputies. The Apostle Paul, in his letter to the Corinthians, made a similar point. He and his partners preached the one who stands crucified. This was a stumbling block (*skándalon*) to the Jews and folly to Gentiles, "but to those who are called, both Jews and Greeks, Christ the power of God and the wisdom of God" (1 Cor 1:23–24). Paul grounded his reasoning neither on self-evident truths nor on conventional tastes but on what God had elected to do in His economy of salvation:

> For the foolishness of God is wiser than men, and the weakness of God is stronger than men. For consider your calling, brothers: not many of you were wise according to worldly standards, not many were powerful, not many were of noble birth. But God

> chose what is foolish in the world to shame the wise; God chose what is weak in the world to shame the strong; God chose what is low and despised in the world, even the things that are not, to bring to nothing the things that are, so that no human being might boast in the presence of God. (1 Cor 1:26–29)

Commenting on this passage, Anthony Thiselton said it "is of critical importance to emphasize that this proclamation of a crucified Christ (v. 23) constitutes the greatest affront (Greek *skandalon*) to all except those who appropriate what is proclaimed."[26] Thiselton referenced Martin Hengel's work, *The Cross*, to recall how the cross could not have been an easy source of pious reflection for the first Christians. The report that "Jesus died on the cross" was not obviously good news for the members of Roman society, where death on a cross was regarded "as brutal, disgusting, and abhorrent." It was

> so offensive to good taste that crucifixion was never mentioned in polite society, except through the use of euphemisms. For Gentiles who might image a "divine" savior figure, and for Jews who expected a Messiah anointed with power and majesty, the notion of a Crucified Christ, a Messiah on the cross, was an affront and an *outrage*.[27]

Thiselton pastorally challenged Christians to "hear afresh the effective reality of the cross as a *reversal* of all 'natural' human values." What the world despises, God chose.

This is in no way a general negative dialectic, by which all that was previously declared to be "evil" is now called "good." God did not choose what was abhorrent in a general way. He chose this particular crucified man. Trusting this man and his chosen deputies "brings self-reliance to nothing and turns attention wholly to Christ as the source and channel of effective reality as God reveals it."[28] But what is the basis for this crucifying call to trust? Sadism? Masochism? Anti-rationalism? No. It is the *storied* rationality proclaimed by the apostles again and again in the sermons of Acts: "God raised him from the dead."[29]

Christians are people who participate in a peculiar story of the world by trusting the God who identified himself definitively in the crucified and

---

26. Thiselton, *1 Corinthians*, 44.

27. Ibid.

28. Ibid.

29. For Peter's sermons, see Acts 2:24, 32; 3:15; 4:10; 10:40. For the collective testimony of "Peter and the apostles," see 5:30; for Paul, see 13:30, 37; 17:31; 26:23.

risen Jesus. Within this story, Christians exercise hope not *because* of but *in spite of* the cross.[30] There is an appropriate way to return and reflect on Jesus' crucifixion as a supreme demonstration of God's righteousness and love for sinners as John did in his Gospel or as Paul did in the third and fifth chapter of Romans. But at least two qualifications must be made. First, this reflection can be done only *after* Jesus' resurrection. Paul maintained that "if Christ has not been raised, then our preaching is in vain and your faith is in vain" (1 Cor 15:14). To trust the crucified Christ, the scandal of the cross must be endured, not redefined. Jesus himself is our example of this.[31] According to the writer of Hebrews, Jesus, the founder and perfecter of our faith, "endured the cross, despising the shame" for "the joy that was set before him" (Heb 12:2).

There is a second qualification for pious reflection on the cross. Though the Christian tradition, especially in the West, has at times taken it in this way, it is by no means clear that Paul, John, or any other New Testament writer transcended the evil of the cross by speculating on cosmic transactions or a necessary logic of salvation. The debate over theories of atonement is complex[32] and I do not wish to engage it here. I only note an implication drawn from our detour. There I observed a common feature that united the four narrative theodicies. They all hoped to resolve their internal conflict in some future state of mind or state of affairs that was independent or unassociated with the appearing of Jesus to raise the dead and render final judgment. At least since the time of the Gnostic sects, Christians have been tempted to transcend their canonical and creedal narrative in search of a "better" solution to evil. But the Christian hope is not directed toward an unseen drama behind the cross.[33] It is directed toward the man who endured the cross.

The story of Jesus and his apostles is displaced when the affront of the cross becomes a theoretical problem to be solved. Anselmian solutions, such as the explanation that God's wisdom had to find a way to satisfy God's justice before God's mercy could be lawfully dispensed, may fit well within a theological system, but they have trouble fitting within the actual story of Jesus. Questions arise like, "How did Jesus forgive sins before he died on the cross?" Or, "If God's justice demands eternal suffering in hell, how did Jesus

---

30. Cf. Forde, *Where God Meets Man*, 32–44.

31. See Yoder, *Politics of Jesus*, 129–30.

32. See McClendon, *Doctrine*, vol. 2 of *Systematic Theology*, 199–213, for a succinct review of the tradition.

33. Cf. Ibid., 215–16, "The explanation of the cross (and of the resurrection) was nothing apart from the concrete account of the cross (as tribulation) and of the resurrection (as eschatological dawn)."

satisfy the requirement by suffering only a few hours?" To keep the integrity of the system, the theoretician might claim Jesus' sacrifice stands "outside of time," or that any suffering from God incarnate, regardless of duration, is sufficient. Answers like these have been convincing to some Christians and offensive to others. Either way, they are typically commended or criticized not by reference to the story of Jesus and his apostles, but by reference to some alleged "story behind the story."[34]

This is not to say that an account of the Christian faith should exclude reflection on how Jesus' death, among other things, fulfills the Yom Kippur narrative from Leviticus 16.[35] This narrative was especially important for the writer of *The Letter to the Hebrews*. The high priest's once-a-year sacrifice may also be what Paul had in mind when he wrote that God put Jesus forward as a hilastērion (Rom 3:25). I am not denying the legitimacy of this account. What I am excluding is a *theoretic* solution to the question of God's trustworthiness in the face of scandalous evil.

The Christian story is scandalized by the question, "Why does God deliver some from evil but not others?" If this question were asked in the case of Jesus' crucifixion, a theoretical solution could be pursued. Question: Why didn't the Father take the cup of suffering from him? (Luke 22:42). Answer: Because God's justice requires that sinners be punished eternally in hell, so Jesus had to suffer hell in our place in order to save us. Q: But why didn't Jesus have to suffer in hell eternally? A: Because he is God. Q: So God is above the law? A: Yes. Q: But if God does whatever he wants, why does Jesus have to suffer at all? Why does God's plan of salvation require a crucifixion? And for that matter, why hell? If our efforts to deliver ourselves from evil, whether theoretically or pragmatically, will always fail, why doesn't God deliver everyone?

Theoretical answers can be given to these questions, but they would not proceed from the storied rationality of the canonical narratives. Well-meaning Christians have done so in the past, and they have often appealed to Scripture to do so. However, these texts needed to be lifted out of the biblical narrative and placed into an idealist-theoretic narrative. Leibniz, a confessing (Lutheran) Christian, authored this form of narrative theodicy (see chapter 6). This was the story told about a conceptual journey to proleptically see the big picture of how everything fits into a pre-established harmony. In this account, the cross and the earth upon which it stood are transcended. Evil is seen to contribute to the overall harmony of the universe.

---

34. Cf. Frei, *Identity of the Jesus Christ*.
35. See Maxwell, "Resurrection of Christ," 22–37.

How might this be done with respect to the question about Jesus' cup of suffering? Portions of the letter to the Hebrews could be employed in a theoretic account. Consider the passage: "without the shedding of blood there is no forgiveness of sins" (Heb 9:22). Should this be seen as part of an explanation as to why God required Jesus' sacrifice on the cross? Or, should it be understood as a description of what God did in his dealings with his chosen people? If we go with the first, we would also need to speculate about some structures of the universe to which even God conforms. If we opt for the second, we would fit this text within the account of what God did to turn Abraham's family away from idolatry toward trust in him.

If Hebrews 9:22 is taken in a theoretic explanation, then the proposition "no forgiveness without bloodshed" would stand in a story of transcending sin and suffering by fitting one's mind to match the structures of the universe. The gospel message heard within this story must primarily be understood as assertive discourse, that is, as speech acts made to fit minds to the world as it is: "This is how God's justice was finally satisfied." Standing alone, such an account of the gospel would have a difficult time explaining how the apostles could preach the gospel in Acts without depicting Jesus' death as a vicarious satisfaction of God's justice system. However, Hebrews 9:22 (and similar statements in Scripture) could also be taken as a plain description of what God elected to do among Israel "under the law" (9:22a). In this case, it would stand in the on-going story of God's words and deeds accomplished through Jesus to turn Israel and all nations to trust Him *in spite of* the cross, without an explanation, but with a promise that our hope is not in vain.

The Scandal of an Electing God

Hearing and participating in the Christian story raises difficult questions. You don't need an academically trained theologian to raise these questions. My five-year old son did just as well: "Daddy, why doesn't God help us?" Challenges are also posed by those who hold to rival stories. The Christian story is scandalized by different forms of the following question: "Why does God choose to deliver some from evil (moral, physical, temporal, or eternal), but not others?" This question can be expressed in at least five ways: (1) Why does God allow evil at all? (2) Why did this particular evil happen to me or to my loved one? (3) Why doesn't the Holy Spirit do a better job sanctifying his church? (4) Why can't I or my loved one overcome this particular sin? (5) Why are some ultimately saved, but not others?[36] All of these queries wrestle, in some way, with the problem of God's election.[37]

The problem of God's election is by no means peripheral to Christianity. "Christian theology must not only recognize the truth of the doctrine of election. It must see election as a central theme in its story and witness."[38] The famous debate between Erasmus of Rotterdam and Martin Luther centered on the question of whether or not God, in his choices, can be trusted. Luther commended Erasmus: "Unlike all the rest you alone have attacked the real issue . . . the question on which everything hinges."[39]

Luther did not deny the reality of that universal human experience of making choices. He simply denied that these choices are free—that is, that they are made independently and apart from the influence of forces beyond our control. All choices are subject to God. An appropriate metaphor to capture Luther's assertion is to say that God is "Author."[40] God stands outside of the perceived contingencies of the world and composes the story just as he pleases.[41] The characters, the setting, the plot, and even the conflict have no existence, no movement, apart from his choices. He alone is Author. And his creation necessarily "cooperates" with his will, with his purpose.[42] As Paul said to the Athenians, "The God who made the world and everything in it . . . gives to all mankind life and breath and everything . . . having determined the allotted periods and boundaries of their dwelling place, that they should seek God" (Acts 17:24–27).

If we opt to remain in the Christian story, Luther claimed that we "cannot comprehend how this God can be merciful and just."[43] The scandal arises from God's apparent choice to deliver some from evil (whether physical or moral, temporal or eternal), but not others. Luther thought that the prospect of eternal suffering in hell "is the greatest possible offense" and confessed: "I myself was offended more than once, and brought to the very depth and abyss of despair, so that I wished I had never been created a man." For this reason there is much "sweating and toiling to excuse the goodness of God." But the construction of theories cannot remove the scandal—"alas

36. These are Robert Kolb's "theodical questions," which he shared in a seminar on "Sin and Evil" at Concordia Seminary in 2011–12. See also, Kolb, "Luther on the Theology of the Cross," 443–66.

37. Cf. Forde, *Theology is for Proclamation*, 30–37.

38. Okamoto, "Christian Mission," 171.

39. Rupp and Watson, *Luther and Erasmus*, 333.

40. Ibid., 223.

41. Ibid., 119.

42. Ibid., 289.

43. Ibid., 138.

then for us wretched mortals in the hands of that God!"⁴⁴ Yet Luther came to see this as a "salutary despair," which brings one "near to grace."⁴⁵

Luther's response to this scandal was not a series of once-and-for-all inferences that stands ready to answer every questioner. This point is lost on those who would claim that Luther taught "double-predestination" as a way of explaining that God reveals his compassion in saving some, but shows his justice in condemning others—as though God wanted to achieve an ideal harmony. It is equally lost on those who think "single-predestination" can be used to theoretically defend God's goodness and demonstrate his trustworthiness.⁴⁶ Luther's response is not a form of case-closed deductive reasoning, but an open path that must be walked. This is the path upon which the faithful children of Abraham have walked for generations—the flight from God hidden in the ordered, yet ambiguous chaos of a cursed creation to "God preached" in Christ.⁴⁷

For Luther, faith and hope in the God of Abraham must come from the outside. The only reason he believed was because this man Jesus was raised from the dead and then sent out preachers to call all people away from their false authorities and to promise them an inheritance among God's people. Luther urged his fellow Christians to trust the reality of this promise over and against every other experience. We must occupy ourselves "with God incarnate, with Jesus crucified," who weeps, wails, and groans "over the perdition of the ungodly," who "has been sent into the world for the very purpose of willing, speaking, doing, suffering, and offering to all men everything necessary for salvation."⁴⁸

Jesus as Paradigmatic Recipient of God's Promise

In the face of this scandalous evil, the story can be rejected or reclaimed. If it is reclaimed, the scandal is endured, lamented, and resisted. At this point, we should include another account of Jesus. Not only is he the speaker-fulfiller

---

44. Ibid., 259.

45. Ibid., 244.

46. Kolb, *Christian Faith*, 82, "We may try to get God off the hook by distinguishing his absolute will from his permissive will . . . This 'solution' tries to pierce the veil of the Hidden God. It neither meets any basic kind of logical criterion for analysis, nor does it meet the need of the sufferer . . . Even when we have posited a permissive will of God, we have not answered the question of 'why' he would permit evil even if he does not cause it."

47. Rupp and Watson, *Luther and Erasmus*, 200. Cf. Gerrish, "To the Unknown God," 263–92.

48. Ibid., 206.

of God's promise to Abraham, but also the paradigmatic recipient. He is the *exemplar* of how God keeps his promises. His life in the Spirit, his crucifixion, death, and resurrection provide the shape of the Christian plot.

I use the term *exemplar* to distinguish from Jesus as *exemplum*, that is, as someone to imitate. Not that this is an inappropriate way to understand Jesus. After he washed his disciples' feet, Jesus himself said that he had given them an *exemplum* (John 13:5, Vulgate) to follow. Also, Peter said that Christ, in his sufferings, left us an *exemplum* (1 Pet. 2:21). But this is not what I refer to when I speak of Jesus as the recipient of God's promise to Abraham and his family. Jesus is our *exemplar*, in the sense that he provides the image into which God the Spirit is conforming the church. As Paul said, God chose for us to be "conformed to the image of his Son, in order that he might be the firstborn among many brothers" (Rom 8:29).

In the account of Jesus as speaker of God's promise, a *forensic*, or declaratory, account of justification was prominent. Jesus—speaking for God—promises, forgives, adopts, and so justifies. As God did for Abraham, Jesus declares the trusting hearer "in the right." Now, with Jesus as paradigm, a *participatory* account of justification is prominent. As Paul told the Ephesian believers, "even when we were dead in our trespasses," God "made us alive together with Christ" and "raised us up with him and seated us with him" (Eph 2:5-6). The believer is justified *with* Christ, by sharing in his resurrection. He was "raised for our justification" (Rom 4:25). A forensic account is not eclipsed here, but magnified. Paul told the Christians in Rome that in their baptism they were co-crucified, co-buried, and co-raised with Christ (Rom 6:1-11).[49] Baptism, a *forensic* act, a promise, an adoption into the people of God—created a *participatory* reality.[50]

Speaking of Jesus in these terms makes room for a third account alongside the categories of *Christus Victor* and *Christus Vicar* inspired by Gustaf Aulèn's influential book.[51] As our *victor*, Christians confess Christ, who liberated us from bondage to Satan, sin, and death. Jesus died in battle to deliver us, but God raised him up never to die again. As our *vicar*, Christians confess that Jesus' cross cannot be universalized. His death was unique. He suffered God hidden in wrath and condemnation alone. He did this for us. As *Christus Exemplar*, Christians confess that while Jesus died alone, we

---

49. See Kolb, "God Kills to Make Alive," 35–56.

50. This is the classic Lutheran position on Baptism. For a recent "anabaptist" account, see McClendon, *Doctrine*, 389, who also described Baptism as a declarative speech act, an "act of God," and "effectual sign."

51. Aulèn, *Christus Victor*.

do not. We pass through God's wrath, punishment, and condemnation with him.[52] He is the prototype into which we are fit. As Paul said,

> I have suffered the loss of all things . . . in order that I may gain Christ and be found in him, not having a righteousness of my own that comes from the law, but that which comes through faith in Christ . . . that I may know him and the power of his resurrection, and may share in his sufferings, becoming like him in his death, that by any means possible I may attain the resurrection from the dead. (Phil 3:8–11)

Jesus, our elder brother, whose Sonship we share by our adoption in the Spirit, is our *exemplar* for enduring our scandal of evil. Leopoldo Sánchez explored how Jesus, in the Garden of Gethsemane, wrestled "with God's will in a tragic world—that is, a world hostile to the Father's love, a world where the innocent suffer."[53] It was there that Jesus finally gave himself into the Father's hands. But "that ultimate self-giving and entrusting to God does not come without intense struggle."[54] After making such a statement, Sánchez had to struggle with how the Christian tradition, especially in the West, has often explained away Jesus' agony by appealing to his immutable, divine nature. At the same time, Sánchez wanted to avoid twentieth century solutions that seek to justify God by explaining that he suffers the tragic world alongside us.[55] Sánchez took on this challenge to help the church find in Jesus "what it means to wrestle with God's will in a world that is surrounded by pain and death."[56]

Sánchez offered an account of Jesus' Gethsemane prayer that moved beyond "the theological bipolarity that in evangelicalism has shaped the current debate between classical and open theism."[57] He explained that classic theists want to protect God's freedom and open theists want to protect not only human freedom, but also defend God's trustworthiness in the face of evil. In this scheme, the debate not only leaves us with an "either/or," it also tends to leave the canonical story behind in favor of theoretic expla-

---

52. Cf. Kolb, *Christian Faith*, 154–55, who described Luther's "Atonement by the Joyous Exchange" in terms similar to what I've called the *Christus Exemplar* account. See also, ibid., 104, "Sinners must die. They must die forever in hell, or they must die in Baptism to be raised to new life in Christ."

53. Sánchez, "Praying to God the Father," 274. See also Sánchez, *Receiver, Bearer, and Giver of God's Spirit*.

54. Ibid.

55. Ibid., 294. Cf. Weinandy, *Does God Suffer?* and Moltmann, *Crucified God*.

56. Sánchez, "Praying to God the Father," 274.

57. Ibid., 275.

nations. Granted, we need some explanation, but this should be directed primarily toward helping us actually participate in the on-going story of Jesus-in-Israel-and-the-church.

A Christian account of divine transcendence should derive from the storied event: the God of Abraham made a world-transforming promise and proleptically fulfilled it by raising Jesus from the dead. As an aspect of their discipleship, Christians should struggle to avoid their own ideal notions about God. Instead, having been confronted and addressed by the emissaries of the risen Jesus, they should reason within the story that God is able to make good on his promises, neither being helped nor hindered by any created being or circumstance. This storied rationality redirects our confidence to God's power and authority to make good on his promises spoken by Jesus, rather than to theoretic explanations about divine attributes. This puts a check on what Sánchez called "an overworked substantialist approach" that relativizes the narrated promise God made to Abraham in favor of a theological system.[58] When the story serves the system, the struggle to consummate the system can become the theoretician's life-organizing story.

Likewise, an account of human *responsiveness* should arise from participation in the story of God's threat and promise in Christ. I use the term responsiveness instead of freedom to indicate the proper Christian conception of humanity's situation before God.[59] As Paul proclaimed in the Areopagus, God calls everyone to repent in response to his announced intention to judge the world in righteousness through Jesus, whom he raised from the dead (Acts 17:31). For those who insist on trusting other authorities, this announcement is a standing threat. But for those who hear, it stands as Jesus' promise to forgive sins and secure for them "a place among those who are sanctified by faith in me" (Acts 26:18). This should be taken as a genuine commissive speech act issued to evoke a response and create a relationship of trust. Appeals to human freedom independent of the God of Jesus can provide a theoretical explanation for why there is sin and suffering in the world. These may even help people toward figuring their lives around an intelligible story. But it won't be the Christian story.

Sánchez sought to leave behind "the God of 'theisms'" (whether classical or open) and "move towards the 'triune' God of the Biblical narratives." The pattern of participation in this story becomes particularly evident "in the Son's life of prayer to God the Father in and by the Spirit."[60] This encourages us to account not only for Jesus' prayer, but also the church's life of

---

58. Ibid., 286.
59. Cf. Bayer, *Freedom in Response: Lutheran Ethics* and Kolb, *Christian Faith*, 63.
60. Sánchez, "Praying to God the Father," 278.

prayer "as a Trinitarian event grounded in the mystery of filial communion between the Son and the Father in the Spirit."[61] Sánchez critiqued Thomas Aquinas's description of Jesus' prayer primarily as a lesson about the two natures of the God-man and as an example for Christians to imitate.[62] In terms of theory, it was instruction. In terms of practice, Christ was "our pedagogue in the ways of humility."[63] This explanation safeguards notions of divine transcendence and the two natures of Christ, but it makes "the incarnate Logos' prayer" something "entirely accidental and external to His *person*."[64] In other words, it disassociates the Jesus of the system from the Jesus of the story. This makes the system liable to be subsumed within a rival story.

The notion of divine "substance" can be a helpful abstraction from the Christian story. It is a way of confessing the difference between God and creation, with no third option in between. But it is a hindrance if we forget that it is not divine substance that is identified in the canonical narrative but divine persons. If we remember that every system is first a storied system, we can recognize how the narrative ascribes to the Son an identity that is distinct from the person of the Father. As depicted in the Gospels, it is proper to identify the Son as the one who, in the power of the Spirit, eternally trusts, depends on, and receives all things from the Father. This is important because Christians are, in time, being conformed into the image of the Son. They are not most properly imitators of the Son, but participants in his unique identity. By their adoption in the Spirit, they are "being made faithful and trusting" children of God, who share "by grace in Christ's own identity as the Son who prays and entrusts Himself to the Father."[65]

By remaining in the story and privileging divine persons over divine substance, Sánchez defined prayer as "a historical expression" of the life of sonship "both for Jesus and the followers of Jesus because both pray to the same Father in and by the same Spirit."[66] Prayer is "an *address* to a personal God"—not meditation on an ideal, not resignation to reality—but speech acts directed toward the God who is "relational in His own triune being and therefore relates to us in a meaningful way."[67] With words of prayer we

---

61. Ibid.

62. Ibid., 283. Cf. Thomas Aquinas, *Summa Theologiae*, Part IIIa, Question 21, article 2.

63. Sánchez, "Praying to God the Father," 284.

64. Ibid.

65. Ibid., 286.

66. Ibid., 287.

67. Ibid., 291.

express *"filial trust,"* which is "not a matter of submitting to an apathetic God or persuading a self-limiting God." Instead, it is a matter of "trusting in a loving Father who has given us the Spirit of His Son to enter a reciprocal I-Thou relation with Him characterized by faith on our side and love on His side."[68]

Christian Hope as Answered Lament

Oswald Bayer said something similar in his proposal for a "theology of lament" or complaint (*Klage*).[69] He argued that lament is a neglected category in Christian theology and that a dogmatics that included the complaint of faith would significantly rework present systems, especially in the doctrine of God, creation, man, Christ, atonement, and eschatology. Bayer noted how through "the influence of Stoic thought, lament was pushed out of the everyday lives of Christians." In contrast, a proper Christian theology of lament stands "in radical contradiction to the Stoic theology of submission."[70] Here, the present distress and suffering of a creation in travail "is not made insignificant or covered up, but it is taken seriously without becoming the ultimate reality or leading to resignation or cynicism."[71]

From Bayer's perspective, systematic theologians are often tempted to consummate their systems and reach "a happy ending too quickly." They do "not take serious the uncertainty and hopelessness along the way." This alienates the system from everyday life because it "takes time to walk the way in prayer, meditation, and affliction (*oratione, meditatione, tentatione*)." Both theoretical cover-ups and Stoic piety distract Christians from "holding God to his given promise and from demanding God's answer with passionate protest and lawsuit like Job." But lament, as an expression of faith, can help keep Christians on the way and in the story. It is different than skepticism or doubt because "no lament exists entirely without remembered trust or, finally, expected answer."[72] The lament of faith "confesses God's lordship and our expectation of his goodness."[73] It comes from a people who have already been adopted in the Spirit, made witnesses to the resurrection, brought home out of exile, settled in the Promised Land, having been res-

---

68. Ibid., 294.
69. Bayer, "Toward a Theology of Lament," in *Caritas et Reformatio*, 211–20.
70. Ibid., 215.
71. Ibid., 218.
72. Ibid., 215–16.
73. Kolb, *Christian Faith*, 74. ". . . we must recognize the difference between the cry of faith, 'God, I am angry with you,' and the cry of unbelief, 'I am angry with God.'"

cued out of slavery in Egypt, and now looking forward to the restoration of all the things the God of Abraham promised by his prophets long ago.

Bayer also suggested what an "eschatology of answered lament" might look like. In the first place, it would need to be grounded on a "Christology of answered lament," with reference to how on the cross Jesus took up the words of Psalm 22, "My God, my God, why have you forsaken me?"[74] As long as Jesus was dead in the tomb, this prayer was unanswered. God's pledge to make the nations his inheritance remained unfilled. God's trustworthiness remained contested.[75] But in the resurrection, his prayer was answered and the promise fulfilled, with Jesus as the "firstfruits" of the full harvest to come (1 Cor 15:20–28). As the church walks toward the promised future of the risen Christ, she prays by the same Spirit, "exhorting and charging God to grant justice to people and all creatures against the enemy (Luke 18:1–8) and thereby remain loyal to his own justice." Bayer described the final judgment as "the world-completing act of the Creator, who in boundless mercy saves from all distress." Therefore, lament "calls on God to establish his promise of life: 'O Jesus Christ, you are tarrying with your Day of Judgment . . . please come.'"[76]

Sánchez's account of Christian participation in Christ's Sonship by the Spirit and Bayer's theology of lament reflect Paul's "description of present Christian existence, rooted in God's past action in Jesus Christ, assured of God's future action for Christ's people and for the whole world, and sustained in the present by the Spirit."[77]

> For all who are led by the Spirit of God are sons of God. For you did not receive the spirit of slavery to fall back into fear, but you have received the Spirit of adoption as sons, by whom we cry, "Abba! Father!" The Spirit himself bears witness with our spirit that we are children of God, and if children, then heirs—heirs of God and fellow heirs with Christ, provided we suffer with him in order that we may also be glorified with him. (Rom 8:14–17)

This has immediate impact on how Christians endure and lament the scandal of evil. Prayer, as "groaning" in the Spirit, is not merely something that Christians are commanded to do. More importantly, it is the Spirit-given response to God's promise to adopt us, to redeem our bodies, and to finally set the entire creation "free from its bondage to corruption." Prayer follows from and returns to the narrated promise that the God of Jesus made to

74. Bayer, "Toward a Theology of Lament," in *Caritas et Reformatio*, 212.
75. Cf. Bayer, *Living by Faith*, 71.
76. Ibid., 212–13. Cf. Bayer, *Gott als Autor*, 161–86.
77. Wright, "Letter to the Romans," in *New Interpreter's Bible*, vol. 10, 590.

Abraham. By the Spirit, we petition, plead, lament, and above all express our trust in the Father. "For in this hope we were saved. Now hope that is seen is not hope. For who hopes for what he sees? But if we hope for what we do not see, we wait for it with patience" (Rom 8:18–25).

SUMMARY

There is more that could be said about Christian hope. If I have succeeded, this will be a helpful account for Christians seeking to offer the reason for their hope in a post-Constantinian context. By helpful, I mean appropriate, leaving the matter of effectiveness to the Holy Spirit. He leads the church into the conflict of interpretations to bear witness to the crucified and risen Jesus. Christians have received a definite strategy for lamenting and struggling against evil. Staying with this life-organizing story as it anticipates the end of evil is the source and distinction of Christian hope.

Conclusion
Zombie Jesus *Redivivus*

I BEGAN THIS BOOK with a conversation in a local coffee shop. I go there on Tuesday mornings with other followers of Jesus to practice Christian discipleship. Because we meet in a public space, these meetings often become an opportunity to bear witness to our faith in Jesus. A dearly loved, long-term guest in our group, Sean, puzzled over our claims: "So you believe in Zombie Jesus?" To him, the hope held out by the New Testament sounded not only impossible, but nonsensical—and a little amusing.

As disciples committed to the teachings of the New Testament, we grieved Sean's unwillingness to receive Jesus—crucified, risen, ruling, and returning to judge both the living and the dead. As Paul described the Ephesian Christians before they believed, we saw Sean as "separated from Christ, alienated from the commonwealth of Israel" a stranger to "the covenants of promise, *having no hope* and without God in the world" (Eph 2:12). But also like Paul speaking to the unbelieving Athenians in the Areopagus, we conversed with Sean as someone who, in his own way, was "very religious" (Acts 17:22).

Like the Athenians, Sean was a participant in a powerful life-organizing story that supplied him with hope. Our challenge was to understand where he was coming from—to embrace him in his present story-formed identity. At the same time, we wanted to profess our hope in the God who "commands all people everywhere to repent, because he has fixed a day on which he will judge the world in righteousness by a man whom he has appointed; and of this he has given assurance to all by raising him from the dead" (Acts 17:30–31). Sometimes, Sean would hear this and "mock"—Zombie Jesus! And yet, he kept coming back—saying implicitly with the Athenians, "We will hear you again about this" (Acts 17:32).

For committed Christian disciples, there is a good reason why "Jesus" is almost always the right answer. Plenty of stories of the world inspire hope for life after death. A few even look for a resurrection of the body. Others hear this as the makings of a B-rated horror movie. Regardless of their peculiarities, most life-organizing, *eschatological* hopes provide psychological stability in walking the all-too-human tension between presumption and despair. But, the Christian difference is and always will be this peculiar Palestinian construction worker who was crucified by order of a Roman procurator during the first half of the first century. In spite of his ignominious demise, his disciples came to confess him as Israel's Messiah and the world's Lord. They took up this outrageous stance because they believed the God of Abraham had raised him bodily from the dead, being the first to rise in a general resurrection God will accomplish on the Last Day. At that time, God will judge the living and the dead and set the world right. Christian hope is distinct because it arises out of this story.

Not too long after these apostolic reports of Jesus' resurrection started coming out of Jerusalem, the name "Jesus" and the experience of "Christ" were lifted out of this story and embedded into others. Such is still the case today. Jesus is claimed as an icon for stories of personal prosperity. He is instrumental for quests for assurance of personal salvation. He is admired for the way he resisted the securities of this passing world and faced death courageously. He is applauded for his non-violent protest against tyranny. Jesus has been fit into these stories and used to support these hopes. He has been made a means to serve something conceived as a greater good: religious assurance, personal fulfillment, existential authenticity, social justice.

But, the story told in the New Testament resists all moves to instrumentalize Jesus, a point that his bodily resurrection makes quite clearly. Jesus is indispensable. He is the Word of Yahweh made flesh. He has come to call Abraham's family to trust him unconditionally. He is the maker and fulfiller of God's promise to give the earth and all creation as their inheritance. He called them by name, forgave their sins, and healed their diseases. They rejected and killed him, but God raised him up so he could complete his mission. Their crucified Messiah restored them to their proper calling as light to all nations. From the beginning of the story, Abraham's family was always to be a family for others. All the families of the earth are to be blessed and favored through them. When Jesus comes again in glory, he will raise bodily all the dead. He threatens to eternally condemn all who have corrupted themselves by trust in idols. But to those who belong to him, he promises a place among those who are sanctified by faith in him (Acts 26:18).

The New Testament expands this account of Jesus: not only does he address Israel and the nations as God in the flesh; he also stands with us as our brother. He stands with us in our distorted, self-spun stories. He embraces us as we endure God's hiddenness in the midst of evil.

The story of Jesus is a *narrative theodicy* because it establishes the righteousness of God in spite of evil. It attests to the God who makes right and thereby demonstrates himself as trustworthy. But, like its rivals, the story is still unfolding. Our continued participation in it is threatened both by the evil we do and the evil we suffer. We confess the God and Father of Jesus as author of all things, but we cannot square this with either the origin or the final end of evil.

The logic of our story compels us to assign blame for evil on the rebellious will of creatures, both human and angelic. God's threat to eternally condemn those who have corrupted themselves by idolatry must be taken seriously. We cannot disregard his address to us in favor of a self-proclaimed ideal of love. His threat of judgment is real and aims to elicit an active response. It is given to turn all people from their idols and toward him in faith. But this storied reasoning does not supply us with the conceptual structures to explain why God, as author of all things, permitted evil in the first place. An appeal to free will is appropriate, if by that we mean we are made responsible to God when he confronts us and calls us to repent. But it is inappropriate if it becomes part of a chain of reasoning used to *theoretically* justify God.

Such a theoretical explanation might begin by declaring an ideal of freedom as the highest good. If God is to have creatures who freely love him, then having some who abuse their freedom is part of the cost of doing business. Thus, all evil is necessary evil and therefore must be seen to serve the greater good. This explanation works reasonably well in a theoretical account, but it follows a logic of resolution (i.e., an eschatology) that is contrary to the Christian account. It seeks to resolve the conflict by fitting one's mind and words to match the world as it already is. At the same time, if someone wishes to actually become a part of God's people, he or she must carry out the directive of self-transformation to become a person who freely loves God. These strategies for overcoming Christianity's scandal of an electing God—that is, the God who is author of all things—achieve success only by abandoning the story in favor of some other narrative theodicy. They exonerate God by removing from him the role of author and assigning it to someone else—either to the assertion-making or directive-fulfilling human being. Eventually, this new story and new agent of emplotment will be accompanied by a new scandal that can only be endured in hope. But it will no longer be Christian hope.

If idealist solutions are rejected, those scandalized by the Christian story could opt for a realist narrative theodicy. This is the story that begins by rejecting all ideals as idolatrous illusions. The world "is what it is." On the one hand, it can be re-described and perhaps celebrated with a form of Stoic piety. On the other hand, it can be pragmatically manipulated to ease our pain. These solutions become self-narrated accounts of growing up to face the world with maturity. Again, the God of Jesus, who made a world-transforming promise to Abraham, is displaced by the authority of assertion-making and directive-issuing human beings. Within these realist narrative theodicies, a continuing scandal of evil must be endured with hope. But it's not Christian hope.

The God of Jesus continues to be God for us by calling us back into his story. There he bears the full weight of evil and promises to establish himself as trustworthy. He vows to remove all scandals to our faith when he brings the world to fit the word of his promise to Abraham. In his *Diatribe* against Luther, Erasmus said that within this story "my mind encounters many a stumbling block."[1] Luther said that the only way to defend God is to dethrone him. The only way to let God be God is to trust him. We must refer "everything to God" and "the difficulties, if not cured, can be endured."[2]

Jesus, our brother, is our *exemplar* for enduring this scandal. This does not mean he is merely an *exemplum* to imitate. He is that, but there is more. His life in the Spirit, his crucifixion, and resurrection are the paradigm for participation in the Christian story. The Holy Spirit, whom we have received by baptism into Christ, has brought us to share in Jesus' unique identity. We are adopted sons and daughters of God. The Spirit continues the work of conforming us into his image. Jesus was once crushed by the awful hiddenness of his God. He trusted his Father, who answered his cry of lament by raising him from the dead. His Spirit draws us forward to the Day when faith will give way to sight. The light of glory in the Advent of Christ will demonstrate the justice and mercy of God. "Until then," Luther told Erasmus, "we can only believe this."[3] Christian hope, like all other forms of life-organizing hope, is always exercised *in spite of* some form of unresolved scandalous evil.

This insight should help Christians humbly, yet boldly engage in public conversations within a post-Constantinian setting. The term post-Constantinian assumes the Christian faith once supplanted a previously dominant way of accounting for the world. It then entered a long period of social establishment, which is now past. Christianity lost social dominance to another account of the world, which, in turn, has begun to lose its

---

1. Rupp and Watson, *Luther and Erasmus*, 87.
2. Ibid., 291.
3. Ibid., 332.

explanatory power to an array of conflicting accounts. This has given rise to much confusion not only about what it means to hope as a Christian, but simply what it means to *be* a Christian. I have argued that being a Christian means participating in the Christian story. Thus, discipleship, witness, hope, and all Christian Theology arise out of this narrative theodicy.

In terms of discipleship, this account of Christian hope has implications for Christian thinking and doing. I address the former here and the latter below. Thinking—reasoning, explaining, and philosophizing—always arises out of a life-organizing story. Since the church confesses that her God is the author of all things and that the setting of her story encompasses the entire spatial-material world, she can always expect some overlap with other storied systems. This insight encourages Christian thinkers to engage other accounts of the world critically, but with a readiness to learn. I attempted to model this by adapting extra-ecclesial concepts to serve thinking within the Christian story. For example, I used Kant's notion of "internal" versus an "external use of attributes" to more clearly express the difference in my approach to eschatology. Also, I adapted Searle's analysis and categorization of speech acts along with his concept of "direction of fit" to explain key differences between rival life-organizing stories. Although I classified both of these men as professing a rival to the storied hope of Christians, my thinking and speaking was enhanced by engaging their stories.

Christian philosopher Boyd Blundell presented the philosophy of Paul Ricoeur as a model for how such critical engagement might be done as "detour and return" to the "main road."[4] Christian thinkers should approach philosophies critically, realizing that systems are always storied systems. They confess a rival eschatology, that is, a resolution to a particular problem of evil that contests Christian eschatology. They imply and express trust in a rival author, that is, a rival god. At the same time, Christian thinkers can engage these rival stories as exploratory detours. By doing so, they will return to their story-of-the-world enriched with new insights. In this book, I followed Ricoeur's lead and pursued such a detour in chapters five, six, and seven.

This account of Christian hope also has implications for Christian action. Throughout, I have focused on verbal action—on speech *acts*. But this approach also applies to non-verbal communicative acts. This includes both the church's gathering for her weekly liturgy and celebration of the Lord's Supper along with the vocational practice of individual Christians. Both practices should be understood within the Christian story, which narrates one theodicy among many rivals. Gathering for the liturgy becomes

---

4. Blundell, *Paul Ricoeur*, 1–12.

the central locus of the Christian struggle against storied evil, which is trust in the authors of other life-organizing stories. In the liturgy, the church assembles bodily and publically to participate in the coming rule and reign of God. This liturgy is in conflict with other liturgies, which incorporate their participants into rival stories.

The rivalry also extends into vocational practice. It is especially tempting for North American Christians to locate their labor within the American, Free-Market Capitalist Dream. This rags-to-riches myth offers a life-organizing hope. It rivals the story that centers on Jesus' life in the Spirit, who led him to sacrificially give his life for the good of his neighbor in need. Also tempting for North Americans and Western Christians in general is the "Myth of Religious Violence" and the so-called triumph of modern democracy. This unquestioned story can deceive Christians into trusting modern democracy as a savior, which requires unquestioned obedience in exchange for peace and security. Telling the Christian story as an all-encompassing plot subsumes modern democracies and all forms and manifestations of government within the coming reign of God. Such an account empowers Christians to serve as citizens, police officers, judges, politicians, and military members in their peculiar, self-sacrificing, enemy-loving, Christian way. From this perspective, the decrees of governmental office-holders can be appropriately challenged and conscientiously objected when they set themselves up as idols. By staying in their story, Christians may be judged as ineffective according to the storied values of others. Yet Christians are distinguished not by their social, economic, and political effectiveness, but by the way they defer all matters of vengeance and final judgment to Jesus.

With respect to mission, this approach enables an understanding of both the gospel and the hearers of the gospel within the context of the story of Jesus-in-Israel-and-the-church. In theologically conservative circles, the Christian gospel is often treated as theoretical, *assertive* discourse. The "good news" about Jesus is conveyed as an explanation about how God found a way to both satisfy his wrath and save sinners without compromising his justice. This presentation of the gospel can leave the hearer either to assent to a description of the world-as-is or to seek out a better explanation. The problem with this account of the gospel is not that it under-emphasizes the narrative aspect of the Christian faith. The problem is much more urgent in that it presumes a rival, idealist-theoretic narrative, which resolves only when our explanations come to match the world as-is. This rivals the Christian gospel, which is a narrated-promise that will resolve only when the God of Jesus conforms the world to fit his word of promise to Abraham. Within the context of the Christian story, the gospel is heard as a *commissive* speech act, not an *assertive* one. Likewise, the word of the Law is not primarily a description of an unachievable moral standard, but a genuine threat of God's continued wrath against all who trust in idols—that is, in authors of rival life-organizing stories.

With respect to the hearers of the gospel, Christian witness should recognize that the story of Jesus remains vulnerable to being subsumed within the hearer's existing life-organizing story. The gospel is the proclamation of forgiveness of sins, but this proclamation occurs within the larger narrated-promise. When the gospel is reduced to "forgiveness" without being grounded in the story of Jesus, it can be colonized by either the realist or idealist version of the pragmatic story. In this case, the hearer enjoys a private assurance or a therapeutic consolation while keeping his or her ultimate loyalties with the reigning public story. But, these would-be standard stories are scandalized when the gospel of forgiveness on account of Christ is proclaimed in response to God's threat to curse those who oppose his promise to give both his favor and his creation to Abraham's family (Gen. 12:3; Rom. 4:13). And when reconciliation is offered to those crushed by this threat, the gospel, through the work of the Spirit, is set to evoke faith and hope in Jesus, the final speaker and paradigmatic recipient of God's promise to Abraham.

This account of hope has been designed for conversations like the one into which our Tuesday-morning group invited Sean. He wasn't ready to be a full participant in our Sunday morning worship in the name of the risen Jesus. Nevertheless, we welcomed him into those Tuesday-morning conversations, which often became a frustrating, yet invigorating mix of discipleship within a common story as well as a witness to those participating in rival stories.

I offer this book as a tool not only for Christians, but also for those who react to the New Testament's claims with some puzzlement, even amusement. My limited, *non-eschatological* hope for this work is that it may help make such conversations in post-Constantinian coffee shops a little more coherent.

Bibliography

Abbott, Daniel. "Divine Participation and Eschatology in the Theodicies of Paul Tillich and Jürgen Moltmann." PhD diss., University of Virginia, 1987.
Allen, Diogenes, and Eric O. Springsted. *Philosophy for Understanding Theology*. 2nd ed. Louisville: Westminster John Knox, 2007.
Aquinas, Thomas. *Summa Theologiae*. 60 vols. New York: Blackfriars, 1964.
Arendt, Hannah. *Eichmann in Jerusalem*. New York: Penguin, 1994.
Auerbach, Erich. *Mimesis: The Representation of Reality in Western Literature*. Translated by Willard R. Trask. Princeton: Princeton University Press, 1953.
Augustine. *On Christian Belief*. Edited by Boniface Ramsey. Translated by Edmund Hill et al. The Works of Saint Augustine I/8. Hyde Park, NY: New City, 2005.
Aulèn, Gustaf. *Christus Victor: An Historical Study of the Three Main Types of the Idea of the Atonement*. Translated by A. G. Hebert. New York: MacMillan, 1969.
Austin, J. L. *How to Do Things with Words*. Cambridge: Harvard University Press, 1962.
Avineri, Schlomo. *The Social and Political Thought of Karl Marx*. Cambridge: Cambridge University Press, 1968.
Barth, Karl. *Church Dogmatics: A Selection*. Edited by Geoffrey Bromiley. New York: Harper, 1961.
Bauckham, Richard, ed. *God Will Be All in All: The Eschatology of Jürgen Moltmann*. Edinburgh: T. & T. Clark, 1999.
———. *The Theology of Jürgen Moltmann*. Edinburgh: T. & T. Clark, 1995.
Bayer, Oswald. *A Contemporary in Dissent: Johann Georg Hamann as a Radical Enlightener*. Translated by Roy Harrisville and Mark Mattes. Grand Rapids: Eerdmans, 2012.
———. "The Doctrine of Justification and Ontology." *Neue Zeitschrift für systematische Theologie und Religionsphilosophie* 43 (2001) 44–53.
———. "Does Evil Persist?" *Lutheran Quarterly* 11 (1997) 143–50.
———. *Freedom in Response: Lutheran Ethics; Sources and Controversies*. Translated by Jeffrey Cayzer. New York: Oxford University Press, 2007.
———. "God as Author of My Life-History." *Lutheran Quarterly* 2 (1988) 437–56.
———. "God's Omnipotence." *Lutheran Quarterly* 23 (2009) 85–102.
———. *Gott als Autor: Zu einer poietologischen Theologie*. Tübingen: Mohr Siebeck, 1999.
———. "Justification as the Basis and Boundary of Theology." *Lutheran Quarterly* 15 (2001) 273–92.

———. *Living By Faith: Justification and Sanctification*. Translated by Geoffrey Bromiley. Grand Rapids: Eerdmans, 2003.

———. "The Plurality of the One God and the Plurality of the Gods." *Pro Ecclesia* 15 (2006) 338–54.

———. "Poetological Doctrine of the Trinity." *Lutheran Quarterly* 15 (2001) 43–58.

———. "Theology in the Conflict of Interpretations—Before the Text." *Modern Theology* 16 (2000) 495–502.

———. *Theology the Lutheran Way*. Translated by Jeffrey Silcock and Mark Mattes. Grand Rapids: Eerdmans, 2007.

———. "Toward a Theology of Lament." Translated by Matthias Gockel. In *Caritas et Reformatio: essays on church and society in honor of Carter Lindberg*, edited by David Whitford, 211–20. St. Louis: Concordia, 2002.

Becker, Ernest. *The Structure of Evil: An Essay on the Unification of the Science of Man*. New York: Braziller, 1968.

Beek, A. van de. *Why? On Suffering, Sin, and God*. Translated by John Vriend. Grand Rapids: Eerdmans, 1990.

Beilby, James, and Paul Eddy, eds. *The Nature of the Atonement: Four Views*. Downers Grove, IL: InterVarsity, 2006.

Bente, Friedrich., ed. *Concordia Triglotta*. St. Louis: Concordia, 1921.

Blundell, Boyd. *Paul Ricoeur between Theology and Philosophy: Detour and Return*. Bloomington: Indiana University Press, 2010.

Bobrinskoy, Boris. *The Mystery of the Trinity: Trinitarian Experience and Vision in the Biblical and Patristic Tradition*. Translated by Anthony Gythiel. Crestwood, NY: St. Vladimir's Seminary, 1999.

Bouchard, Larry. *Tragic Method and Tragic Theology: Evil in Contemporary Drama and Religious Thought*. University Park, PA: Pennsylvania State University Press, 1989.

Braaten, Carl, and Robert Jenson. *The Futurist Option*. New York: Newman, 1970.

———. *The Last Things: Biblical and Theological Perspectives on Eschatology*. Grand Rapids: Eerdmans, 2002.

Bradshaw, Timothy. *Trinity and Ontology* . Edinburgh: Rutherford House, 1988.

Bultmann, Rudolf. *New Testament and Mythology and Other Basic Writings*. Edited and translated by Shubert Ogden. Philadelphia: Fortress, 1984.

———. *The Presence of Eternity: History and Eschatology*. New York: Harper, 1957.

Camus, Albert. *The Plague*. Translated by Stuart Gilbert. New York: Knopf, 1960.

Cavanaugh, William. "A Fire Strong Enough to Consume the House: The Wars of Religion and the Rise of the State." *Modern Theology* 11 (1995) 397–420.

———. *The Myth of Religious Violence: Secular Ideology and the Roots of Modern Conflict*. New York: Oxford University Press, 2009.

Crites, Stephen. "The Narrative Quality of Experience." *Journal of the American Academy of Religion* 39 (1971) 291–311.

Crossan, John. *Dark Interval: Towards a Theology of Story*. Nile, IL: Argus, 1975.

Cullmann, Oscar. *Christ and Time: The Primitive Christian Conception of Time and History*. Translated by Floyd Filson. London: SCM, 1962.

Cunningham, Conor. *Darwin's Pious Idea: Why the Ultra-Darwinists and Creationists Both Get it Wrong*. Grand Rapids: Eerdmans, 2010.

Daley, Brian. *The Hope of the Early Churh: A Handbook of Patristic Eschatology*. New York: Cambridge University Press, 1991.

Deane, David. *Nietzsche and Theology: Nietzschean Thought in Christological Anthropology.* Burlington, VT: Ashgate, 2006.
Dennett, Daniel. *Darwin's Dangerous Idea: Evolution and the Meaning of Life.* New York: Touchstone, 1996.
———. "Darwin's 'strange inversion of reasoning.'" *Proceedings from the National Academy of Sciences* 106 (2009) 10061–65.
Dibelius, Martin. *Studies in the Acts of the Apostles.* Edited by Heinrich Greeven. Translated by Mary Ling. London: SCM, 1956.
Dostoevsky, Fyodor. *The Brothers Karamazov.* Translated by Constance Garnett. New York: Macmillan, 1948
Edwards, James. *The Plain Sense of Things: The Fate of Religion in an Age of Normal Nihilism.* University Park, PA: Pennsylvania State University Press, 1997.
Fackre, Gabriel. *The Christian Story: A Narrative Interpretation of Basic Christian Doctrine.* Grand Rapids: Eerdmans, 1984.
Felluga, Dino. "Modules on Greimas: On the Semiotic Square." *Introductory Guide to Critical Theory.* Accessed on Feb 12, 2014 at http://www.purdue.edu/guidetotheory/narratology/modules/greimassquare.html.
Fergusson, David, and Marcel Sarot, eds. *The Future as God's Gift: Explorations in Christian Eschatology.* Edinburgh: T. & T. Clark, 2000.
Feuerbach, Ludwig. *The Essence of Christianity.* Translated by George Eliot. Amherst, NY: Prometheus, 1989.
Fish, Stanley. "How to Do Things with Austin and Searle: Speech Act Theory and Literary Criticism." *Modern Language Notes* 91 (1976) 983–1025. Accessed on June 20, 2013 at http://www.jstor.org/stable/2907112.
Ford, David. *Barth and God's Story: Biblical Narrative and the Theological Method of Karl Barth in the "Church Dogmatics."* Frankfurt am Main: Lang, 1981.
Forde, Gerhard. "Caught in the Act: Reflections on the Work of Christ." *Word and World* 3 (1983) 22–31.
———. *A More Radical Gospel: Essays on Eschatology, Authority, Atonement, and Ecumenism.* Edited by Mark Mattes and Steven Paulson. Grand Rapids: Eerdmans, 2004.
———. *On Being a Theologian of the Cross: Reflections on Luther's Heidelberg Disputation, 1518.* Grand Rapids: Eerdmans, 1997.
———. *The Preached God: Proclamation in Word and Sacrament.* Edited by Mark Mattes and Steven Paulson. Grand Rapids: Eerdmans, 2007.
———. *Theology is for Proclamation.* Minneapolis: Fortress, 1990.
———. *Where God Meets Man: Luther's Down-to-Earth Approach to the Gospel.* Minneapolis: Fortress, 1972.
Frei, Hans. *The Eclipse of the Biblical Narrative: A Study in Eighteenth and Nineteenth Century Hermeneutics.* New Haven: Yale University Press, 1974.
———. *The Identity of Jesus Christ: The Hermeneutical Bases for Dogmatic Theology.* Philadelphia: Fortress, 1975.
———. *Types of Christian Theology.* Edited by George Hunsinger and William Placher. New Haven: Yale University Press, 1992.
Freud, Sigmund. *The Standard Edition of the Complete Psychological Works of Sigmund Freud.* Edited by James Strachey. London: Hogarth, 1957–74.
Frey, Jörg. "New Testament Eschatology—An Introduction: Classical Issues, Disputed Themes, and Current Perspectives." In *Eschatology of the New Testament and Some*

Related Documents, edited by Jan van der Watt, 3–32. Tübingen: Mohr Siebeck, 2011.

Fukuyama, Francis. *The End of History and the Last Man*. New York: Free Press, 1992.

Gerrish, Brian. "'To the Unknown God': Luther and Calvin on the Hiddenness of God." *Journal of Religion* 53 (1973) 263–92.

Gibbs, Jeffrey. *Matthew*. 2 vols. St. Louis: Concordia, 2006–10.

González, Justo. "Hispanic Worship: An Introduction." In *¡Alabadle! Hispanic Christian Worship*, edited by Justo González, 20–29. Nashville: Abingdon, 1996.

———. *Mañana: Christian Theology from a Hispanic Perspective*. Nashville: Abingdon, 1990.

Graham, Gordon. *Evil and Christian Ethics*. Cambridge: Cambridge University, 2001.

Grenz, Stanley, and Roger Olson. *20th Century Theology: God & the World in a Transitional Age*. Downers Grove: InterVarsity, 1992.

Griffiths, Paul. "A Properly Christian Response to Religious Pluralism." *Anglican Theological Review* 79 (1997) 3–26.

Hauerwas, Stanley. *The Hauerwas Reader*. Edited by John Berkman and Michael Cartwright. Durham: Duke University Press, 2001.

Hauerwas, Stanley, and L. Gregory Jones, eds. *Why Narrative? Readings in Narrative Theology*. Eugene: Wipf and Stock, 1997.

Hauerwas, Stanley, and William Willimon. *Resident Aliens: Life in the Christian Colony*. Nashville: Abingdon, 1989.

Hays, Richard. *The Faith of Jesus Christ: The Narrative Substructure of Galatians 3:1–4:11*. 2nd ed. Grand Rapids: Eerdmans, 2002.

Hess, Carol Lakey. "'Come Here Jesus . . . Wonder what God Had in Mind:' Toni Morrison and F. Scott Fitzgerald as Narrators of (Anti-)Theodicy." *Religious Education* 104 (2009) 354–76.

Hinlicky, Paul. *Paths Not Taken: Fates of Theology from Luther through Leibniz*. Grand Rapids: Eerdmans, 2009.

Hong, Christopher. *A History of the Future: A Study of the Four Major Eschatologies*. Washington, DC: University Press of America, 1981.

Horton, Michael. *Covenant and Eschatology: The Divine Drama*. Louisville: Westminster John Knox, 2002.

Hovey, Craig. *Nietzsche and Theology*. New York: T. & T. Clark, 2008.

Hume, David. *Dialogues Concerning Natural Religion*. Edited by Stanley Tweyman. New York: Routledge, 1991.

Irenaeus. *Against the Heresies*. Translated by Dominic Unger. 3 vols. New York: Paulist, 1992–2012.

Jacoby, Russell. *Social Amnesia: A Critique of Conformist Psychology from Adler to Lang*. Boston: Beacon, 1975.

Jameson, Fredric. *The Political Unconscious: Narrative as a Socially Symbolic Act*. Ithaca, NY: Cornell University Press, 1981.

Jaspers, Karl, and Rudolf Bultmann. *Myth and Christianity: An Inquiry into the Possibility of Religion without Myth*. New York: Noonday, 1958.

Jenson, Robert. *Story and Promise: A Brief Theology of the Gospel About Jesus*. Philadelphia: Fortress, 1973.

———. *Systematic Theology*. 2 vols. New York: Oxford University Press, 1997–2001.

Jones, Ernest. *The Life and Word of Sigmund Freud*. 3 vols. New York: Basic, 1953–57.

Just, Arthur. *Heaven on Earth: The Gifts of Christ in the Divine Service.* St Louis: Concordia, 2008.
Kant, Immanuel. *Critique of Pure Reason.* Translated by Paul Guyer and Allen Wood. Cambridge: Cambridge University Press, 1998.
———. *Introduction to Logic.* Translated by Thomas Abbott. New York: Philosophical Library, 1963.
———. *Logik: Ein Handbuch zu Vorlesungen.* Königsberg: Nicolovius, 1800.
———. *Religion and Rational Theology.* Translated and edited by Allen Wood and George Di Giovanni. Cambridge: Cambridge University Press, 1996.
———. "Was ist Aufklärung?" In vol. 7 of *Sämmtliche Werke*, edited by Friedrich Schubert, 143–54. Leipzig: Voss, 1838.
Kearney, Richard. *On Paul Ricoeur: The Owl of Minerva.* Burlington, VT: Ashgate, 2004.
Kermode, Frank. *Sense of an Ending: Studies in the Theory of Fiction.* New York: Oxford University Press, 1967.
Knight, Douglas. *The Eschatological Economy: Time and the Hospitality of God.* Grand Rapids: Eerdmans, 2006.
Koester, Craig. *The Word of Life: A Theology of John's Gospel.* Grand Rapids: Eerdmans, 2008.
Kolb, Robert. *Bound Choice, Election, and Wittenberg Theological Method: From Martin Luther to the Formula of Concord.* Grand Rapids: Eerdmans, 2005.
———. *The Christian Faith: A Lutheran Exposition.* St. Louis: Concordia, 1993.
———. "God Kills to Make Alive: Romans 6 and Luther's Understanding of Justification (1535)." *Lutheran Quarterly* 21 (1998) 35–56.
———. "Luther on the Theology of the Cross." *Lutheran Quarterly* 16 (2002) 443–66.
Kolb, Robert, and Charles Arand. *The Genius of Luther's Theology.* Grand Rapids: Baker, 2008.
Kolb, Robert, and Timothy Wengert, eds. *The Book of Concord: The Confessions of the Evangelical Lutheran Church.* Minneapolis: Fortress, 2000.
Künneth, Walter. *The Theology of the Resurrection.* Translated by J. Leitch. St Louis: Concordia, 1965.
Ladrière, Jean. *L'espérance de la raison.* Leuven, Belgium: Peeters, 2005.
Lash, Nicholas. *A Matter of Hope: A Theologian's Reflections on the Thought of Karl Marx.* Notre Dame: University of Notre Dame Press, 1982.
Leibniz, Gottfried. *Dissertation on Predestination and Grace.* Translated by Michael Murray. New Haven: Yale University Press, 2011.
———. *Theodicy: Essays on the Goodness of God, the Freedom of Man and the Origin of Evil.* Edited by Austin Farrer. Translated by E. M. Huggard. London: Routledge, 1951.
Lindbeck, George. *The Nature of Doctrine.* Philadelphia: Westminster, 1984.
Linder, Douglas O. "State v. John Scopes ("The Monkey Trial")," Speech on the Occasion of the 75th Anniversary of the Scopes Trial, July 10, 2000. Accessed at on Aug 18, 2016 at http://law2.umkc.edu/faculty/projects/ftrials/scopes/evolut.htm.
Loemker, Leroy. *Struggle for Synthesis: The Seventeenth Century Background of Leibniz's Synthesis of Order and Freedom.* Cambridge: Harvard University Press, 1972.
Long, Thomas. "The Life to Come: Preaching with Hope." *Concordia Journal* 22 (1996) 352–59.
———. "Preaching God's Future." In *Sharing Heaven's Music: The Heart of Christian Preaching*, edited by Barry Callen, 191–202. Nashville: Abingdon, 1995.

Löwith, Karl. *Meaning in History: The Theological Implications of the Philosophy of History.* Chicago: University of Chicago Press, 1949.

Luther, Martin. *Luther's Works.* American Edition. Edited by Jaroslav Pelikan and Helmut Lehman. 82 vols. St. Louis: Concordia, 1955–.

MacIntyre, Alasdair. *After Virtue: A Study in Moral Theory.* 3rd ed. Notre Dame: University of Notre Dame, 2007.

———. *Whose Justice? Which Rationality?* Notre Dame: University of Notre Dame, 1988.

Magee, Bryan. *Karl Popper.* New York: Viking, 1973.

Marx, Karl. *The Essential Marx.* Edited by Ernst Fisher. Translated by Anna Bostock. New York: Herder and Herder, 1971.

———. *The German Ideology: Parts I & II.* Edited by Roy Pascal. New York: International Publishers, 1947.

Marx, Karl, and Friedrich Engels. *On Religion.* New York: Schocken, 1964.

Maxwell, David. "The Resurrection of Christ: Its Importance in the History of the Church." *Concordia Journal* 34 (2008) 22–37.

McClendon, James. *Systematic Theology.* 3 vols. Nashville: Abingdon, 1986–2000.

McClendon, James, and James Smith. *Understanding Religious Convictions.* Notre Dame: University of Notre Dame Press, 1975.

McLellan, David. *Karl Marx: His Life and Thought.* London: Macmillan, 1973.

Metz, Johann Baptist. "A Short Apology of Narrative." In *The Crisis of Religious Language,* edited by Johann Baptist Metz and Jean-Pierre Jossua, 84–96. New York: Herder and Herder, 1973.

Meyer, Joel. "Christian Justification After Nihilism." PhD diss., Concordia Seminary, 2012.

Milbank, John. *Theology and Social Theory: Beyond Secular Reason.* Cambridge, MA: Blackwell, 1990.

Miles, Jack. *God: A Biography.* New York: Knopf, 1995.

Moltmann, Jürgen. *The Coming of God: Christian Eschatology.* Translated by Margaret Kohl. Minneapolis: Fortress, 1996.

———. *The Crucified God.* Translated by R. A. Wilson and John Bowden. Minneapolis: Fortress, 1993.

———. *Ethics of Hope.* Translated by Margaret Kohl. Minneapolis: Fortress, 2012.

———. *God for a Secular Society: The Public Relevance of Theology.* Translated by Margaret Kohl. Minneapolis: Fortress, 1999.

———. *God in Creation.* Translated by Margret Kohl. San Francisco: Harper, 1985.

———. *Theology of Hope: On the Ground and Implications of a Christian Eschatology.* Translated by James Leitch. Minneapolis: Fortress, 1993.

———. *The Trinity and the Kingdom: The Doctrine of God.* Translated by Margaret Kohl. Minneapolis: Fortress, 1993.

———. *The Way of God in Jesus Christ.* Translated by Margret Kohl. London: SCM, 1990.

Moore, Russell. *The Kingdom of Christ: The New Evangelical Perspective.* Wheaton, IL: Crossway, 2004.

Morse, Christopher. *Not Every Spirit: A Dogmatics of Christian Disbelief.* Harrisburg, PA: Trinity International, 1994.

Nafzger, Peter. *These Are Written: Toward a Cruciform Theology of Scripture,* Eugene, Oregon: Pickwick, 2013.

Neiman, Susan. *Evil in Modern Thought: An Alternative History of Philosophy.* Princeton: Princeton University Press, 2002.

———. *Moral Clarity: A Guide for Grown-up Idealists.* Princeton: Princeton University Press, 2009.

Nietzsche, Friedrich. *The Anti-Christ, Ecce Homo, Twilight of the Idols, and Other Writings.* Edited by Aaron Ridley and Judith Norman. New York: Cambridge University Press, 2005.

———. *Beyond Good and Evil: Prelude to a Philosophy of the Future.* Edited by Rolf-Peter Horstmann and Judith Norman. Translated by Judith Norman. Cambridge: Cambridge University Press, 2002.

———. *The Portable Nietzsche.* Translated by Walter Kaufman. New York: The Viking, 1954.

———. *Werke in Drei Bänden.* Zweiter Band. Munich: Hanser, 1960.

Nygren, Anders. *Agape and Eros.* Translated by Philip Watson. New York: Harper, 1969.

O'Donnell, John J. "Pannenberg's Doctrine of God." *Gregorianum* 72 (1991) 73–88.

———. *Trinity and Temporality.* New York: Oxford University Press, 1983.

Okamoto, Joel. "Christian Mission among a World of Religions." *Missio Apostolica* 14 (Nov 2005) 163–74.

Olson, Roger. "Trinity and Eschatology: The Historical Being of God in Jürgen Moltmann and Wolfhart Pannenberg." *Scottish Journal of Theology* 36 (1983) 213–27.

Pannenberg, Wolfhart. "Der Gott der Geschichte: Der trinitarische Gott und die Wahrheit der Geschichte." *Kerygma und Dogma* 23 (1977) 76–92.

———. *Systematic Theology.* Translated by Geoffrey Bromiley. 3 vols. Grand Rapids: Eerdmanns, 1991.

Peterson, Michael, ed. *The Problem of Evil: Selected Readings.* Notre Dame: University of Notre Dame Press, 1992.

Pinches, Charles. "Christian Pacificism and Theodicy: The Free Will Defense in the Thought of John H. Yoder." *Modern Theology* 5 (1989) 239–55.

Piper, John. *The Justification of God: An Exegetical and Theological Study of Romans 9:1–23.* Grand Rapids: Baker Book House, 1983.

Placher, William C. *The Domestication of Transcendence.* Louisville: Westminster John Knox, 1996.

Plantinga, Alvin. *God, Freedom, and Evil.* New York: Harper, 1974.

Plato. *Phaedrus.* Translated by R. Hackforth. Cambridge: Cambridge University Press, 1952.

Plotinus. *The Enneads.* Translated by Stephen MacKenna. London: Faber, 1956.

Prenter, Regin. *Spiritus Creator.* Translated by John Jensen. Eugene, OR: Wipf and Stock, 1999.

Rahner, Karl. *The Trinity.* Translated by Joseph Donceel. New York: Crossroad, 1997.

Ratner-Rosenhagen, Jennifer. *American Nietzsche: A History of an Icon and His Ideas.* Chicago: University of Chicago Press, 2012.

Ratzinger, Joseph. *Eschatology.* Translated by Michael Waldstein. Chicago: Catholic University of America Press, 1988.

Reagan, Charles. *Paul Ricoeur: His Life and Work.* Chicago: University of Chicago Press, 1996.

Reuther, Rosemary Radford. "Eschatology and Feminism." In *Lift Every Voice: Constructing Christian Theologies from the Underside*, edited by Susan Brooks Thistlethwaite and Mary Potter Engel, 111–24. New York: Harper, 1990.

———. *Sexism and God-Talk: Toward a Feminist Theology*. Boston: Beacon, 1983.

Ricoeur, Paul. *The Conflict of Interpretations: Essays in Hermeneutics*. Edited by Don Ihde. Evanston, IN: Northwestern University Press, 1974.

———. "Evil: A Challenge to Philosophy and Theology." *Journal of the American Academy of Religion* 53 (1985) 635–48.

———. *Figuring the Sacred: Religion, Narrative, and Imagination*. Edited by Mark Wallace. Translated by David Pellauer. Minneapolis: Fortress, 1995.

———. *Freud and Philosophy: An Essay on Interpretation*. Translated by Denis Savage. New Haven: Yale University Press, 1970.

———. *Oneself as Another*. Translated by Kathleen Blamey. Chicago: University of Chicago Press, 1992.

———. *The Symbolism of Evil*. Translated by Emerson Buchanan. New York: Harper, 1967.

———. *Time and Narrative*. Translated by David Pellauer, and Kathleen McLaughlin (Blamey). 3 vols. Chicago: University of Chicago Press, 1984–1988.

Reiff, Philip. *The Triumph of the Therapeutic: Uses of Faith after Freud*. Wilmington, DE: ISI Books, 2006.

Robinson, Robert. "Narrative Theology." In vol. 3 of *The Encyclopedia of Christianity*, edited by Erwin Fahlbusch et al., 689–93. Grand Rapids: Eerdmans, 1999.

Rodin, R. Scott. *Evil and Theodicy in the Theology of Karl Barth*. New York: Lang, 1997.

Ross, G. MacDonald. *Leibniz*. New York: Oxford University Press, 1984.

Roth, Michael. *Psycho-Analysis as History: Negation and Freedom in Freud*. Ithaca, NY: Cornell University Press, 1987.

Rühle, Otto. *Karl Marx: His Life and Work*. Translated by Cedar Paul and Eden Paul. New York: New York Home Library, 1943.

Rupp, E. Gordon, and Philip Watson, eds. *Luther and Erasmus: Free Will and Salvation*. Louisville: Westminster John Knox, 2006.

Ruse, Michael. "Darwin and the Problem of Evil." In *Darwin's Nemesis: Philip Johnson and the Intelligent Design Movement*, edited by William Dembski, 139–50. Leicester: Intervarsity, 2006.

Sánchez, Leopoldo. "Praying to God the Father in the Spirit: Reclaiming the Church's Participation in the Son's Prayer Life." *Concordia Journal* 32 (2006) 274–95.

———. *Receiver, Bearer, and Giver of God's Spirit: Jesus' Life in the Spirit as a Lens for Theology and Life*. Eugene, Oregon: Pickwick, 2015.

Sauter, Gerhard. *Eschatological Rationality: Theological Issues in Focus*. Grand Rapids: Baker, 1996.

———. *What Dare We Hope?* Harrisburg: Trinity International, 1999.

———. *Zukunft und Verheißung: Das Problem der Zukunft in der gegenwärtigen theologischen und philosophiscen Diskussion*. Zurich: Zwingli, 1965.

Sauter, Gerhard, and John Barton. *Revelation and Story: Narrative Theology and the Centrality of Story*. Burlington: Ashgate, 2000.

Schleiermacher, Friedrich. *The Christian Faith*. Edited by H. R. Mackintosh and J. S. Stewart. Edinburgh: T. & T. Clark, 1928.

Schopenhauer, Arthur. *The World as Will and Representation*. Translated by E. F. J. Payne. 2 vols. 2. New York: Dover, 1966.

Schwarz, Hans. *Eschatology*. Grand Rapids: Eerdmanns, 2000.
———. *Evil: A Historical and Theological Perspective*. Translated by Mark Worthing. Minneapolis: Fortress, 1995.
———. *The God Who Is: The Christian God in a Pluralistic World*. Eugene, OR: Cascade, 2011.
———. *The Search for God: Christianity, Atheism, Secularism, World Religions*. Minneapolis: Augsburg, 1975.
———. *The Theological Autobiography of Hans Schwarz: A Multi-cultural and Multi-denominational Christian Ministry*. Lewiston, NY: Edwin Mellen, 2009.
Schweitzer, Albert. *The Quest for the Historical Jesus*. Edited by John Bowden. Minneapolis: Fortress, 2001.
Schwöbel, Christoph. "Last Things First? The Century of Eschatology in Retrospect." In *The Future as God's Gift: Explorations in Christian Eschatology*, edited by David Fergusson and Marcel Sarot, 217–41. Edinburgh: T. & T. Clark, 2000.
Scott, Mark Alan. "Theodicy: Failure and Promise within the Thought of Karl Barth, David R. Griffin, and Jürgen Moltmann." PhD diss., Southern Baptist Theological Seminary, 1987.
Searle, John. *Intentionality: An Essay in the Philosophy of Mind*. New York: Cambridge University Press, 1983.
———. *Mind, Language, and Society: Philosophy in the Real World*. New York: Basic, 1998.
———. *Mind: A Brief Introduction*. New York: Oxford University Press, 2004.
———. *Speech Acts: An Essay in the Philosophy of Language*. Cambridge: Cambridge University Press, 1969.
Sheehan, Jonathan. "The Poetics and Politics of Theodicy." *Prooftexts* 27 (2007) 211–32.
Sinclair, Peter. "Narrative and Eschatology: Graham Greene, Evelyn Waugh, Muriel Spark and the Theology of Narrative." PhD diss., University of Connecticut, 2009.
Smith, Ronald. *J. G. Hamann: 1730–1788: A Study in Christian Existence with Selections from His Writings*. New York: Harper, 1960.
Stackhouse, John G. *Can God Be Trusted? Faith and the Challenge of Evil*. New York: Oxford University Press, 1998.
Stackhouse, Max, et al., eds. *God and Globalization*. 4 vols. Harrisburg, PA: Trinity, 2000–2007.
Stephenson, John. *Eschatology*. Confessional Lutheran Dogmatics vol. 13, edited by Robert D. Preus. Fort Wayne, IN: Luther Academy, 1993.
Sternberg, Meir. *The Poetics of the Biblical Narrative*. Bloomington: Indiana University Press, 1985.
Stiver, Dan. "Ricoeur, Speech-Act Theory, and the Gospels as History." In *After Pentecost: Language and Biblical Interpretation*, edited by Craig Bartholomew, Colin Greene, and Karl Möller, 50–72. Grand Rapids: Zondervan, 2001.
———. *Theology after Ricoeur: New Directions in Hermeneutical Theology*. Indianapolis: Indiana University Press, 2010.
Stock, Konrad. *Annihilatio Mundi: Johann Gerhards Eschatologie der Welt*. Munich: C. Kaiser, 1971.
Surin, Kenneth. *Theology and the Problem of Evil*. New York: Blackwell, 1986.
Sutton, Robert. "The Human Question: Reflections on the Problem of Evil." *Drew Gateway* 53 (1983) 47–55.

Tannehill, Robert. *The Narrative Unity of Luke-Acts: A Literary Interpretation.* Vol. 2, *The Acts of the Apostles.* Minneapolis: Fortress, 1994.

Tappert, Theodore, ed. *The Book of Concord: Confessions of the Evangelical Lutheran Church.* Philadelphia: Fortress, 1959.

Thielicke, Helmut. *Modern Faith and Thought.* Translated by Geoffrey Bromiley. Grand Rapids: Eerdmans, 1990.

Thiemann, Ronald. *Revelation and Theology: The Gospel as Narrated Promise.* Notre Dame: University of Notre Dame, 1985.

Thiselton, Anthony. *1 Corinthians: A Shorter Exegetical and Pastoral Commentary.* Grand Rapids: Eerdmans, 2006.

———. *Life After Death: A New Approach to the Last Things.* Grand Rapids: Eerdmans, 2012.

Tilley, Terrence. *The Evils of Theodicy.* Washington, DC: Georgetown University Press, 1991.

———. "Incommensurability, Intratextuality, and Fideism." *Modern Theology* 5 (1989) 87–111.

———. *Story Theology.* Wilmington, DE: Glazier, 1985.

Tracy, David. *The Analogical Imagination.* New York: Crossroad, 1981.

———. "Ricoeur's Philosophical Journey: Its Import for Religion." In *Paul Ricoeur: The Hermeneutics of Action,* edited by Richard Kearney. Thousand Oaks, CA: Sage, 1996.

Vanhoozer, Kevin. *The Drama of Doctrine: A Canonical-Linguistic Approach to Christian Theology.* Louisville: Westminster John Knox, 2005.

Voelz, James. *What Does This Mean? Principles of Biblical Interpretation in the Post-Modern World.* St Louis: Concordia, 2003.

Vogel, Dwight, ed. *Primary Sources of Liturgical Theology.* Collegeville: Liturgical, 2000.

Wainwright, Geoffrey. *Eucharist and Eschatology.* London: Epworth, 1971.

Walls, Jerry, ed. *The Oxford Handbook of Eschatology.* New York: Oxford University Press, 2008.

Weber, Timothy. *Living in the Shadow of the Second Coming: American Premillennialism (1875–1982).* Grand Rapids: Zondervan, 1983.

Webster, John, Kathryn Tanner, and Iain Torrance, eds. *The Oxford Handbook of Systematic Theology,* 306–22. New York: Oxford University Press, 2007.

Weinandy, Thomas. *Does God Suffer?* Notre Dame: University of Notre Dame Press, 2000.

Wiesel, Elie. *Night.* Translated by Marion Wiesel. New York: Hill and Wang, 2006.

Wiggins, James, ed. *Religion as Story.* New York: Harper, 1975.

Wilkinson, David. *Christian Eschatology and the Physical Universe.* New York: T. & T. Clark, 2010.

Willimon, William. *Sighing for Eden: Sin, Evil and the Christian Faith.* Nashville: Abingdon, 1985.

Wilmore, Gayraud. *Last Things First.* Philadelphia: Westminster, 1982.

Wolterstorff, Nicholas. *Divine Discourse: Philosophical Reflections on the Claim that God Speaks.* New York: Cambridge University Press, 1995.

———. "The Promise of Speech-act Theory for Biblical Interpretation." In *After Pentecost: Language and Biblical Interpretation,* edited by Craig Bartholomew, Colin Greene and Karl Möller, 73–90. Grand Rapids: Zondervan, 2001.

Wright, N. T. *Christian Origins and the Question of God*. 3 vols. Minneapolis: Fortress, 1992–2003.
———. *Evil and the Justice of God*. Downers Grove: InterVarsity, 2006.
———.*The Letter to the Romans*. In *The New Interpreter's Bible*, Vol. 10, edited by Leander Keck, 395–770. Nashville: Abingdon, 2002.
———. *Suprised By Hope: Rethinking Heaven, the Resurrection, and the Mission of the Church*. New York: Harper, 2008.
Yoder, John Howard. *The Original Revolution: Essays on Christian Pacifism*. Scottdale: Herald, 1971.
———. *The Politics of Jesus*. Grand Rapids: Eerdmans, 1994 .
———. *The Priestly Kingdom*. Notre Dame: University of Notre Dame Press, 1984.
Young, Julian. *Friedrich Nietzsche: A Philosophical Biography*. Cambridge: Cambridge University Press, 2010.

www.ingramcontent.com/pod-product-compliance
Lightning Source LLC
Chambersburg PA
CBHW062025220426
43662CB00010B/1478